Speaking in Thumbs

Speaking in Thumbs

A Psychiatrist Decodes

Your Relationship Texts

So You Don't Have To

MIMI WINSBERG, M.D.

 DOUBLEDAY | NEW YORK

Copyright © 2021 by Mirène Winsberg

Jacket image: Sunflowerr/Shutterstock
Jacket design by Emily Mahon

Names: Winsberg, Mimi, author.
Title: Speaking in thumbs : a psychiatrist decodes your relationship texts so you don't have to / Mimi Winsberg, M.D.
Description: First edition. | New York : Doubleday, [2021] | Includes bibliographical references.
Identifiers: LCCN 2021006579 (print) | LCCN 2021006580 (ebook) | ISBN 9780385546966 (hardcover) | ISBN 9780385546997 (ebook).
Subjects: LCSH: Man-woman relationships. | Couples. | Online dating. | Interpersonal communication. | Internet—Social aspects.
Classification: LCC HQ801 .W743 2021 (print) | LCC HQ801 (ebook) | DDC 306.7—dc23
LC record available at https://lccn.loc.gov/2021006579
LC ebook record available at https://lccn.loc.gov/2021006580

MANUFACTURED IN THE UNITED STATES OF AMERICA

First Edition

1st Printing

Contents

Introduction

If a pair of Bottega Veneta ballet flats could stomp, then I would say Agnes stomped down the long hallway and into the cavernous room that is my office. Instead of flinging herself onto the gray sectional, she leaned stiffly against a drafting chair, clutching her phone like a sacred tablet. Her nails were the color of the accent wall, the carpet, and the cigarette pack peeking out of the purse slung low against the thigh of her white capri pants: celadon.

I had acknowledged her arrival and was waiting for a response. At thirty-two, Agnes was used to being the smartest person in the room, and it showed in the way she carried herself. She was an MIT graduate and a level-six engineer at Facebook, making more money than a surgeon or a top corporate lawyer. Now she was wearing a mixture of scowl and pout.

"I don't get it," she said, thrusting the ridiculously dim screen of her phone at me. I put on my glasses, which I seldom do around my patients. A text message from a man named Jason read, "Let's talk when you are back from your trip."

"What's the matter?" I ventured.

They had met online recently and had just spent a lovely weekend together, talking, hiking, cooking, *feeling*. She was hurt and annoyed by his text and wasn't sure why. "What does this mean, how should I respond?" she asked. I could read the subtext: Why isn't the relationship developing the way I think it should?

"You know about sharks, how they have to stay in motion?" I said.

"Otherwise they die," she replied.

"Exactly. People assume relationships are like sharks—that they need to move forward to survive. Well, they're not; they move in mysterious ways, or sometimes not at all."

Agnes slumped into the drafting chair, rolled it beside me, and handed me her phone. We began to dissect her online chats with Jason to see if we were dealing with a shark, or perhaps an animal with a better chance of survival.

I've got a story for you.

It's my own story, but I've been a psychiatrist long enough to know that it's a common one. Over twenty-five years of practice, my couch has provided me with a window into people's intimate lives—their hopes, their dreams, and their worries. It has shown that we are all creatures of romantic attachment, not to mention the victims of epic dating fails. I have listened to countless colorful accounts of my patients' online dating—just like Agnes's—their heartening successes and their heart-stopping failures. The thrill of connection, and the agony of rejection.

So if I've got a story, it's only because you've had so many stories for me.

Those narratives themselves have always been psychiatry's bread and butter. While medicine continues to grasp for the biological and genetic underpinnings of mental illness—which neurochemicals cause us to be depressed, anxious, compulsive—our stories remain a quick and reliable tool for understanding ourselves, available to one and all.

In psychiatry we call it the heuristic approach. A heuristic is a problem-solving method that uses shortcuts to come to quick conclusions. We can't analyze every synapse, download every experience, and sum up a person. We likely never will. But the heuristic approach offers us something else. Through stories and the way we make them meaningful, we can engage in a fruitful process of learning and discovery.

Scientifically speaking, stories have a bad rap. Anecdotal evidence is considered by science a lesser form of knowledge when compared with cold, hard data. Feelings, impressions, unsupported theories—they abound in the writings of psychiatry's forefathers, largely dismissed today. Freud himself acknowledged that his case histories should read like short stories; they lack the emphasis on data that we've come to expect, the serious stamp of science. He focused instead on the connection between our narratives and our symptoms—the idea that our psychiatric conditions could be understood by analyzing the stories we tell ourselves about life events.

I witnessed firsthand the role that stories can play in understanding symptoms when I was in medical school. I had elected to do some work in refugee camps in Asia, as well as a rotation at a local clinic that served Southeast Asian refugees. Many of the patients had not only been displaced but suffered significant trauma. Their stories, relayed through an interpreter, were both tragic and compelling. One Cambodian woman described a psychosomatic blindness—losing her sight after watching her husband being stabbed to death with sharp sticks. As Freud suggested, her symptoms could only be understood through her recollections; no eye exam or CT scan could do them justice. This experience brought my interest in mental health into sharp focus. Even when I was a young medical student, my willingness to listen to people's stories could be powerful and life changing, for them and for me.

It is what we do as humans, after all. We tell stories about ourselves and the people in our lives. Some of the stories are true, some distorted, some frankly false. As a psychiatrist, I am trained to listen to patients' stories in a specific way: to draw out their histories, their family backgrounds, their symptoms and struggles. Some of what I do is to help patients tell a new story about themselves.

And of course many of the stories I have heard in my practice have been about love—love being one of the greatest stories, one that gives our lives meaning. Love is always a story we tell first to ourselves and then to each other.

For three years, I did my listening at the very place that is credited (or blamed) for inventing the predominant means of online human communication today. At Facebook, I listened to Silicon Valley's alpha and beta testers, its disrupters and innovators. The inventors and shepherds of *the algorithm*—that impenetrable sequence of code that promises deeper and more profound connection with our fellow humans—they were and still are my patients. Those geniuses who know how you tick? I know how they tick.

Now, I should admit that for all this talk of stories and their primacy, I'm not immune to the lure of technology. At Facebook and beyond, I've seen the power of data firsthand. In the age of Big Data and measurable outcomes, now even psychiatry—founded on the intangibles of emotion—has felt the pull. The field has gone digital. I've been fortunate enough to be at the center of it, helping to lead the charge as digital health companies attempt to apply data science, measurement-based care, and even artificial intelligence to the study of human behavior and its associated illnesses. I co-founded Brightside Health, a digital behavioral health company at the convergence of technology and mental health. At Brightside we treat depression and anxiety over telemedicine, using state-of-the-art technology to help patients and providers select treatment plans and manage care. While patients have long relied on trained clinicians for diagnostic impressions and treatment selections, we are now more and more turning to machines, which can help us recognize patterns that humans routinely miss.

The past five years of my work in digital health have centered on training machines to recognize symptom clusters in text messages—in other words, using technology to pore over our digital communication and reveal crucial facts about behavioral health. As a leader in mental health, Brightside has pioneered advances in both diagnosis (recognizing the telltale signs of mental illness) and triage (judging how urgent a patient's illness is), as well as the selection of appropriate psychiatric treatments. Effectively, we're wrangling data to understand both internal psychology and external behavior, training machines not only how to think but how to "shrink."

Alongside all this Big Data, I've seen the rise of Big Dating. Any technology of real value has always been quickly adapted to suit our most primal desires. So with the advent of personal and mobile computing, it's perhaps inevitable that online dating has, in a matter of a decade or two, gone from the fringes to the norm. More than fifty million American adults say they either have used or continue to use a dating app in the pursuit of romance. Tinder alone processes 1.6 billion swipes per day. In less than a single generation, Big Data has upended the courtship process.

I've felt its effects firsthand. Shortly before I began my tenure as Facebook's resident psychiatrist, my marriage of sixteen years ended. Our partnership had become all about the business of running a family, and while we could still connect intellectually, we had drifted apart romantically. And so we amicably parted ways.

I knew what was in store for me—dating apps—and I was fine with it. In no time I was swiping daily, looking to find that special someone . . . or just looking. What I discovered was something I hadn't expected: that all my training had prepared me extraordinarily well for this. My clinical practice informed the way I approached dating, and vice versa. My familiarity with data analysis seeped through too. Soon I was sifting through bursts of text messaging to find the golden nuggets of information hidden within. I found myself with an uncanny ability to see through (even sometimes, if I'm being honest, to provisionally *diagnose*) those I engaged with on these dating apps, often after exchanging just a few messages.

It was here at the intersection of psychology, tech, and romance that I began to see the human condition up close, in high resolution. It is where I truly, and literally, had skin in the game. I started developing my own heuristic approach, translating intimate exchanges like a text whisperer.

"U still up?" an incoming message reads.

Up for what? What do they really mean?

We've all done it: obsessively parsing the words from a prospective partner. Looking for clues in their response times, whether too fast or too slow. Wondering why that three-dot ellipsis came . . . and went. To inject meaning into these fleeting moments is a romantic comedy cliché.

Well, it turns out that this cliché, like so many others, is grounded in reality. The changes in the way we communicate accompany a broader fact: romantic relationships have become more complicated. Now it's not just "Whom should I be dating?" but "How many people should I be dating at once?" "How do I define myself along lines of gender and orientation?" We wonder who is going to initiate the conversation and who will be the one to deepen it. We wrestle with the nuances of the past, overlaid with shifting gender norms and our complex, evolving identities. We seek contact. We crave connection. We are talking about stuff that we have never talked about before.

And we are doing it over text. Texting is now the dominant mode of communication. It forces us to rely exclusively on our written language (and of course our emojis). Word choice, semantics, and grammar have to communicate ever more meaning in the absence of the cues we derive from body language, eye contact, and stance, to say nothing of vocal cues like tone, cadence, and volume. Now our words alone do the heavy lifting. The act of writing—with just our thumbs, no less—forces the compression of these emotional cues into tiny chat bubbles, which then require a new skill set to unpack and understand.

The word "data" derives from the Latin verb *dare*, "to give." The French word for data is *les données,* "the givens." Let's not forget, in our technology-ridden lives, that with every thumb tap and keystroke we are giving away little pieces of ourselves. We leave behind contrails of digital exhaust, signatures of ourselves, our desires, our states of mind, even our character.

Does online *dating* translate into online *data*? Can the thumbprints encoded in individual text messages help us make sense of our online conversations as a whole and shed light on our subsequent courtships, on-screen and in person?

Sometimes our clearest, most unbiased view of a person is in our first meeting with them. It's before the storytelling aspects of our brains have begun to spin a narrative about them, before we've become attached, our noses pressed up against the glass of our budding relationship, without our objectivity or perspective. What better first glimpse of a person than their initial text messages? Armed with the right tools, these chat bubbles offer peepholes into the psyche.

Our text messages also reflect key factors in the creation of healthy communication patterns throughout the courtship process. The unique features of an individual, and even a couple, are sitting there on our phones, visible to the trained naked eye. The narcissism of the guy who broke your heart was evident in his use of possessive pronouns. The guy who had the attention span of a puppy cursed too much from the start. When the man who eventually shows up for dinner looks nothing like his profile picture, or when a delightful connection disappears like a ghost, traces of those fatal flaws might have been hiding in plain text.

This book is a guide to analyzing dating and relationship text threads. It will provide tools to help you avoid the bad experiences that pollute our dating world and the clarity to better understand and identify key elements of personality, attachment style, and even psychopathology.

I'll be honest, transparent, revealing. We'll look over my shoulder at text exchanges, and I'll show you how to read between the lines. We'll examine the chats that you've probably had, the ones you will have, and the ones you will want to have. These are private conversations, but they are part of our collective yearning to communicate, to comprehend the frustrations, pains, and joys that we endure in finding romantic connection.

Based on my real-life experience and professional expertise, we'll gather insights on finding the person with the right psychological profile for you, one chat bubble at a time. The first section of the book examines what text can reveal about the traits of the individual; the second section is focused on uncovering traits of the pair-bond; and in the third section we'll use text exchanges as the written medical record of the arc of the relationship so that we can recognize important inflection points—as well as breaking points. We'll decipher the real meaning of our romantic text messages.

Together, we'll go from speaking in tongues to *speaking in thumbs.*

PART 1

Swiping

Mixed Emojis

OUR LOVE/HATE RELATIONSHIP WITH ONLINE DATING

Sinead: My app says we are a 94% match!

> **Rosalyn:** Mine too. Maybe our profiles should go out on a date while we just keep texting here 😜

The pictures are cute. The bio clever. The face that beams up at you from the open app on your phone seems to want all the same things you do. Someone somewhere, or maybe it was an algorithm, determined that you're 94 percent compatible—whatever that means. Your finger is poised to swipe right, with all the anticipation that they'll swipe right as well; I mean, 94 percent compatible, surely they noticed that too. You'll match, meet, and the rest will be history.

If only it were so easy.

Endless strings of texts, fleeting trysts, an online crush on the person you imagine will be the future love of your life—they all form the mainstays of the online dating experience. There is excitement, anticipation, and enthusiasm. There is also ennui, alienation, and just plain exhaustion. If there is one thing that can be said about online dating, it's that it's rife with contradictions.

Even though it's my job to understand human behavior, I too have felt buffeted by the ups and downs of online dating. We can't help but embark on the journey with inflated expectations.

We're promised a whirlwind of choices, a crowd of suitors, a wondrous wizard of technology pulling the strings behind the curtain. But knowing that the process can be a drag, we simultaneously brace ourselves for disappointment. It's a story of mismatched expectations, a journey rife with paradoxes.

I once had a text exchange start like this:

> **Me:** Hi Mark
>
> **Mark:** Hello Mimi. Nice to connect with you
>
> **Me:** Likewise. Always fun to meet interesting people.
>
> **Mark:** I'll certainly try not to disappoint you.

I led with "fun" and "interesting"; Mark countered with "disappoint." Right out of the gate, he called out this tendency that many of us share, to brace for disappointment in the face of hope. He did so in a facetious way, flirtatiously acknowledging that the hand was his to lose—explicitly calling a low-stakes game as he diminished my expectations. Still, Mark was pointing to a truth about romance: the most perilous aspect is certainly its uncertainty. We say that we "fall" in love because the process feels inherently out of control.

One patient, after a nasty breakup, described to me her secret desire to "win at dating apps." While this is a nice fantasy, the reality is more akin to walking into a casino, where we might entertain ideas of life-changing jackpots, but it's the house that always wins. Online dating involves chance; players face unavoidable risk when they follow the usual advice to "put yourself out there." Bracing for disappointment may just be the price of admission for using the app.

Because online dating involves technology, and technology has reduced friction in so much of our lives, from ordering a pizza to calling a cab, we expect, consciously or not, that dating apps should somehow spare us all this uncertainty. Once our expectations are permitted to soar, no outcome is likely to please.

When I listen to people talk about their experiences with dating apps, I hear a litany of complaints: about conversations going nowhere, not getting second dates, ghosting, the notorious "bad algorithm." I also find a relentless pursuit of perfection, coupled with a lot of churn. "Men are like buses," said one of my patients. "There's another one every few minutes." Matches sound oddly disposable, rather than representations of actual human beings; chats are treated as transactional and fungible. People form an index of false assumptions, cognitive distortions, and puzzling conclusions. We are prisoners of the paradox.

In this chapter, we'll dig into the contradictions that surround online dating, how they affect us, and the neuroscience behind them. We'll also discover how the app that sits in the palm of our hand can be used as our tool, and not the reverse. Along the way we'll look at real-life examples, showing how we can put our words to work for us. It is only once we've grappled with our mixed feelings about the *medium* that we can get to the *messages*.

The Paradox of Familiarity

What are we most attracted to, the familiar or the novel?

> **Duncan:** Hi there—loved your profile. It was very authentic!
>
> **Duncan:** Has London always been your home?
>
> **Duncan:** I really want to hear back from you!

Sarah: Hey . . .

Sarah: No, London has not always been my home, I'm originally from California

Duncan: Ah, I lived in California for ten years. Loved it.

Duncan: What are you up to tonight?

Sarah: I'm going out. Having a few drinks with friends

Duncan: well, I'd love to buy you a cocktail . . .

Duncan: is it a girls night?

Sarah: it is a girls night . . .

Duncan: I'll be grabbing a lovely dinner at the Hawksmoor

Sarah: Oh no, not a lovely dinner at Hawksmoor. At least the steak is good company 😆

Duncan: I'll be in Soho in the AM, if you are close we could grab a coffee

Sarah: Ah, thank you, very kind but I have plans tomorrow.

Duncan: I guess I'll just have a cosy Sunday at home then.

Sarah: A cosy Sunday at home . . . how Sundays are meant to be spent. I'm a Sunday morning with a cup of coffee and paper kinda girl. I look forward to it all week. Haha

Sarah: Was just putting the kettle on

Duncan: Are you making tea?

Sarah: Um yes, I'm a 90 year old woman in a 32 year old body. Such a homebody. Love cooking, Love reading. Love listening to records. Love a hot drink.

Duncan: So cute. I love electric blankets! It's the best when you wake up . . . and it's cold . . . then you turn on the blanket. Bliss!

Sarah: This is killing me. I used to actually put an electric blanket under my mattress topper. So you could turn it on before getting into bed, and then get into a warm bed. That was bliss.

Duncan: Same same! See, we both like to be cosy. Of course, cuddling is the #1 best warm feeling. 😍💕

Sarah: But. When life does not permit . . . an electric blanket and a cup of tea will do.

Duncan: . . . lol, you're cute. So British

Duncan and Sarah are off to a tepid start. Actually, they have quite a few degrees to go before reaching tepid. But with all the chat about electric blankets and hot tea, Sarah is slowly warming up. One does have the sense that had Sarah said she was a vegetarian, Duncan would have immediately let go of his steak house dinner plans and gushed instead about his love of zucchini. Nonetheless, she is reassured by their shared delights in the small things. Her texts suggest someone who values comfort over excitement.

Everyone falls somewhere on the spectrum. On one end is what's known as novelty seeking; on the other is harm avoidance. The psychiatrist Robert Cloninger has elaborated on the subject. Those high in novelty seeking, he argues, will be consistently more attracted to the unfamiliar and less risk averse. At the extreme, their bucket lists might include skydiving, mountaineering, or even extreme sexual practices. More moderate novelty seekers will be satisfied with trying a new recipe or visiting a new store at the mall. Those high in harm avoidance, meanwhile, will seek security and familiarity, rarely roaming out of their comfort zone. In the next chapter we will explore how to identify where the person you are texting with falls within these categories, using only their text messages as clues.

For now, let's consider a more adventurous pair. Brittany and Kevin, both in their twenties, get right into fantasy and risk taking in their initial text exchange. They both clearly prefer the excitement of the unknown to the quotidian and familiar.

> **Brittany:** Why do I feel like your fantasy is chloroforming unsuspecting women, only for them to find themselves handcuffed in your sex dungeon

> **Brittany:** If that's the case, the safe word is pamplemousse

> **Kevin:** You missed the important part where I was unknowingly given a ketamine injection and walk in, lose consciousness, and wake up tied to a 4 corner bed

> **Kevin:** Plot twist!

> **Kevin:** I hope that pamplemousse is still the safe word

Familiarity comes in different flavors.

So we vary in the way we're drawn to novelty. But how much do we even *want* to know about a stranger as we decide whether to embark upon the next step? Are we more likely to swipe right the more we know about a person? In other words, does information help or hurt our first impressions? One body of research indicates that the more we know about a person up front, the less likely we are to like them. Another says that familiarity leads to liking and attraction. How do we reconcile these contradictions?

Michael Norton, a member of the Behavioral Insights Group at Harvard Business School, has spent his career finding answers to questions about our behavior as it concerns love, money, and happiness. He sought to understand whether knowing more about a person (or their dating profile) would lead to greater feelings of attraction. He and his colleagues Jeana Frost and Dan Ariely had noted that users' satisfaction and engagement with online dating as a whole plummeted quickly after an initial spike. They wanted to understand why. So they did what all curious researchers do: they designed a study.

Norton and his colleagues showed hundreds of online daters a series of potential matches along with anywhere from one to ten personality traits that were randomly chosen from a list of two hundred typical profile traits—such as age, income, athleticism, or religion. The study participants then rated the profiles. Interestingly, the more traits the participants were shown, the lower they rated the profiles. In other words, the more they were told about a potential date, the less appealing that date became.

Norton tells me his team wasn't particularly surprised by the results but that dating app users usually are. "We *think* that if we know more about someone, we will like them more," he says, "because all the people that we love in our life are people that we know a lot about.

"But," Norton adds, "that's because there are a whole lot of people we never gave the chance to. We hand select the ones we like, and choose to get to know them better."

Their study concluded that ambiguous or vague information about a person leads to interest, whereas, as the old saying goes, familiarity breeds contempt. On average, the authors showed, the more you learn about any new random prospective partner, the less excited about them you will be.

"There is nothing worse," said my friend Margaret, who has been on enough first dates to have co-authored this book with me, "than when a guy can't maintain some sense of mystery at the outset." I couldn't agree more. Consider my initial text exchange with Doug, where my interest quickly evaporated:

Me: Where in WI are you from?

Doug: Stevens point (in the middle)

Me: How can a point be in the middle?

Doug: Good question. It's the point where the Wisconsin river bends.

Me: Ah, I lived in Minnesota during medical school. Followed my college boyfriend there.

Doug: Nice—how's the online dating world treating you? Been single for awhile or recently may I ask

Me: Well I was married for a long time. And now enjoying not being married. Why do you ask?

Doug: Just inquisitive I guess. I find this process so much work.

Doug's final text bubble is the romantic equivalent of moaning at a job interview about the fact that you had to shave that morning in order to look presentable. Even if it's true, that is not what's going to land you the job. *Sprezzatura* is an Italian word that means studied carelessness, or graceful nonchalance. Essentially, it means making it look easy. While it would not have occurred to me to put *sprezzatura* on a list of qualities I was looking for, if I'm honest with myself, I can say that without a bit of *sprezzatura* at the outset, there is no seduction. Learning about Doug was starting to feel like a chore.

Why would knowing more about someone repel us from

them? Norton and his colleagues found that people tend to latch on to something in a profile that they disagree with or find unappealing, and their interest plummets from there as expectations begin to sag under the weight of the accumulated information. With only vague information, we can still project imaginary qualities onto a person and maintain high expectations. Too much information only bursts our bubble of hope.

They went a step further. In their next experiment, the researchers surveyed two groups of online daters. One group responded to questions about a future planned date, and a second group responded to questions about a date that had already taken place. Expectations far exceeded outcomes; pre-date scores were wildly higher than post-date scores. Imagining a future date was more satisfying than the date itself!

Norton described another discouraging finding: "People who had been on more dates with online matches felt worse about their most recent date." So having more points of comparison—more experiences to think back on—made people more critical. The more options they'd had, the pickier they got. Paradoxically, Norton noted, these same people continued to be just as optimistic about their next date as they'd been at the start. They were souring on past dates, but they weren't learning to adjust their expectations for the future.

So does familiarity in fact breed contempt? In real life, or IRL, probably not. Once people have passed our initial screening, Norton suggests, and we've decided we want to truly interact and get to know them, more interaction will encourage affinity and affection.

Harry Reis, a professor of psychology at the University of Rochester, looks at a different side of the relationship coin. He studies the factors that influence the frequency and closeness of our social ties, particularly how they can help predict intimacy, attachment, and emotional regulation. Among Reis and his colleagues' revelations is that having confidence that a person will respond to you, increased comfort during your interactions with them, and greater perceived knowledge about the other person (feeling that you are getting to know them) leads to liking and attraction.

These factors may seem intuitive enough. For some of us, though, there is another paradox at play. Many of us find comfort in identifying *flaws* in the person we are chatting with. Perhaps we prefer to see a few faults at the beginning—an endearing tendency to misspell, a crooked facial feature in a profile picture— rather than thinking someone is perfect and having them let us down later.

Bennet touches on this notion of imperfection in our initial conversation:

> **Bennet:** That is a fine looking bike. I must confess a slight love for slightly less than perfect gear. As the Japanese 16th century tea master Sen no Rikyu said "In the tea room, all the utensils should be slightly less than adequate" Perhaps this is why I don't do ironmans?

> **Me:** I watched a movie about the Japanese philosophy of the imperfect. I subscribe to that with my wrinkles. Perfectly imperfect, right?

> **Bennet:** It is the whole wabi-sabi concept: the beauty of the imperfections and the beauty of age. And what wrinkles? I don't see any

> **Me:** Hmm—you might need to get your eyes checked. Reading glasses?

> **Bennet:** Yes indeed. And I'm wearing them

Me: I just got some reading glasses for the first time in my life and I'm now amazed at the wrinkles on my face that I had no idea that I had!

Bennet: There's a nice softness now to life when I don't wear mine.

Bennet: it makes the world look like a 1970 Vogue pictorial. So you could do worse.

Do faults make a person seem more accessible? IRL dating so often evolves as a process of disillusionment as that gem we spied online starts to show some cracks. It may be that it's appealing to start from a place of reality, and to enjoy a process of gradual *illusionment* as you fall in love.

Whatever the reason, this trade-off—between the comfort in what we know and the thrill or disappointment in what we don't—will always be at play in our online dating. Seeking new experiences will always involve risk taking; we must trade some sense of security in order to find it. This inherent tension pervades our romantic pursuits as we vacillate between the familiar and the foreign.

The Same but Different

There's a curious wrinkle in all this discussion of comfort and novelty, one that I've observed over the years with my patients. When they are attracted to someone who is not their usual type, I sense that they may be unconsciously sniffing out an essence of something familiar—or even familial. Attraction might be best summarized as something novel that *resembles* something familiar. We are less attracted to fully familiar people because, we presume, we know all their flaws. Familiarity, however, remains important in our relationships because it allows us to identify with another person. The potential of an online profile seems only greater if it matches our previous criteria of what a partner should be like. So we are likely most attracted to what is only *incrementally* new. It's familiarity but with a twist.

When I began chatting with Paulo, we had much in common: interests, political views, tastes. Then he surprised me:

Paulo: Question—somewhat of a touchstone question, at that . . . do you have any interest in shooting pistols?

Me: Who were you planning on shooting?

Paulo: Well, it pays to practice before choosing WHO . . .

Me: Are you a gun owner?

Paulo: I recently became one.

Paulo: No really rational reason.

Me: Impending zombie apocalypse

Paulo: There might be that in the backfield.

Me: Whatcha got?

Paulo: 9mm

Me: Ammo?

Paulo: Range only

Paulo: I only have about 100 rounds . . . CA is quite strict.

Me: I know

Me: There is Nevada

Paulo: But we could do 50 each.

Me: I have to go there to get Fois gras too

Paulo: Now you're talking!

Paulo: Thelma & Louise & Julia . . . Natural Born Gourmands!

Me: Some might not encourage me to go off on a remote weekend with a stranger that involves guns.

Paulo: True.

Paulo: I'll give you the key.

Me: Lol—to what?

Paulo: The lockbox

Me: Shoot, I thought you meant your heart

Paulo: Piano, piano . . . Lentamente, carina.

I can't say I had been planning to become a member of the NRA. Still, I found myself attracted to Paulo. He was well read, had lived in many countries, was emotionally sensitive. He also owned a gun and could chop wood for me. He was familiar, but with a twist.

The psychologist Sheena Iyengar, author of *The Art of Choosing,* studied this notion when her research group looked at how people embrace new things. They showed subjects items such as shoes or sunglasses from a set of choices, then asked them to rate the items on two scales: how much they liked them, and how unusual they were. She found that most people *think* they like things that are more unusual than what everyone else likes. In fact, people largely liked the same things and liked things they perceived to be slightly unusual. Most didn't choose the really standard shoes or sunglasses, nor did they choose the really offbeat ones. What they wanted was something with a little bit of a kick. The same but different.

Let's look at the first text exchange between Solange and

James. Solange, a savvy psychologist in her thirties, is an enthusiastic online dater. She and James quickly connect over text because of their perceived similarities in philosophy and lifestyle. But their conversation is also spiked with excitement about the unknown.

Solange: Hi James. The personality that comes through your photos is fantastic. I share your love of joy and playfulness, not to mention burgers on brioche buns and committed polyamory (not necessarily in that order). And Karaoke! What songs do you sing?

James: Hi Solange. I super appreciate your thorough and well-worded message. It's so rare in dating apps! Journey and Chicago are at the top of the list. Can you believe I was at a karaoke bar and they had a rule: no ballads! What a terrible rule. I mean, seriously. I'm excited that you are also polyamorous. What's your experience so far?

Solange: Hi James, How can a karaoke bar possibly have a rule against ballads?! Ballads are "made" for karaoke. Or karaoke was made for ballads. One of those. As for me and polyamory, long story. I've had both monogamous and polyamorous relationships, mostly the latter. What I've discovered for myself is that polyamory is a mindset, a philosophy, not just a different set of rules. I like that each partner is responsible for managing their own jealousy and insecurities rather than treating these things as indicators of love and commitment. I like the idea that love is abundant rather than scarce, that there is enough for everyone. How about you?

> **James:** I've been polyamorous for awhile too. I started when I was in a phase of reinventing myself, and was open to exploring new things. But I'm past the exploration phase. I also know what I want and am looking for that. Something I tell people is that it's easy to find things when you're not sure of what you're looking for. It's very hard to find what you're looking for, when what you want is very specific. What I've found about polyamory is a lifelong journey into my own barriers to love, and separating a lot of concepts that I've conflated together. Would you be up for meeting soon? I think at the very least we could have a very connected vulnerable conversation.

Solange and James draw on common experiences to create a sense of familiarity. They reverberate in the tone of their messages and echo each other's language from the start. But the subject of polyamory, and the possibility of other partners in their lives, seems to inject some intrigue into the chat for each of them. They're coming from a place of similarity, but with the thrill of something new.

It's not only familiar personalities that we're drawn to. We are even attracted to people who look a bit like ourselves. One study demonstrated that Norwegian couples rated their partner's photograph as more attractive when it was digitally morphed to look ever so slightly more like themselves. ("Slightly" being the operative word: after greater than 22 percent resemblance the partner was deemed gross.) Similarly, couples with matching speech styles are more likely to stay together than those who speak differently. In Solange and James's text exchange, they almost sound like the same person.

There are some other revealing features tucked inside their

texts. You'll notice they sometimes read like a treatise on polyamory. There is little banter. Yes, there is the brief back-and-forth about karaoke, but other than that it's all personal disclosure. And while they are talking about sex, the conversation isn't actually sexy per se. It's as if they were taking a shortcut to intimacy by talking about intimate things, rather than creating their own version of it. They clearly both want to be perceived as sexual beings and to determine if their sexuality is compatible; that's a worthwhile pursuit. But the chat lacks some spark or, dare I say, chemistry. Having a connected conversation does not happen by *talking about* having one!

My hunch about the two was borne out IRL. Solange accepted James's invitation, and they met for a drink a few days later. James sat stiffly on his barstool, much less comfortable with the encounter than Solange had imagined he would be. He did not attempt to make even slight physical contact, and what had been a text thread about abundant love became, in person, a staid and pinched conversation. They never met again.

This outcome is all too common. While dating sites are in widespread use, a Pew Research Center study recently showed that only one in ten Americans say they have been in a committed relationship with someone they met on a dating app. A full 45 percent of recent users said their experience made them feel frustrated.

Take this initial text exchange between forty-two-year-old Dana and Dale. Dana works as a nurse, has two kids, and would like to meet someone, but she's been single for a while and trapped in what feels like a vortex of online dating chats that never really seem to go anywhere. Their conversation until this point has been playful and flirty, until Dana unexpectedly decides to bow out:

> **Dana:** I'm probably not the one for you. I'm fearful, middle-aged and mundane. There are some exciting moments, and there could be some rocking sex, but mostly what you get is the domesticity of a single mom with all that brings. Yuck.

> **Dale:** Hey, I'm more middle-aged and mundane and have been a single parent for longer. Not that this is a competition. And I'm really enjoying our chat.

> **Dana:** Well, I'm working like 17 hours a day and there are other reasons too. After I had the twins I lost a ton of weight and have way more damage to my body than a woman my age should have. I don't think your idea of sexy is a date that badly needs a tummy tuck.

Dana's self-deprecating words may betray some central character traits, as well as an underlying tendency to self-sabotage. We will explore what texts can reveal about character in the next chapter. But notice for now how badly she needs to safeguard against disappointment and rejection. The chasm between flirting over text and the reality of a relationship is just too big a leap for her to take. To many of us who have online dated, her feelings are all too real, whether or not we've ever divulged them to a stranger. It's an experience rife with hope, fear, and frustration.

And yet for all that, one recurring contradiction emerges: while people generally complain about the experience, they also can't put down the phone. There is something about online dating that keeps people, even Dana, coming back for more.

Sheila's chat with Neal sums this up in a nutshell. Sheila is thirty-one and has been burned more than once by online dating. But that doesn't stop her from trying. She's matched with

Neal, and they've launched into a long conversation about their relationship histories. Neal reveals a tendency to rescue women who seem to need help and then to worry he has no way out.

> **Sheila:** Do you think that is why you keep getting stuck in bad relationships?

> **Neal:** Could be. Never really told anyone this before. It's great talking to you. Really intimate.

> **Sheila:** Well, I just spent two weeks developing emotional intimacy with some guy who finally revealed that he has a regular girlfriend he's planning to move in with but is also beginning a relationship with another girl.

> **Neal:** That's awful! 😣 So glad I didn't move in with my girlfriend

> **Sheila:** Girlfriend? 🧐

> **Neal:** I mean my ex girlfriend.

It isn't clear whether that was a Freudian slip on Neal's part, or whether he was referring to a relationship he had in fact moved on from. Either way, Sheila will persist, with Neal or without him.

DA Stands for Dating Apps

"I had to uninstall my apps off my phone," said Chris, a twenty-eight-year-old private equity investor. "It's too easy to get sucked in, and then, before I know it, hours have gone by and I'm chatting with a belly dancer from Belize."

Are dating apps the new slot machines?

Like any addictive behavior that results in a chemical rush, dating apps are designed to hook you into receiving tiny jolts of pleasure. When a person is about to experience some kind of reward, the neurochemical dopamine is released into the brain. It's not the dopamine itself that makes you feel good; pleasure and euphoria are actually mediated by opioids that our brains produce (like endorphins). But dopamine helps the brain recognize incentive or imminent pleasure. The dopamine signal is the brain's way of saying, "Pay attention, you are about to get a reward—you need to remember this, so you can do it again." That reward can be anything from food, to kissing, to drugs, to gambling. It can even be playing or watching sports. Dopamine, which neuroscientists refer to as DA, is about learning and reinforcing what will feel good.

DA mediates behaviors that involve desire, motivation, hard work, passion, perseverance, novelty, and reward. These behaviors take on even more significance when the reward is uncertain. Give a rat a lever that it can press to receive a food treat, and you'll observe a burst of DA just before it gets the treat. Over time, as the rat consistently receives treats with each press of the lever, the DA response will attenuate. The food is still pleasurable, but it has become a known and certain reward, and so DA takes a backseat and no longer plays a driving role in the rat's brain circuitry. But if that treat is given intermittently and only random lever presses result in a reward, the brain's DA circuitry lights up like a Christmas tree when the reward is presented. Like a slot machine addict, the rat will abandon other pursuits and spend most of its time pulling the lever to see if a reward is coming. For the brain, a gamble holds much more interest than a sure thing.

What makes social media and dating apps so addictive is the unpredictable element that random human behavior so naturally provides. Your post is liked a lot or a little. Your swipe reveals a match or it doesn't. A new message awaits, bearing excitement or disappointment. Like in a casino, you are surrounded by flashing lights and ringing bells. Everyone is winning—intermittently and unpredictably.

Most of us, at any given moment, can reach for our phones without moving our feet. At night, we keep our phones at our bedsides. Dating apps may be the last thing we engage with before drifting off to sleep and the first when we wake up. There is even a faux-Greek word for the feeling of withdrawal from our phones—"nomophobia," or "fear of no mobile." In a 2011 study, one-third of Americans polled said they would rather give up sex than their phones. And the phones have only gotten better since then! (The sex, who can say?) We can only imagine what pursuits are being abandoned or neglected in favor of the screens in our pockets.

There can be a fine line between habit and addiction. A habit is just a behavior done with little thought involved. It develops because we reinforce it, both consciously and unconsciously. Habits can be healthy, like flossing and exercise, or unhealthy, like smoking and snacking. They are considered addictions when the behavior becomes so persistent and compulsive that it hurts the user or takes away from important aspects of their lives, impairing their ability to function.

Can swiping become an addiction? It certainly can. It all depends on what toll it takes on your life and relationships. Dating apps are yet another addictive offshoot of the tech industry, designed to hook the user into a mentality of "but wait, there's more." The cost of all that choice and connection is the ensuing lack of attention to, and disconnection from, what might be right in front of you.

The Paradox of Choice

"After I've been dating someone for a while, it's almost like the dating app knows our phones have been hanging out in the same location together," says my patient Graham, a forty-year-old creative director who moves from one intense short-term relationship to the next every few weeks. "The app starts to notify me of all the new possibilities," he says. "It's hard not to start swiping and see what might be better."

I'm not sure if this surveillance feature is actually built into dating apps, but I do know this: Graham is dogged by choice.

With scores of swipeable faces at the tip of our thumbs, dating apps can leave us less decisive than ever. Apps give us access to so many more choices than we would otherwise meet in daily life. But it turns out our brains are not built to process so many alternatives. Once faced with double digits of choices, we reach cognitive overload.

Research out of Temple University's Center for Neural Decision Making has shown that when people are given complex information, activity in the dorsolateral prefrontal cortex ramps up, but only to a point. After too much information is presented, this executive area of the brain switches off, much like an overloaded circuit breaker. In addition, areas responsible for anxiety in the brain become more active. Our dopamine systems may go into overdrive and ultimately shut down, paralyzed. In these states, we don't and can't make a choice.

Professor Barry Schwartz of Swarthmore College has spent years advancing his argument about "the paradox of choice": that too much choice leads to poorer outcomes and makes us less happy. In one famous experiment, dubbed the jam study, shoppers presented with too many gourmet jam choices were unable to complete their purchase. The ones who did purchase were unhappier with their purchase than people presented with fewer choices.

Schwartz thinks there is value to limiting our choices and, beyond that, that one of the secrets to happiness is mitigating our expectations. More choices come with more agonizing over those choices, more responsibility for them, and more potential for regret. Schwartz's lectures are often peppered with cartoons. One that he likes to show to illustrate this point is of a college student wearing a sweatshirt emblazoned with "Brown but my first choice was Yale." Another is of a couple at the altar in which the bride is uttering the phrase "You'll do" instead of "I do."

Joe's text to Allie sums up the sentiment:

Joe: You da bomb.

Allie: Aww . . . I think you're really great too.

Joe: and if I hadn't just started chasing this redhead I'd probably have tried to seduce you. 😊

Allie: Gotcha. Guess I'll take that as a compliment?

Is choice overwhelming us in our dating lives? Schwartz thinks so, but with higher stakes than any jar of jam. His collaborator Sheena Iyengar agrees. "Oh, it's a huge problem, right? It's what we call FOMO [fear of missing out]. Barry Schwartz and I first identified it in the domain of job search. And the same thing is happening at a much larger level when it comes to dating," she says. "You have so many options, and, in many ways, these are incomparable options because you're comparing humans."

Mandy learned this all too well when she found herself texting with several women after first joining a dating app. After hooking up with the woman who is now her partner, she had the following exchange with another woman, who also held some appeal:

> **Hallie:** Can we set up a time now to meet? What's good for you? PS your dog is so beautiful (your kids too!) I have a hankering for a dog. Yum!

> **Mandy:** Hi Hallie—I don't mean to be hard to pin down, I'm just still figuring out how to do this whole online dating thing! How about we meet up live & low key somewhere?

> **Hallie:** Sure I'm game. What do you suggest?

> **Mandy:** Hi Hallie—apologies for the slow response, my dance card has kinda filled up, and I'm wanting to hit pause on connecting live with any new folks. If you're willing, we could possibly check in again in a few weeks, but for now . . . Be well, and best wishes, Mandy

It isn't just choosing between people that poses challenges. By continuing to browse and swipe on a dating app, we are also making a choice not to invest in any one match or relationship. "When there are lots and lots of options," Schwartz says, "people are less inclined to do the work." The work, when it comes to dating, is of course the hard and vulnerable effort involved in navigating a relationship. And as we've seen above, it's often the work of really learning about a person that makes you like them and attach to them over time. If you don't do so, you may find yourself stuck, like my patient Graham, in a cycle of fleeting, insignificant relationships.

In *The Paradox of Choice*, Schwartz uses the following quotation (which he admitted to me is probably wrongly attributed to

Camus): "Shall I kill myself, or have a cup of coffee?" The quotation especially resonated with me as a doctor who often works with suicidal patients; in therapy, I find it helpful to bring them back to life's small actions and pleasures. But Schwartz points out that the quotation underscores a simple fact: suicidal or not, we are always making choices, whether we know it or not. When we have a cup of coffee, we are unconsciously choosing not to commit suicide (also not to drink tea).

Presented with too many choices, the pleasure of choosing right is canceled out by the fear of making the wrong choice. The impulse to keep swiping on potential partners will inevitably win out.

We don't do ourselves any favors when we set unrealistic standards for our partners-to-be. In her book *Marry Him: The Case for Settling for Mr. Good Enough,* the psychotherapist Lori Gottlieb talks about the long list of requirements her future spouse would need to possess. When she brought this list to a traditional matchmaker, the matchmaker laughed and warned her that there were probably only three people in the world who met these criteria and *they* might not be into *her.*

Such lists can also fail to acknowledge subtle but important factors in attraction. Not long ago one of my patients described a guy she had met. He seemed perfect: tall, handsome, athletic, smart, accomplished, and wealthy. There was one problem, she said. "What, he hasn't written a concerto?" I said. No, she didn't like the sound of his voice.

Even if we were able to generate the ideal mate through a list that could be fed into an algorithm and matched, what are the chances we'd actually be attracted to that person? And what are the chances that person would be attracted to us? That brings us to the final paradox of online dating.

The Paradox of Learnability

In 1931, the Austrian mathematician and philosopher Kurt Gödel published his incompleteness theorem. Simply put, the theorem states that there are properly posed mathematical questions that cannot be proved from already self-evident propositions. These questions are thus deemed undecidable. In other words, some mathematical statements cannot be proved true or false using mathematical axioms, even though those mathematical axioms themselves cannot be proved false. Therein lay the paradox.

The idea that math is insufficient to understand some aspects of the universe may not seem shocking to non-mathematically minded people, but it was certainly shocking to the mathematical world of Gödel's time. Other mathematicians tried to challenge the theorem without success.

The theorem remains relevant to this day, particularly as it applies to machine learning and artificial intelligence (AI). Machine learning supposes that with a large enough data set and a sophisticated enough algorithm a machine can make accurate predictions. Show a computer enough images of a bird, devise a rule set for the computer to be able to identify certain features of a bird (a beak, wings, wide-spaced eyes), and over time the computer should be able to reliably distinguish birds from other animals. It has proven enormously effective in such fields as video surveillance, facial recognition, and medical diagnostics.

But you can't simply identify an ideal partner, reduce them down to a set of features, and run them through a machine. What the extension of Gödel's theorem shows is that no matter how powerful the computer or AI, a data set may never be enough to make certain predictions reliably. This was dubbed the learnability paradox. It's the notion that machine learning itself has an unsolvable problem at its core.

This abstract principle intersects with the world of dating precisely at the place where daters today congregate, on dating sites and apps—and specifically under the hood, in the much-vaunted *algorithms* that power those apps. Old-school online dating sites, like matchmaking services before them, led clients to believe in them through a process of refinement. Hundreds of questions were answered; an individual's profile could be pages long. With so many keystrokes up front, people necessarily felt invested and dependent on the outcome of the process. It is questionable whether much of this data was actually used; the sites and services likely just tossed available profiles your way. But it lent an air of seriousness, a patina of science, to the match-making. There could be a self-fulfilling prophecy to it all: you believed that your matches were well suited to you, and so you were more likely to give them a fair shot.

Over time, all the window dressing went, well, out the window. Now the strategy has evolved to maximize and optimize choice. Users who receive lots of right swipes will be ranked higher than those who don't, and they will be presented in turn with more desirable choices. A popularity contest, in other words.

There are other features beyond simple rank. Dating algorithms also learn from a user's prior swiping behavior. They operate under the same collaborative filtering principles that power your Facebook, Google, Netflix, and Amazon suggestions. Your prior decisions inform predictions about your preferences. If you haven't previously engaged with white people, for instance, the app may stop showing you images of white people. So the algorithms aren't actually predicting who might be compatible for you, but rather the likelihood of your right swipe. This may lead to users only being presented choices based on superficial criteria. Just because you swiped left on a bunch of people with tattoos doesn't mean you don't ever want to be shown someone with a tattoo, or that there is not a tattooed person out there who might be a good fit for you.

Might the concept of "the right match" fall into Gödel's learnability limbo, where no human-curated data set of right-swiped profiles is large enough to predict whom we might actually fall in love with? By focusing on a list of desired traits—like a degree from a prestigious college, or a person's taste in music, or their athletic lifestyle—might we miss important red flags? Could we be obscuring glaring personality traits, psychiatric diagnoses, or even the larger and more elusive question of "Could you really be into this person?"

Technology and artificial intelligence have begun to offer us the hope of knowability; whether they achieve it none of us will probably live to see. But in the meantime, they've also fueled our deepest existential fears. Killer robots, online propagandists, virtual reality that eclipses our real lives—these are features not just of Hollywood sci-fi but of our day-to-day existence. Almost everyone who has used a dating app has at some point wondered if they were chatting with a bot.

Take this dating app exchange that I once entered into. Well, not an exchange exactly . . .

> **Brian:** Hi Mimi, nice to connect. Brian.
>
> **Brian:** Mimi?
>
> > **Me:** Hi Brian. Looks like I missed this msg some time ago. Hope you had a good weekend.
>
> **Brian:** Hi Mimi. Let's try again.
>
> **Brian:** Hello
>
> **Brian:** Mimi?

Brian: Missed again 😎

Brian: Mimi, Harvard in common, how r u?

Brian: Mimi?

Brian: Hi Mimi

Brian: Hi Mimi. How r u?

Brian: 😊

Brian: Mimi? 😗

Brian: Mimi are you still around?

Brian: Mimi?

Brian: ??

Brian: So . . .

Brian: Hello . . .

Looking at this thread, it's hard not to wonder if Brian is a bot—a piece of lazily designed code. Then again, one would expect more sophisticated programming for a bot. This is likely just a faulty human.

So while dating apps certainly grant us choice and ease of communication, their algorithms are likely not their most useful feature. A pivotal study by Eli Finkel and colleagues at Northwestern University found that algorithms were very limited in their ability to predict compatibility and that the best predictors of a lasting relationship came from responses to "unpredictable and uncontrollable events that have not yet happened."

Michael Norton of Harvard Business School says that dating algorithms get a bad rap. "Yes, their claims may be overstated," he says, "but what they do is give you options that you wouldn't otherwise have. They present you with lots and lots of vaguely acceptable options. They are not going to provide you with a soul mate on the first try."

To put it another way, think of how a child interacts with a plastic toy. It can be the departure point for a wonderful session of play, becoming a magical universe in the small hands of the child. Or it can be an inert chunk of plastic. Likewise, dating apps offer you only a portal. Creating the magic and mystery is your job.

If, as Finkel's study concluded, "the best-established predictors of how a romantic relationship will develop can be known only after the relationship begins," then when does a relationship begin? With the very first text exchange, of course!

That is, if you know how to interpret it. As the comedian Chris Rock says, "When you meet somebody for the first time, you're not meeting them. You're meeting their representative." We'll look next at how to get past all the agents and managers and get to the person themselves.

CHAPTER 2

Can I Get Your Numbers?

FROM DATA SCIENCE TO DATING SCIENCE

Ian: OK, lets grab coffee . . . I'm downtown during the week. U able to get close?

Linsay: I work right there.

Ian: Meet at Caffe Illy?

Linsay: Would love to.

Ian: How about Tuesday?

Linsay: Great. Free at noon. You?

Ian: Just a strange time for coffee.

Ian: I usually have a cup in the AM and then another one around 3

Linsay: OK I can make 3pm work to adapt to your caffeine dosing. As long as you are flexible about when I smoke my crack. Because while I'm flexible with my caffeine intake, I have a strict schedule for that.

The first meeting over coffee. A true Norman Rockwell moment.

While Linsay might enjoy drinking coffee and picture herself with a coffee drinker—she probably even listed cappuccino as one of her favorite things—Ian's rigidity might be more telling than his caffeination habits. Because dating profiles reduce people to searchable attributes, like whether they drink coffee, daters may miss the more ineffable qualities, such as their flexibility and sense of humor. Does liking coffee really mean very much, given that 64 percent of American adults do? Who doesn't like long walks on the beach at sunset? And does saying that you are "funny," "easygoing," or "genuine" really mean very much, when we are hard-pressed to find a dating profile of a self-described boring, uptight, or disingenuous person. These are vacant data points.

In the case of "funny" or "genuine," showing is better than telling. My dear friend Andy, whom I met online, wrote in his bio, "I will make you laugh." He quickly did.

Andy: Hi Mimi. How could you hate Trump? He's got such great hair! And what kind of medicine do you practice?

Me: I'm a psychiatrist. Though I'm doing more work in digital health now.

Andy: Shrink-wrapped apps?

The last chapter highlighted the paradoxes that permeate online dating. We discovered that some aspects of the apps serve us well, such as giving us more options, while other aspects fall short, such as giving us options based on lists or choices that may not reflect our true desires. Dating apps are designed as marketplaces. What marketplaces do, economically speaking, is allow people to save time while finding what they want. But with dating, as we've seen, when we generate ideas of what we want or like, we are often looking for an experience that doesn't easily translate into a list of codable traits.

Just because the dating apps themselves tend to disappoint, we needn't gnash our teeth like Wild Things. There are other ways to capitalize on the choice dating apps offer us and extract from them the information we need. It simply requires taking creative steps to *find* that information.

In the text exchange that started this chapter, Linsay recognizes the possibility that Ian's coffee schedule represents a sign of rigidity, or lack of openness. She teases him by joking about the rules for her fictitious drug use. Ian is missing the point: it's a date, not a coffee break. Making an issue about what time they have coffee may foretell a lack of flexibility in his approach to relationships and an overly concrete way of approaching the world in general. With her teasing, Linsay, in turn, reveals her direct, slightly brash, risk-taking personality. That may not be Ian's cup of tea.

Snippets of a text conversation can help us make predictions about an individual's temperament, personality, and other dynamics that may manifest themselves throughout a relationship. These elements are often visible during our earliest texts exchanged with an individual, so it's useful to learn how to spot them. In this chapter we will look at what it means to extract meaningful data from such short bursts of conversation: the art and science of thin slicing.

"Thin slicing" is a term used in psychology to describe pattern recognition from narrow windows of experience, or a small subset of data. Typically, these conclusions are drawn subconsciously, as Malcolm Gladwell famously described in his book *Blink*. Part of what makes our brain so impressive is its ability to come to a sophisticated judgment in a very short reaction time. Brilliant examples of this are the hockey player Wayne Gretzky and his ability to "see" the ice, to take in all the players' positions and visualize shots with all of their angles in a single glance. Or the chess champion Garry Kasparov, who could envision future moves on a chessboard without having to explicitly calculate them. Likewise, a trained psychiatrist can learn to read and deduce a history of trauma, despair, or suicidal intent in a patient through a fleeting facial expression.

None of these seemingly innate and subconscious superpowers

came without intense training and practice. Gretzky famously spent countless hours as a child with a pen and paper in hand watching *Hockey Night in Canada,* tracing the movement of the puck, learning to intuitively recognize patterns others might not. Studying the masters enhances our own ability to thin slice.

Kasparov and Gretzky might have been masters in their own fields, but there are also masters of thin slicing as applied to behavioral science. One of these masters is Paul Ekman, a professor at the University of California, San Francisco Medical School, who has succeeded in thin slicing emotion through the recognition of what are known as facial microexpressions. By thoroughly cataloging the muscles involved in fleeting expressions, movements that last less than one-fifth of a second, Ekman can perceive the suggestions of fear, anger, or disgust that an untrained eye would miss.

A more pedestrian form of thin slicing takes place when we form first impressions from observing just a few seconds of a person's behavior. We've all done it—judged someone by their handshake, eye contact, or mannerisms. Frank Bernieri, a professor of psychology at Oregon State who specializes in social perception and judgment, is an expert in thin slicing as it applies to first impressions. He argues that first impressions are "prerational"; in other words, they happen at a gut level. They draw on our unconscious ability to find patterns in situations and behavior based on very narrow slices of experience.

They may also tap into bias and prejudice. The trick then is to make those first impressions as accurate as possible. That's where training comes in. With the right preparation, conclusions based on thin slicing can be as accurate as, or even more accurate than, ones based on more information. While most untrained people won't do better than a coin toss when it comes to deciphering if someone is lying, take a lie detection course such as the one taught at the FBI National Academy and you will improve your odds significantly.

Obviously, we can't rely on facial expressions, or any other visual cues for that matter, when it comes to thin slicing texts. But the technique applies just as effectively. Whether we are extracting important information from a first glance, a fleeting facial expression, or a few text messages, we are drawing broad conclusions from a small data set. By using initial text messages as a form of thin slicing, we can learn a great deal about a prospective date.

Before we jump into more of those all-important first texts, let's look at two more examples of thin slicing in behavioral science that rely more heavily on language. They'll help light the way as we move forward.

This Is Your Relationship Thin Sliced

A notorious example of thin slicing in the romantic arena is Dr. John Gottman's predictive work on relationship success. In his "Love Lab," Gottman records couples involved in spontaneous verbal conversations and arguments. He has collected decades' worth of data of couples' interactions while they are wired to sensors that record heart rate, sweat, and movements, and observing cameras document body language, facial expressions, and words. By coding the exchanges and modeling patterns, he's able to predict with 93.6 percent accuracy which couples will divorce and under what time frame. This, using only three minutes of a single conversation. Imagine, early in your courtship, being able to see the writing on the wall. Some couples might prefer not to know.

Yet knowing would be helpful and even actionable. Gottman argues that while there is no magic formula for love, there is useful advice hidden within the data. Much of his recipe for relationship success boils down to having a solid friendship, building trust, allowing your partner to influence you, and being gentle. Successful couples also make each other feel good physically; their blood pressure lowers during conversation rather than rising.

What's astounding is the way these macro concepts can be made visible in even the most micro of exchanges. Sometimes, for instance, a first text exchange is pure delight:

Me: Hi Damien. How are you?

> **Damien:** Holà Mimi! I am well. My map radius tool indicated that you are in Tahoe. Or Fresno. Or Legget. I'm voting heavily for Tahoe. Drop me a line when you repatriate.

Me: Strong work! Tahoe it is. Another great weekend of skiing. Home later today. I've never been to Legget. Have you?

> **Damien:** I have been to Legget. As a cosmopolitan polyglot, I find it a must. Unfortunately I have also been to Fresno.

Me: Yes, the 'no is to be avoided. What does a polyglot do on the eel river? Be in silence? I do love riding my bike up the north coast. There are some killer climbs out of Mendocino.

> **Damien:** I speak tree. Those pygmy pines on the road out of Mendocino have particularly wicked senses of humor. How is your week shaping up? Would you like to go down to the fountain and share a pop?

In my first exchange with Damien, it felt as if we were already speaking our own language, one that others might not easily understand. I suspect that if this exchange had taken place in

Gottman's lab, he would have captured the click in our conversation as playful attunement. Open-ended questions and deepening statements are certainly there. I can attest that Damien's texts made me smile and feel good on a physical level. For lack of a better word, I guess we grokked.

Thin Slicing in Mental Health

Gottman studied live interactions, but reliable predictions can be drawn from text alone. One powerful example comes not from the study of romantic relationships but from the world of mental health. Crisis Text Line (CTL) is a company founded by Nancy Lublin, a serial entrepreneur known for her persistence and grit. Crisis Text Line's trained counselors volunteer their time to field millions of text messages from individuals who reach out in need. The company emerged from another nonprofit of Lublin's called Do Something, designed to mobilize teens to volunteer for worthy causes. The best way to reach teens was through text messaging, of course, and as Do Something was successfully reaching millions of teens, it would also get texts back in reply. Scattered among the largely positive messages that were coming in were a few upsetting texts, like "I'm being bullied" or "My friend is addicted to crystal meth."

Then there was the single disturbing text message that compelled Lublin to action. One day, her team received a text that said, "He won't stop raping me. It's my dad. He told me not to tell anyone." Followed by "R U there?"

And so Lublin built Crisis Text Line. Since then, the company's counselors have provided daily lifesaving interventions to people with depression, with anxiety, in abusive situations, or struggling with suicidal thoughts. Sometimes all four at once. To field and triage the millions and millions of messages that CTL receives, the company has created algorithms using key words and word pairings that can serve as markers of acuity. Using words like "die," "suicide," and "overdose," of course, bumps you to the front of the queue. But in their analysis of the data, they have also found some less expected correlations between text content and the risk it presents. Want to take a guess at the most lethal words found in a text message, the words most likely to lead to an active rescue? Most of us would guess that "suicide" and "die" would rank high, but in fact "Excedrin," "ibuprofen," and "800 mg" top the list. The word "ibuprofen" was sixteen times more likely to predict that the person texting would need emergency services than the word "suicide."

It's a different kind of thin slicing, based on data science and the parsing of text language, but it allows the service to get back to high-risk texters in under five minutes, with an average response time of under one minute. Velocity like this would be impossible without sophisticated data science humming in the background.

Crisis Text Line has managed to collect one of the largest health data sets in the world from diverse cross sections of society. These learnings help inform the company's own interventions, naturally, but they also reflect the state of American mental health as a whole. Where doctors see individual cases, Crisis Text Line can see trends.

So, Ekman can read intent from a fleeting facial expression, Gottman is able to predict a relationship's success from a snippet of conversation, and Crisis Text Line is able to make risk assessment predictions from a text message. What about predicting someone's personality or character from their dating texts? Are there certain words that telescope "serial killer"? Are there word combinations that communicate "bunny boiler"?

In order for us to talk about personality, we need to establish a shared vocabulary. So let's look at how scientists measure and characterize it. We'll be using this language throughout the chapters that follow as we encounter personalities big and small.

Personality Quantified

You've probably come across many different varieties of personality tests. Companies commonly use the Myers-Briggs Type Indicator in the hiring or team-building process, business coaches sometimes use the Enneagram, and bizarre clickbait quizzes have popped up in your Facebook feed—everything from which Disney princess you are, to which Harry Potter house you should live in based on your preferred Taylor Swift tune. While these personality tests may be entertaining, some may be as useful as your daily horoscope.

One test stands above the others in both scientific validity (it measures what it says it will measure) and reliability (it produces consistent results), and that is the Big Five personality test. The Big Five, otherwise known as the Five Factor Model (FFM), describes personality along five dimensions: openness, conscientiousness, extroversion, agreeableness, and neuroticism. (Think of the acronym OCEAN.) Researchers have argued for the biological basis and universality of the Big Five, and that it transcends language and cultural differences, though in fairness it's mostly been validated in literate, urban populations.

The Big Five personality dimensions emerged from research done on the words people used to describe themselves, and they have been used to predict many things, from academic achievement to dating behavior. With the FFM, people aren't categorized or boxed into distinct personality types; instead, each person falls somewhere on a spectrum. So, for example, instead of proclaiming me an ENFP (as the Myers-Briggs did), the Big Five test tells me that I am very high both in extroversion and in openness to experience, high in conscientiousness, while low in neuroticism and only moderately agreeable.

People high in **openness to experience,** as the name implies, are curious and imaginative. High scorers tend to be artistic and appreciate diverse views, ideas, and experiences. People low on this scale are more traditional, dislike change, and may struggle with abstract thinking.

Conscientiousness relates to responsibility and productivity. High scorers tend to be organized and persevering. These individuals are also extremely reliable and tend to be high achievers, hard workers, and planners. At the other end of the spectrum, those low in conscientiousness dislike structure and have a tendency to procrastinate or fail to complete tasks.

Those high in **extroversion** have stronger friendship ties and support systems. They tend to be more outgoing, amicable, and assertive. Friendly and energetic, extroverts draw inspiration from social situations. In contrast, introverts enjoy more solitary experiences and dislike small talk. They produce less dopamine in response to human faces.

Agreeableness can be broken down into compassion, respectfulness, and trust in others. People high in agreeableness tend to be cooperative, helpful, nurturing. They are the peacekeepers and are generally optimistic and trusting of others. Those very low in agreeableness take little interest in others and may be insulting, callous, or manipulative. But being somewhat low in agreeableness can also confer some advantages. These individuals will find it easier to work alone, make difficult decisions, and set boundaries for themselves.

Finally, people high in **neuroticism** are more likely to suffer from depression, anxiety, and substance abuse; they will experience more worry, fear, anger, guilt, and even jealousy. They can be insecure, sensitive, moody, and tense and easily tip into negative emotions. Those low in neuroticism tend to be emotionally stable and handle stress well. Those lowest would be likened to a tall, cool glass of water.

The refreshing thing about the Big Five personality test is that rather than categorizing people as purely extroverted or purely introverted, for example, it rates them on a scale of 0 to 100, for their propensity toward one pole of each of the five dimensions. Most people will fall somewhere in the middle.

How do Big Five scores predict our romantic life? High neuroticism scores seem to be particularly hard on relationships. Neurotics will experience more worry, mood swings, and irritability, and this seems to take a toll on long-term relationship satisfaction. An interesting exception: if a couple is having a lot of sex, that seems to offset the negative impact of neuroticism. So if you are going to pick a neurotic, pick one with a strong libido. The bad news is that neuroticism also appears to generally interfere with healthy sexuality. In more than one study, neuroticism predicted both lower relationship satisfaction and lower sexual satisfaction.

High levels of conscientiousness and agreeableness lend themselves to relationships high in trust. People high in these dimensions tend to be more successful in long-term relationships. Low levels, in contrast, predict novelty seeking, which may also correlate with sexual risk taking. In one study of sixteen thousand people from fifty-two countries, it predicted infidelity. In a meta-analysis, researchers out of the University of Kentucky found that low agreeableness also predicted casual sex with strangers, failure to use condoms, and a large number of partners.

Openness to experience seems to predict, at least among

women, more frequent and varied sex. And, as we've seen among the neurotics, sex seems to help only long-term relationships. Extroverts are generally happier and more charismatic, have better developed relationship skills, and are better adjusted sexually. Being with an extrovert is fun, but understand that they will likely be more adventurous and may have more difficulty with relationship exclusivity.

The Big Five results are generated by collecting subjective responses to a variety of statements. So they are based on *our own* impression of ourselves. But what happens if the way I see myself is different from the way others see me? We'll take a deeper dive into self-knowledge, self-awareness, and insight in the next chapter.

The Big Five in Textspeak

For now, let's think about the way text allows us to reveal ourselves and discover others'. There is a long history of research at the intersection of language usage and personality, but new developments in data science have powered this analysis to new levels. Previously, it was hard to get someone to sit down and write thousands of words. Now, as posting, texting, and tweeting feature more centrally in communication, we can analyze at large scale, and it's suddenly possible to discover trends that were harder to see in small writing samples. Just as Crisis Text Line was able to see trends because of the size of its data set, the power of computing has made it possible to thin slice texts and tweets for personality traits.

The inherent value in text messages, in particular, is that they exist in the space between spoken language and formal writing. With texts and tweets, people are less bound by the rules of grammar, punctuation, and syntax. Free from those constraints, they can express themselves in personal and unique ways that reveal their character and style. To experts like Celia Klin, a professor of the psychology of language at Binghamton University, texting looks more like speaking and less like writing. The words are important, but so is the social information they convey.

"Because many of those visual social cues are missing in text"—the eye contact, inflection, facial expressions—"people have adopted brilliant new language uses in their texting to convey meaning," Klin told me. "It's not surprising," she says, "because language is one of the things we do best in life." But there is potential for misunderstanding. "Even when people proofread their texts, they tend to hear their own voice in their head with tone and nuance and believe that is exactly how it is heard by the reader."

Still, word choice can be telling. Even single-word analysis is interesting: extroverts use the word "mouth" more frequently, along with "drinks," "other," "restaurant," and "dancing." Those high in neuroticism, in contrast, are drawn to using the words "awful," "though," "lazy," and "depressing."

The masters of long-term relationships, those high in the agreeable dimension, will use the words "wonderful," "together," "morning," and "spring" with greater frequency. Those extremely conscientious types will pepper their language with "completed," "stupid," "boring," and "adventure." Those *actually* open to adventure—the ones high on the openness scale—will favor the words "folk," "human," "poetry," "universe," "art," and "always."

Take my first words with Charlie, who showed immediate signs of openness in his language:

Me: Hi Charlie

Charlie: Mimi!

Me: Don't think I've seen the tooth brushing bathroom selfie before—very innovative.

Charlie: I like to push the boundaries of life :)

Charlie: It's also my way of cleaning up the bathroom selfie

Me: It's good. I'll be sure to credit you when it goes viral. How was your week? Mine has been brutal. Imagine my disappointment upon realizing that today is only Thursday.

Charlie: You've had a tremendous victory in losing track of time. Mine has been a poignant and precious week.

"Push the boundaries," "life," "poignant and precious," and "losing track of time" all appeared within four text bubbles. My own highly "open to experience" dimension was curious to learn more about Charlie, whose words evinced an equal openness to experience, even though I was a bit grumpy at the time ("brutal" and "disappointment," anyone?).

As I chatted with Charlie further, his agreeable nature had a chance to emerge. I had learned he was a psychologist and joked that my Australian shepherd should hire him.

Me: I have a crazy dog who needs your help. She is afraid of men with beards and baseball caps and also skateboarders. Can you blame her on the latter?

Charlie: I am afraid of all those things as well.

Me: You guys are two peas in a pod. She is an awesome runner and swimmer—will follow me for two miles in open water and will bleed for me on trails.

Charlie: Yes, I will follow you for two miles and bleed for you on trails.

Me: Wow! That was a quick commitment

> **Charlie:** I'm not concerned, except for the bleeding part

> **Me:** I'll bring bandaids. And take care of your ego.

> **Charlie:** OK thank you. My ego is soft and squishy and very flexible.

Besides being funny and endearing, Charlie uses empathetic language. He makes sure to relate not just to me but also to my dog. He indicates his willingness to trust by jokingly volunteering to "bleed" for me. And he's confident enough to use the words "soft and squishy," not words many men use in their initial texts (though in his photos he looks lean and muscular).

Single words are useful, but the magic comes in word pairings. IBM came up with a personality insights tool for its Watson supercomputer that it boldly claimed could make an accurate personality assessment based on a writing sample of just a hundred words. IBM's published correlations are far from perfect, but they represent a reasonable start for certain use cases such as dating apps, and a good preview of the potential for what has been precociously called artificial intelligence.

The Fingerprints of Illness

Digital behavioral health companies have leveraged this kind of data analysis, as well as what we refer to as augmented intelligence, in order to make a **provisional diagnosis,** that is, one that has not been confirmed by a face-to-face encounter. We say "augmented" rather than "artificial" intelligence, because it is important to keep in mind that the human cannot be fully removed from these equations, just as it is important to point out that any diagnosis based on text messaging is necessarily provisional. The notion is less to predict psychiatric diagnoses than to look at attributes in text that predict personality traits and psychological tendencies.

Nonetheless, what we say and write can be indicators of our mental health, and writing analyzed by sophisticated cognitive systems can provide insight into personality traits but also early-stage mental illness. For example, MIT researchers trained a computer to recognize depression and accurately predict it in context-free, natural, flowing text conversation. Using text messages, the model accurately detected depression using an average of seven question-answer sequences without ever requiring certain questions such as "Are you feeling depressed?"

One study looked at 6,202 Twitter users who tweeted words like "alone" or "lonely" more than five times during the study period. It then compared the entire Twitter timelines of these users with a matched group who did not use similar language in their posts. Users who used this language also reflected themes about difficult interpersonal relationships, substance use, body complaints, their need for change, and insomnia. Not surprisingly, the words "alone" and "lonely" have an extremely high association with depression and anxiety.

A Czech study asked 124 female students attending psychology seminars to write an essay about their deepest thoughts and feelings about college. The students also completed a clinically validated depression inventory scale that divided them into groups of currently depressed, formerly depressed, and never-depressed people. Depressives were found, predictably, to use more anger words, anxiety words, and negative emotion words. But the authors also discovered that more use of the word "I" (pronouns in the first-person singular) correlated with depression and that depressives had significantly scarcer use of the pronouns in the second and third person.

In larger-scale studies that have been conducted to examine both text and tweet content, patterns emerge. Mentions of one's work suggest conscientiousness and openness. Mentions of money can indicate lack of agreeableness. So, in turn, do terms of achievement like "win" and "earn." Language centered on illness, like "clinic," "flu," and "pill," correlates with introversion, and a lot of focus on bodily sensations and functions indicates neuroticism and a lack of openness.

There are certainly text exchanges that don't require sophisticated programming or a psychiatrist to understand. Sometimes you can read a thread and know a person is eccentric, for example. But eccentric in what way? Likewise, you don't need an expert to tell you when someone is behaving like a plain asshole. But most texts are more subtle. The goal, as you embark upon your initial exchanges with your dates and dates-to-be, is to recognize the suggestions of someone's personality tucked within the more overt messages.

In the following exchange after an initial date, Rob demonstrates both his conscientiousness and his lack of openness:

Rob: Hi Helen—nice to meet you—back at home and knocked out my excel spreadsheets. Let me know if we can see each other again before your trip.

Helen: Hi Rob. Nice to meet you too and appreciate your thoughtfulness. It sounds like you want to move forward with immediacy and I'm not sure I'm able to bring that intensity to the equation, given my upcoming travel.

Rob: Hmm I usually come to the date with the blueprints, open to changes. But my intensity and I had a chat, and she's going to take some time off;-) I hope you have a good trip.

Rob: But I do wonder what you think? I don't believe in chemistry, to me it's just a buzz word, a person deserves to know why he/she is liked or not . . . facts. Would you rather go for intense and decent or fun and trashy?

Helen: I'll sleep on it. Tomorrow my roommate will be home, perhaps we could all cook together and then ask if he thinks we're compatible? Get some outside perspective??

Rob: Well, I'm expecting you to know what's good (or not) for you. Full disclosure, I've had a few bad experiences with ex's family and friends, to the point of wondering how many of us were in the relationship.

Rob has some insight: he knows he is intense, albeit in a decent and committed way. But he doesn't seem to understand why this might scare Helen. His references to spreadsheets, blueprints, and facts are signs of both his conscientiousness and his rigidity—his lack of openness. These features might be appealing to some, off-putting to others, but they are likely intimidating to someone with Helen's neuroticism. Her inability to trust her own choices, looking to others to guide her decisions, indicates some underlying anxiety. The chances for this relationship are distinctly less than average.

The Grammar Detective

What about our grammar and the structural aspects of our sentences? What can we learn from those? Quite a bit, as it turns out. People who frequently use second-person pronouns like "you" and "your" will tend to be more agreeable and conscientious. On the other hand, those who bandy about negations (like "no" and "never"), revert to the future tense (for example, "will" and "gonna"), and draw on cognitive discrepancies—differences between the actual and the ideal, like "shoulda," "coulda," "woulda"—will likely be less conscientious.

Let's look at a text exchange and see if we can recognize some key personality features related to grammar and syntax. Conrad, a banker, wrote in his profile, "I am good to myself, smile a lot, and don't see the need to be anything but young." Marie is a therapist.

Marie: Hi Conrad. Nice to meet you.

Conrad: Hey! Sorry for the slow response. Life intervenes

Marie: No worries! I hope you're having a good day.

Conrad: Yeah, super busy today

Marie: Aren't the markets closed?

Conrad: What, really? Is that why there are no numbers on my computer? Busy with other stuff. Gotta clean house—Mom is visiting this week. Should've done it earlier.

Marie: Awww, sweet. Do you only clean the house when your mom visits?

Conrad: Hahaha. It's like when you go on a date. You clean better.

Marie: Hmmm, interesting. You talk about your mom and dating. What would Freud say?

Conrad: Sorry but after we matched I decided I never should've swiped right. We would never get along.

Marie: I see—why is that?

Conrad: I don't believe in therapy. Treatment for me would be like a broken pencil. Pointless. Hahaha.

> **Conrad:** People pay someone to listen to them then they just say nice things about themselves to try and impress. It's like cleaning better before a date. Good luck to you.

Yes, this is one conversation at one point in time, but many telltale features of personality can be thin sliced from this text exchange. Marie's use of "Hmmm," "Awww," and "sweet" indicates an agreeable nature. She also uses question marks and second-person pronouns a lot. She seems interested in others. Conrad, in contrast, asks questions only sarcastically and uses negations ("never," "pointless") and cognitive discrepancies galore ("should," "would"). Many aspects of his texts point to a lack of conscientiousness and agreeableness. A more traditional psychoanalyst might interpret his reference to a broken pencil as anxiety about his own sexual prowess, but we'll leave that for the therapy couch, should he ever decide to sink into it.

Characters in Characters

In text messages, we see all sorts of nonstandard forms of communication: omitted punctuation, added punctuation, all lowercase letters, and, of course, emojis. Jessica Bennett suggests in her *New York Times* column "When Your Punctuation Says It All (!)" that in texts too much punctuation can appear overeager, while not enough can be dismissive. Given the lack of spoken inflection in digital communication, it's no surprise that we have to pay more attention to punctuation to decode messages' meaning.

Can punctuation itself reveal personality? Perhaps. Analysis of tweets in conjunction with Big Five assessments has shown question marks to be a sign of extroversion. Presumably extroverts are more interested in asking questions. Colons correlate with conscientiousness, perhaps because they can be found in organized lists. Commas, conversely, correlate with a lack of conscientiousness.

Celia Klin's research group looked at the period and found that when people received a text message that ended with one, it was perceived as angry or rude. With no period to cap off the sentence, it was seen as friendlier. The formality of the period, especially at the end of a short text, created emotional distance for people and was consistently rated by readers as less sincere, more sarcastic, and perhaps passive-aggressive.

I have two friends (both of whom I met on dating sites) who assiduously use periods. They are both writers. When I asked one, early in my texting history with him, why his texts were always punctuated with a period, even if it was just a "Yes," he replied, "Without a period, the letters might fall off the end of the sentence."

What can we say about these period users in our life? They are picky people—maybe a tad overweening. They are adhering to their own standards and values, probably more willing to confront social norms with their own individual style. As we ourselves get closer to such types and grow to love them, we may be influenced by their style.

Gertrude Stein had strong feelings about punctuation. She apparently hated the exclamation point. F. Scott Fitzgerald reportedly said, "An exclamation mark is like laughing at your own joke." The pseudonymous Italian writer Elena Ferrante goes as far as to call the exclamation point a "phallic display." Ernest Hemingway also preferred a more flattened style. One study showed that overuse and abuse of exclamation points correlate with higher levels of neuroticism and a lack of openness. Take this first exchange I had while I was in Hawaii for the Ironman:

> **Jim:** Hi Mimi! Great pics! Here for the race?
>
> **Me:** Yes but not racing this year. Have raced here the last 9 years so taking a year to chill. You?
>
> **Jim:** Rockstar! Yeah I'm racing.
>
> **Me:** Your number? I'll be cheering
>
> **Jim:** 425!! I dig a liberal chick!! My kind of girl!

Are all these exclamation points necessary? They come off as amateurish, even insecure. Their excess in text messages has indeed become more standard; they are used for emphasis when words seem insufficient. But they have an anxious, excitable, "pay attention to me" quality, especially when they are used as replacements for the period. These days, a single exclamation point may not suffice to communicate enthusiasm. Now it's two, three, four, or more. Strong emotion or hyperbole is no longer required to use them; they can simply represent warmth. My friend Daniel describes them as "the original emoji."

Ethan also uses the exclamation point liberally, along with some other interesting character repetition:

> **Ethan:** Heyyyy we still haven't met Sieraaaa!!
>
> **Sierra:** Will have to wait until the next time our moons align
>
> **Ethan:** You are such a wonderful bundle of hotness and funnnn!! Wildo!
>
> **Sierra:** I'm in a work meeting and your text made me smirk

Ethan: . . . willdo we'lldo wildOhhhhhhh
myyyy

> **Sierra:** One of those:-) Thanks for reaching out.

Ethan: You around to talk later 2day? I want to find a time to be surrounded by your awesome aura.

Ethan: Who: you and me. What: Simply a good conversation. When: at your convenience, ideally before Saturday.

While Ethan might come across on the surface as a very open, relaxed guy, you'll recall that exclamation points, at least in one study, correlated with a *lack* of openness and *higher* levels of neuroticism. Ethan also uses "affective lengthening"—those are the extra letters in "heyyyy," "ohhhhhhh," and "funnnn"—which conveys emotional intensity. Along with the exclamation points, his "who, what, when" message betrays a more rigid personality.

Parentheses, those enclosed aside comments, correlate with both a lack of openness and extroversion. They are couched statements that may not rise to the occasion of relevance, and so they are wrapped in punctuation, as though to appear a gift. (I'm not sure this is worth saying, so I'll wrap it in parentheses for you.)

The ellipsis leaves much open to interpretation. In her book of essays, *Incidental Inventions,* Elena Ferrante says that ellipses are "flirtatious, like someone batting her eyelashes, mouth slightly open in feigned wonder." No wonder online dating messages are rife with ellipses, a medium that is often used to convey innuendo, possibility, and . . . promise.

What about the person who intentionally uses lowercase where we expect uppercase? It offers the allure of humility, but is it a faux humility or a true one? It has always seemed to carry a certain affectedness to me, especially because, with autocorrect, using a lowercase *i* requires an explicit effort. I suspect there's a hint of the antiestablishment at play, a thumbing of the nose, you could say.

Digital Body Language

Emojis are such a complicated subject that a discussion of them might merit its own chapter. Gretchen McCulloch has elaborately documented their history and function in her book *Because Internet: Understanding the New Rules of Language,* and she concludes that emojis are largely a substitute for gestures, and thus add nuance and clarity to text exchanges. When we communicate verbally, we rely heavily on facial expressions and hand movements.

Facial expressions and hand movements have cultural boundaries and differences. Americans, for instance, smile with much greater frequency than people in many other cultures. My mother was French and divided her time between Paris and New York. She would often joke that in Paris she could distinguish Americans and French from across the room, or from across an outdoor café, simply by their facial expressions as they spoke. While Americans will smile through a conversation, the French stay straight-faced, reserving their smiles for more special occasions.

How do we communicate things like eye contact, facial expression, and hand movements over text? How do we interpret irony and sarcasm? An algorithm would need both linguistic and semantic information to do so—that is, the actual meaning of the words and the writer's intended meaning. In the sixteenth century, sarcasm was indicated with a reversed question mark, or a "percontation point"; nineteenth-century French poets used it as an "irony mark." Similarly, an upside-down exclamation point is found in Ethiopic languages. In modern emojis, this tone is denoted with an upside-down smiley face.

Emojis can add clarity to your intended meaning, but do they suggest a lack of trust in the written language? And do they rob us of the joy of feeling completely understood? I have always found emojis to be shortcuts in our self-expression—the frozen food of language, rather than language cooked from scratch. While their use now extends well beyond teenage girls' texts, they still feel canned to me. "Work harder," I want to say to the texter. "Tell me what you really mean."

So often they are inserted where extra meaning isn't needed. Is it to add color? To bring joy? To play, as if tossing a ball that the other can toss back? Regardless, these are stylistic choices that may say more about the person texting than anything about our need for gestures to accompany our textspeak.

A large-scale study out of the University of Rochester showed that frequent users of emojis have low extroversion scores, with introverts using emojis the most. Highly agreeable scorers will also favor emojis, while users with low neuroticism scores use emojis the least often. These data lines would seem to explain quite neatly my own aversion to emojis.

It's not easy telling people that you are a psychiatrist who doesn't always understand emojis. My teenage daughter likes to test me:

Kyra: What does this mean:
☹️☹️⛄🔒🔒🏠✏️

> **Me:** It means that you are hiding behind emojis and not showing up emotionally for your mother.

Kyra: No, it actually means I'm sick at home and feel stuck there because it's a snow day and all there is to eat is an old burrito. Because my mother forgot to go grocery shopping.

So Emojional!

While emojis may be intended to add clarity to words, researchers have also found that the same emoji can be interpreted differently by different users, so emojis themselves can lead to confusion and misunderstanding. Creating sentences out of emojis is an art form of its own, and Alison makes a game of it in this initial dating app chat:

Alison: Once my friend and I designed a game and the objective was to use all the overlooked emojis in our texting which led to some interesting conversations

Eric: By all means send some examples!

Alison: Well there are overlooked bad pun opportunities, eg "I've 🎲 hell and back" "You want a 🍕 this?" Then there are ones I have no context for but will build a sentence around just to use them like 🖊. And then there is this overlooked gem 😵, is that derpiness, embarrassment, or inebriation?

Eric: That could also be post really good sex natural high face. At least that's what I've always thought.

Alison: I will now forever think of it as a just-had-sex-so-good-I-can't-even-think-face.

While emoji use can certainly seem random and idiosyncratic, specific emojis can indeed indicate personality features. For instance, extroverts will be more likely to use 👍 or 😊, and they will seldom use the 😭 or the 😐, which represent negative or ambiguous emotion. Agreeable people use hearts in all of their forms ❤️ 🖤 💕 and rarely use the 😖. Those high in neuroticism prefer the exaggerated facial expressions of the 😭, 😨, 😐, and 😳. As the authors of the University of Rochester study note, "These emojis have little positive correlation with other personality traits which represents a unique emoji usage pattern for neuroticism users as well as their distinct emotional characteristics." Openness, in contrast, shows no relationship to emoji use whatsoever.

This text exchange between Tom and Melanie dragged on for many months before an initial date. Tom seems to have developed a strong online crush, and he punctuates his texts with emojis:

> **Tom:** I am REALLY interested in getting to know you. I reread your earlier messages and also your profile . . . and I really like that you weren't afraid to post photos of yourself without makeup! Or at least not gobs of it! 😁

> **Tom:** Okay so I was just thinking about you at the gym this morning and I am going to throw caution to the wind and give you my full name. You can then "Googleize" me and get a better feel for who I am. After that we can further discuss dinner plans (assuming there is still interest) 🌹 Tom D

> **Melanie:** Thank you for outing yourself. I'm Melanie G . . . headed to Boston through Sunday—I have a couple of big presentations to give.

Tom: Thanks for writing. I thought you might have decided to "pursue other interests" after learning more about me. Ciao bella 🌹

Tom: Good luck with your presentations . . . although I am starting to get the impression that luck is not a major element in your life. 🌹

Melanie: Let's have dinner.

Tom: Did you receive my LinkedIn stalker message? All go well with your presentations?

Tom: What are you doing Saturday night?

Melanie: Do you want to meet my dad on our first date? Because he is visiting this weekend. What a great story that would be . . .

Tom: I haven't met a dad on a first date since high school!! It would make me feel very young . . . and very nervous, but, it would also be something unique and different! Haha! I don't think it would be appropriate for you to leave him.

Tom: Was just thinking about you . . . as I am occasionally apt to do . . . and hoping you're having a wonderful weekend with your dad. I am sure your father remembers every little detail of the day you came into his life . . . as if it were moments ago. 🌹

Melanie: Hi—busy week. I hope you are doing well. Try to call this week? [She gives her phone number.]

Tom: So very happy to hear from you. I leave Saturday for Europe so if you would like to speak, hopeful we can connect before I depart. I would really enjoy exchanging voices and making dinner plans! 😊😁🌹

Tom: Let's talk. You may find my voice repulsive and decide dinner would just be a bit too much. Otherwise after my trip but that feels like such a long time to wait! 🌹

> **Tom:** Okay . . . I rang the number you gave me but did not leave a message. Texted you as well. Won't text bomb you. I promise.

> **Tom:** So I am in total violation of all the rules of online dating by writing so much but I figure you can handle it . . . and I promise I am not a psycho stalker. Just wanted you to know I watched one of your online videos and really enjoyed seeing and hearing you speak (facial expressions, smile, etc.) Have a spectacular day 🌹

When Melanie and Tom finally found a time to have dinner, it was a disaster. She had unconsciously responded to all the flattery and thought she might enjoy herself. In doing so, she missed some important signals in his text messages.

On their date, Tom first asked Melanie to choose a bottle of wine. She did, and he said, "Thank God you did not choose the most expensive wine on the menu. All the women I date do that. They just seem to be after my 401(k)." If it's possible, the date went downhill from there. Melanie was kicking herself for wasting an evening. But as she was quick to point out, "It's not as if his texts were not full of red flags . . . er, roses . . . !!"

Beyond his tendency to lay it on thick, what can we surmise about Tom from his punctuation, emoji use, and dating message content? He is likely introverted (emoji use), insecure ("pursue other interests," "stalker"), high in neuroticism ("repulsive," "psycho stalker"), low in openness ("not appropriate," "violation of all the rules"), not to mention very persistent. Not what Melanie, a highly extroverted, confident, and open person, was looking for.

It's not that there are, objectively speaking, ideal partners and suboptimal ones. There is someone for everyone, and what is right for one person is wrong for another. If being with a narcissist makes you feel good, great, just go in knowingly, and be aware of the risks and benefits of involvement with one. If the shy, quiet, and predictable type makes you feel most secure and comfortable, then by all means, choose that. As Catwoman says in *Batman Returns*, "It's the so-called normal guys who always let you down. Sickos never scare me. Least they're committed."

It's up to each of us to take the time to self-examine and decide what we are looking for and will enjoy. We must also respect those desires and pay attention to the signals we're being sent as they emerge. In the next chapter, we'll look not only at would-be dates but also at ourselves. We'll talk about awareness, self-knowledge, insight, and overcoming the obstacles to understanding what you are looking for. Because the only thing worse than not knowing is not wanting to know.

CHAPTER 3

Working Out the Kinks

HOW TO KNOW WHAT YOU WANT

Jared: Well, obviously the first question we need to tackle is what is the name of your stuffed animal?

> **Brooke:** Wadsworth . . . obviously

Jared: Of course because he's an elephant?

> **Brooke:** Oh I like the idea of Wadsworth the elephant. This one's a bear.

Jared: Much more dominant. So Wadsworth is obviously from England?

> **Brooke:** Wadsworth the bear is obviously British. The clever, soothing British Baking Show kind of British NOT the judgy or Brexity kind. I could never sleep with that.

Jared and Brooke dance around their partner preferences with a discussion of the stuffed animal Brooke says she sleeps with. Power, personality, and political allegiance are introduced early into their playful and affiliative banter. Jared may be hinting that he wants someone more dominant, and Brooke has found a way to cleverly insert her personality and political preferences (open, not judgy; liberal, not Brexity) into a flirtatious repartee about a stuffed toy.

Regardless of our stated preferences, finding the right partner entails grappling with what we really want. It can be easy to let fear, shame, pride, or worry cloud our search. By taking the time to understand ourselves—to work out our own kinks—we can take braver action to seek what we really want. Greater awareness will lead to clearer, and ultimately better, choices.

Most online daters match with people who bear little resemblance to the person they claim to be looking for. A large-scale study of forty-one thousand Australians showed that daters routinely make contact with people on dating sites who in no way resemble the Mr. or Ms. Perfect they claimed to prefer. Which might lead you to wonder, which is the true north—a person's behavior or their stated preferences? Are they matching with people that they're unconsciously drawn to, or are their actions at odds with their true desires?

As expectations around romantic relationships have evolved, decisions have become more complex. In the past, the only question was "*Whom* should I marry?" Now relationships are less likely to follow a straight-and-narrow set of rules; they're more likely to bend in response to paradoxical needs. The central question is just as likely to be "*What* sort of relationship am I committed to?"

Here we will take a short detour from *others* in order to try to shed light on *ourselves*—our own expectations, confusions, desires, and kinks, the features that surround our romantic endeavors. This will allow us to clarify what we're really looking for, before we dive even further into dating. Understanding what we want and need starts with self-awareness, and as we'll see, shedding light on ourselves is not always so easy.

Strangers to Ourselves

The popular wisdom is that we simply don't know what we want. It's a notion that echoes through our halls of academia, chambers of Congress, courtrooms, churches, and sanctuaries. It rings the bell on Wall Street and clatters across Madison Avenue. These institutions are intent on filling a perceived void of self-knowledge with their version of what we *should* want. With the cacophony of opinion and doctrine, there's little incentive to investigate what truly moves us. We're being told what to want—constantly.

At the center of this uproar are questions that have bedeviled humankind forever: Who are we? Why do we do what we do? And are there reliable ways of finding out? The social sciences emerged to answer these questions, and only raised more of them along the way.

In his seminal book *Strangers to Ourselves*, the psychologist Timothy Wilson traces the history of the quest for self-knowledge while laying out practical pathways for achieving it. The core issue is that most of what goes on in our mind is unconscious. "When Freud said that consciousness is the tip of the mental iceberg, he was short of the mark by quite a bit," Wilson says. "It may be more the size of a snowball on top of that iceberg." Does that mean that who we actually are is entombed in an area of the mind that's inaccessible to us? Not exactly.

Freud gave us the unconscious with a capital *U*. In his theorizing, it was a vault that snapped shut after infancy and remained shut for life, requiring years of psychoanalysis to unlock. It was only then that we could access the repressed memories that drove us. The notion was sexy and dramatic: Who knew what craven desires lay within, what dark secrets populated our dreams? Only your psychiatrist, it turned out. (And possibly your hairdresser.) Hollywood loved it; pulp fiction ate it up. But the psychoanalytic approach was ultimately deemed unscientific, rejected by modern psychology. Behaviorists stalked the landscape, proclaiming that what was in the mind mattered not;

only our behavior revealed our true selves. Does "being" motivate "doing," or vice versa? The conflict of the era was irreverently summed up by Kurt Vonnegut Jr.:

"To be is to do"—Socrates.
"To do is to be"—Jean-Paul Sartre.
"Do be do be do"—Frank Sinatra.

Today, the study of the mind and the study of behavior are both thriving, the two threads inextricably tied. The unconscious is considered no longer a single impregnable monolith but a complex system of interwoven departments, all with discrete functions. Behavior, meanwhile, remains the single best way to gain insight into how our unconscious mind operates. And although we can't readily access the contents of our unconscious, ways have been found to consciously alter them.

The latest iteration of the unconscious—called the adaptive unconscious or the cognitive unconscious, also implicit or automatic thinking, among other terms—is the new playground for psychologists of every stamp. In scientific papers it is almost always associated with unscientific words like "mystery" and "intuition" and described as a liminal zone between dreams and reality. Who knew that social science could be so poetic? I tend to favor "adaptive unconscious," because, beyond describing how the unconscious evolved with us and is crucial to our survival, the term echoes our constant struggle to understand it.

It is now a given that the lion's share of our mental processes occur without our awareness—that in many departments our autopilot is constantly engaged and that in others it can be turned on and off. Thank goodness for that. Our days would be very long if we were constantly recalculating how to tie our shoes or put one foot in front of the other. Our minds would be a mess if we had to scan every image in our memory in order to recognize a face. Communication would be impossible if we had to retrieve words and build phrases from scratch every time we spoke. The brain has conscious areas we can easily access, subconscious ones that require keys, and unconscious zones that are mostly off-limits. But like a warehouse, things don't always get stored in the right place. Therein lies the rub.

I have long described a portion of my role as a psychotherapist as an elaborate card game of concentration. When a patient reveals a jack to me from their deck of experiences and thoughts, I have to remember the last time they turned over a jack, make the connection for them, and remind them where that other jack was metaphorically stored.

Nowhere was this more evident than with a patient of mine, D.W., whom I saw for several years following the end of his marriage (and who agreed to let me tell his story). He had a very negative view of online dating. Women on those sites must have some fundamental flaw, he reasoned, because it would be so easy for them to meet men in real life. His circle of friends spoke glowingly of the convenience of online dating, but to him the ease of use meant he would be meeting women who were lazy or lacking in social skills. They showed him the multitude of choices available; he saw a gallery of rejects. They emphasized that he could text and get to know women before dating; he predicted endless boring conversations.

In the end, he relented and downloaded an app, and for about a year all of D.W.'s predictions were on the money. His stories were sad and funny: a date falling asleep in his car as he drove her home; another spending two hours talking about all of her terrible dating app experiences; yet another, on a first date, asking him to spend the night because she was afraid of being raped by an intruder. These and others he found unattractive, dull, and neurotic. Half jokingly, I asked him why he was dating unattractive, dull, and neurotic women. "Because," he said, "that's all that is available online."

He persisted, and over time D.W.'s dating experiences improved, although, paradoxically, his outcomes did not. He dated a slew of attractive, successful, and outgoing women. He reported excellent compatibility and fantastic sex. But in every case, some minor detail would throw him off, and he would abruptly leave the relationship.

This could be attributable to any number of factors: we spent time examining his attachment style and fears around emotional intimacy. But D.W. had started off with an extreme bias against online dating, followed by a long period of subconsciously dating women who only confirmed his bias. The preponderance of data that he collected seemed to confirm his initial stereotype, that women on apps were suboptimal partners, perhaps even suboptimal human beings. This notion had become a schema— a mental structure of preconceived ideas that, once reinforced, becomes automatic and unconscious. It was one that he then felt compelled to repeat.

Schemata (as they are plurally known) are essential to the function of an organized mind. They are mental categories that allow us to classify our environment. They can also be rigid structures, hard to override consciously once they are entrenched. We may be told by someone that a dog, snarling and tugging at its chain, is actually quite friendly. Our biting-dog schema would reject that notion, and we would be wary of petting it. Simultaneously, another schema, perhaps one of disliking a particular breed of dog—for entirely different reasons—might be reinforced. And so on. Schemata can become so powerful that any data that contradicts them will be deflected as an exception, a mistake, or an illusion.

John: I've enjoyed our dialogue and I wanted to share with you that I am separated and have been for about a year. It is something I initiated. If that is a concern for you, I would understand and respect that. All answers are good.

John: I'm not looking for emotional support from another woman to finalize my divorce. With all that said, I felt transparency is good. It is what I would want.

Elisabeth: Thanks for your note. Sorry I was busy this past weekend. I'm happy to try to connect by phone or meet up. As for the separation issue, I appreciate the transparency. I will say "separated not yet divorced" has not worked out well for me in the past.

Elisabeth: Please don't take any of the above as overly dramatic . . . just to say I'm trying to avoid being the rebound person ☺

John: I'm very centered on the reality that some folks may have had a less than ideal experience in this area in the past. And that's ok. I might feel the same way depending on what my experiences may have been.

John: You should feel great about speaking your truth. I don't know how that can be read as overly dramatic. I'm inclined to say maybe trust your instincts here. It was nice to match with you, and perhaps our paths cross again at another time. From my perspective, our messages have been interesting and pleasant. Virtual hugs. ☺

In this text exchange, Elisabeth's and John's references to past relationships can be read as evidence of existing schemata. Elisabeth acknowledges that she hasn't had great experiences with men who are not yet divorced. Although she says she is open-minded and willing to meet, her comment seems to have foreshortened the conversation. It is unclear from John's formal style of speech whether he is avoiding rejection (perhaps he's been dumped for his separated status in the past?) or if he really believes that Elisabeth should trust her intuition. Each may be correctly or incorrectly connecting the dots of their past experiences; both would benefit from gaining insight into their actual fears.

From Introspection to Insight

Scientifically defined, introspection is an act of observing an object when that object is the observation itself. If that sentence gave you a bit of whiplash, then you can imagine how difficult it can be to make conclusions based on such a process. Introspection is a mainstay of therapy, mostly with the purpose of accessing the "true self" or the unconscious, which we now know is generally impervious to the proddings of self-examination. When people introspect, they can find themselves adrift in a sea of **confabulation.**

Nature abhors a vacuum, and so does the mind. There is increasing evidence that in the absence of an explanation for our own unconscious behavior our conscious mind tends to create one. Confabulation is a way of rationalizing behaviors we don't understand by making up stories about them. When faced with an action or a statement of our own that we can't explain, one that seems to have no history or reason—why we swiped right on him, ended things with her, and so on—we confabulate, creating sometimes incredibly detailed and complex stories to explain ourselves. We all confabulate to some degree, sometimes consciously, perhaps to enhance the parts of a story we don't remember well; just as often unconsciously, for reasons that elude us. We can't change the facts, but we can alter the supporting narrative to express a more palatable outcome.

D.W. couldn't say, for example, that his attachment patterns were causing him to withdraw emotionally from romantic relationships. He didn't yet have access to that information. Instead, his conscious mind created perfectly rational explanations for why he rejected his dates, based on trivial details. In one case, he broke things off with a woman who remarked on a text message she had glimpsed on his phone, which he had left unlocked and in plain sight. He reasoned that she was all "up in his business" and would make his life miserable. Privacy violation, he said, was his only "one strike and you're out" rule. Until he came up with another. And another.

Confabulation is the act of creating a narrative to connect the dots when we don't understand how they are actually connected. These narratives can be useful, even therapeutic. Sometimes a crack in the narrative reveals our true thoughts and motives. Those "I can't believe I just said that" moments are a sort of verbal wardrobe malfunction: your Freudian slip is suddenly showing. In general, when it comes to probing our own unconscious, the emperor is not only wearing clothes, he's wearing everything in the closet.

Kieran's motivations are relatively unguarded in his conversation with Andrea:

> **Andrea:** Not sure how this app works. Does this mean that we're dating now?

> **Kieran:** Dating? DATING? I'm almost pregnant, and you're having commitment issues?!?!

Andrea: Cool. I'll update my relationship status on MySpace. Do you actually live here or are you just passing through SF on a pandemic holiday like everyone else on this app?

Kieran: I come from Mars (Bar)

Kieran: I live here. DO YOU?

Kieran: Cut to chase: meet for so-called witty banter manana (that's Spanish for tomorrow)?

Andrea: Yup. I live here. Are you from Spain or are you just practicing your high school Spanish with me?

Andrea: I'd be up for meeting—but we should probably talk over the phone first to make sure we won't bore each other to tears.

Kieran: You're a Jewish Aquarian I'm a Jewish Catholic

Kieran: No I mean I'm a Catholic aquarium

Kieran: behind the perfect hair on my chest are tiger guppies

Kieran: We're not gonna bore each other

Kieran: If it gets boring we start kissing until it's boring no longer.

Forget wearing the wardrobe; Kieran just walks into the party bare-chested in flip-flops and shorts. He is all id—no analysis required. For most of us, though, our motivations are assiduously defended and not so easily accessed.

When our true motives do peek out from under our garments, we have a tendency to rationalize them away. In a famous experiment by Michael Norton of Harvard Business School, male college students were given a choice of two subscriptions to sports magazines—one that included a swimsuit edition and another that included a "Year's Top 10 Athletes" edition, but that were otherwise essentially the same. They consistently chose the one with the swimsuit issue. When asked why they made the choice they did, they tended to explain away their preferences on the basis of some feature of the articles therein. This study, along with many others, supports the notion that when people behave in ways that are incongruent with how they want to see themselves, they justify their behavior with rational excuses. ("I swiped right on him because he volunteers at the animal shelter," rather than "I liked the shirtless photo of him at the beach.") It's much easier to go with an easy, palatable answer than to confront a harder, less appealing one.

When people are asked to list the reasons for the dating choices they've made, their feelings and attitudes shift; the more reasons they list, the greater the observable change. So an indescribable feeling of comfort that we get from the sound of our partner's voice will evolve into a sentiment such as "I like my partner's voice because . . ." and that "because" will become the reason; the initial feeling of comfort will be overshadowed. Our brains are lazy. Once we latch on to a particular reasoning, we stop looking for what we actually feel.

I once had a guy break up with me several weeks into a relationship because, he explained, my hips were too narrow. So often with online dating and other romantic pursuits, we override the strong intuitive signals our brains send us about what we really want. Had this man truly wanted someone with wide hips, it should have been clearly visible to him in our first encounter. Or maybe, like D.W., this was just an explanation he latched on to—perhaps to mask an inability or unwillingness to commit to a longer-term relationship. Whether he needed to prioritize the *hips* in relations*hips,* or whether he wanted to do away with "relations" altogether, he would have done himself, and me, a favor by recognizing it up front. We've all done it—ignored the screaming signals and forged ahead. We rationalize: that a person is a great match because they meet a set of criteria, or check a series of boxes from a prefabricated list, one that bears no resemblance to our *true* desires (be they wide hips, a series of short intimate liaisons—you name it).

Yolanda inquires about Dieter's height as she considers whether to graduate the text to an in-person meeting. Dieter toys with her in his response, not so subtly poking fun at her potential checklist:

> **Yolanda:** And now, to the more mundane . . . What's your last name? And generally how tall are you? I'm curious if we will stand face to face or if I will look up to you or down at you ;)

> **Dieter:** I just sent you a pic of my drivers license. TMI?

> **Yolanda:** Not TMI. I guess I'll look up at you. And maybe I'll look up to you. And you'll look down at me, but hopefully not down on me. And I'm glad that you weigh more than me. Though I am considerably curvier. Here's my DL.

> **Yolanda:** Btw, you look like a serial killer in that photo.

> **Dieter:** I've never done this before. Something oddly erotic about exchanging DL pics.

> **Yolanda:** Sorry about the serial killer comment. I hope that won't give you bad dreams or bad ideas.

> **Dieter:** I resent 'serial' killer. I always do them one at a time with great care.

You might imagine that through introspection, we better understand what we seek, and why, and can therefore reach new heights of happiness. You might be wrong. Research by the professor of behavioral sciences Rick Harrington and his colleagues at the University of Houston-Victoria shows that people who do a lot of introspection are more stressed, depressed, and anxious; are more self-absorbed; and feel less in control of their lives and choices.

By contrast, the psychologist Anthony Grant showed that people high in *insight* had stronger relationships, were more in control of their choices, and experienced greater self-acceptance and happiness. So how can we distinguish between introspection and insight? How can we go from *thinking about* ourselves to *knowing* ourselves? To get to knowing, we have to let go of the myth that Freud perpetuated: that extracting information requires an archaeological dig of the psyche. There are some practical pathways at our disposal.

The first technique, as Tasha Eurich outlines in her book *Insight,* is to ask yourself *what* you are feeling, rather than *why* you are feeling it. That is, *naming.* Observation of your own feelings is likely to produce better self-knowledge when it's non-judgmental, and people get stuck when they have feelings they can't explain. When they are gently guided toward naming feelings, the sensation of "being blocked" is lifted, and the underlying feeling is identified. By asking ourselves what we like from a partner, putting aside the question of why we like it, we can more easily identify the thing we seek.

Julian has indicated that he is married and seeking an open relationship. Rita matches with him on a dating app, and she leads with this:

> **Rita:** Tell me, the wifey ain't satisfying hubby? Or does she know—r u two poly?

Julian: Yes we are poly. Have been for about 10yrs. It is good to have needs met by more than one person. We use it more as a way to create balance and avoid overly depending on one person to fulfill all needs, especially in intimacy. Supportive for scheduling, diversity of interests/ orientations . . .

Julian: What are you looking for?

Rita: Sorry I can't do married ppl. Although I bet you're amazing in bed and you're super Duper cute. Too bad for me. I guess I'm one of the rare uptight people here in *sinful* San Francisco 😇 😈

Rita: P.S. I am looking for a good fuck.

Give Rita credit: She is seeking something casual and knows she doesn't want to negotiate approval from another person's spouse before having sex with them. She is clear about what she wants and where she is going to get it.

All the text-whispering tools in the world (and in this book) are useless if we can't be straight with ourselves about what we want. If a particular kink is important, it might be helpful to come to grips with that, rather than seeing it as something that needs to be concealed, controlled, or corrected. If a personal need for independence or distance in a relationship is essential to you, to not feel threatened or smothered, that can encourage you to seek out partners who don't need to spend every waking moment together. Merely exercising a policy of containment toward our desires will create a chasm between your persona (the character we present to others) and your true personality. Real insight involves shining a light on our thoughts and our feelings, the welcome and the unwelcome.

Persona, Grata or Non

Rachel came into my practice like a tornado. Her intensity was such that to say she was merely driven would be to call a Ferrari a Pacer. Rachel was an accomplished physician, held an adjunct professor role at a major medical school, served on two boards, worked out at least two hours a day, and, of course, was dating up a storm because she wanted to settle down with someone and raise a family. Her mind and body were liquid steel.

Moments after our sessions began, she would, like clockwork, burst into tears.

Rachel had approached twelve years of graduate and postgraduate study like an academic mountaineer, ever reaching for the higher degree, residency, fellowship, award, always accompanied by her placeholder boyfriend, whom she summarily dumped when she entered the real world. Because much of her adult life had been consumed by research and study, and she'd spent those years cradled in the comfort of a nurturing relationship, she was at times emotionally naive in our sessions, despite otherwise being so worldly and sophisticated.

After spending the first ten minutes of our sessions emptying my Kleenex box, Rachel would compose herself, let her hair cascade onto her sculpted deltoids, straighten out her skirt, and begin the tale of her latest heartbreak. The story would be some variation on an ongoing theme. She had met a guy on a dating app, usually an über-masculine, brushes-his-teeth-with-testosterone type. Their attraction had been immediate, with the first few days spent in an amatory whirlwind. She had catered to his every need and pleased every part of him, from *Kama Sutra* to Kierkegaard. He stormed the keep like a plundering knight.

Within a few weeks, though, things would wind down. Her

tomcat would turn into a teddy bear, preferring cuddling to sexing, making her dinner instead of making out, and sleeping, actually sleeping, when they went to bed. Days later the inevitable would come crashing down on her: there was too much intimacy—or too little—for his taste. She reminded him of his sister, or his mother. It wasn't the right time/moment/season. The outlets in her bathroom weren't code compliant. And off he went.

As she regaled me with her stories, the notion of her playing the subservient geisha always seemed at odds with the person before me, her firm tone of voice, direct gaze, ramrod posture. Although she thought of herself at times as submissive, wanting nothing more than just to sink into life with an equal partner, she also admitted that she liked to be in control. She always initiated sex and wanted it often, usually on demand. When not having sex, she preferred either intellectual conversation or exercise. Anything else would make her anxious and fidgety. Her life was lived in tight compartments, like a film with only action scenes. Men who didn't share an interest in these compartments were less than perfect in her eyes.

Rachel's *persona* had little to do with her *personality,* and she was largely unaware of the discrepancy. She was attracted to a certain type of man, and her persona had unconsciously developed around attracting that type. But her persona was insufficiently fleshed out for it to be maintained for very long, and as her true personality emerged, her erstwhile John Wayne chose not to wait for his dismissal. He bolted for the door.

As we consider, in the pages ahead, the conscious and unconscious motivations that compel us, it's important to note that neither is, strictly speaking, the right one. Both can inform us, and both deserve consideration. Part of Rachel's work, as we'll see, was to reconcile her explicit and implicit selves.

Me, Myself, and I

It may be the subject we think about most. Ourselves. There is a construct of "me" that sits in our heads, and it seems both persistent and immutable. But we are possessed with, or possessed by, two personalities: our conscious, constructed self, and our unconscious one. They exist relatively independent of each other. While the conscious persona fusses lazily over appearance and protocols, the unconscious self is fast, effortless, unintentional, and uncontrollable. As we read the room, it has already read the room. As we open our mouths to speak, it has already spoken. At various times and to varying degrees we become aware of this Russian doll problem, our self within a self. When we do, it results in self-consciousness, an experience embraced by some and rejected by others. Where we live on the spectrum between these two extremes can say a lot about how we relate to other people—especially our significant other.

There has been much study of personality self-knowledge, or the differences between our explicit and implicit selves. One interesting discrepancy that has emerged is the chasm between how *we think* our friends, colleagues, and family view us and the way they actually do. When the difference is quantified on a scale of 0 to 1, where 0 represents no similarity whatsoever and 1 represents a perfect match, it's about 0.17. In other words, if we're poor judges of our own personality, we're even worse judges of how our peers see us. In contrast, our peers have a fairly decent idea of our own self-view (0.45 on the same scale).

This isn't altogether surprising. We are strongly motivated to get the people in our lives to see us as we see ourselves. Peers can be helpful in understanding our own behavior, simply because they have front-row seats to the way we behave, past and present, and thus are well equipped to predict how we might act in the future. Their view of our unconscious in action has few obstructions, as does their investment in our happiness and success.

It points toward a second practical pathway toward insight, beyond putting a name to our feelings: soliciting *feedback*. Now, with as much openness and agreeableness as we can muster, we can take another simple step: ask a friend. Feedback on how others perceive us is readily available from those we trust, and it is often more trustworthy than our self-assessments.

It can also, of course, be addressed in therapy. As a psychiatrist, I grow to care deeply for my patients. I get to bear witness to their innermost feelings, after all. Part of my job is to straddle the threshold, with one foot in the door (empathizing with their reality) and one foot out (being able to provide them objective feedback). I have to admit that many aspects of the hard-charging Rachel reminded me of a younger version of myself, which made it easy to see her both objectively and subjectively (in particular her dread of slowing down). For Rachel to change, she had to acknowledge her fears of hitting the pause button. So often, overcoming the barrier to self-reflection involves confronting the anxiety or threat that will arise from that reflection.

As the therapist James Hollis, author of *Living an Examined Life,* explains, being able to reflect on our inner reality can lead to awareness in the form of a sudden epiphany. Sometimes, he says, we need to be stunned into reflection by a loss, breakup, or series of breakups that force us to reexamine our provisional conclusions about ourselves.

Barring such life-changing events, there are three further steps to self-awareness beyond naming and soliciting feedback. These steps can be a quick trip or a lifetime journey. Your mileage may vary.

Minding the Gap

Mindfulness, an extension of the naming technique, means simply noticing what you are thinking, feeling, and doing in response to certain triggers or circumstances, without reacting, explaining, or overthinking. Sometimes it means looking at those thoughts and feelings from a new vantage point. While action and productivity are excellent coping skills to buoy mood—I recommend them to patients early and often—if overused, they can be a defense, serving as foils to self-examination. Our constant smartphone use, social media presence, and even dating app addictions might all be evidence of mindlessness, rather than the mindfulness that leads to meaningful self-awareness.

Sometimes we will do anything to avoid being alone with our thoughts, as Aimee is well aware:

Aimee: I'm back in the predicament of needing to sit at my altar since I didn't finish my meditation this morning. And here we are bantering again.

Terrance: Chatting with you seems to be my priority too. But I'm intrigued by the notion of pausing meditation and resuming hours later. I have much to learn.

Aimee: Glad to know my lack of discipline intrigues you. I made a commitment to completing some very specific meditations. But my favorite pith metta (loving kindness meditation) is "Never mind; start again!"

Terrance: Go meditate. Then we can start again.

Aimee: Very kind of you.

The University of Virginia psychologist Timothy Wilson studied our penchant for mindlessness by asking subjects to sit in a room with no cell phones, books, pens, or any other diversions—nothing to occupy them but their own thoughts. People felt very uncomfortable. He upped the ante by offering them the option to self-administer electric shocks while they sat. Given the choice between doing nothing and receiving small electric shocks, the majority of the participants elected to receive shocks. Wilson concluded that people would rather experience pain (in small quantities) than sit with themselves.

Somehow this isn't shocking. Our conscious minds are wired for any time but the present as we stew over the past and quiver over the future. An under-recognized truth is that self-fulfillment, serenity, well-being, and even happiness can only be felt *in the moment*. Otherwise, they are either memory or hope. We *want* to be in the present; we just don't know how.

Unfortunately, the path to mindfulness is scattered with platitudes. "Mindfulness" is one of the latest buzzwords to feature prominently in the pop psychology vending machine, with 209 billion Google search results on the day of this writing and seventy thousand books in print on the topic. It is now available in flavors ranging from Mindful Dog Ownership to Mindful Veganism. There is nothing wrong with mindfulness—as a subject, as a process, as a way of life. The shortcuts of commodified mindfulness, though, can lead us to gloss over unexamined personal issues. True mindfulness requires practice, or *a* practice, tailored by each individual to themselves, not prescribed in a generic package.

Both feedback and mindfulness can run up against what Timothy Wilson and Harvard professor of social psychology Daniel Gilbert refer to as the psychological immune system. Like our defenses from bacteria, viruses, and fungi, this system defends us from psychological abuse, stress, and criticism. It makes us feel good about ourselves by corralling negative thoughts that threaten our perception of self. It helps us to overcome disappointment, be more accepting and tolerant, and maintain a reasonable balance of optimism. An extension of Wilson and Gilbert's analogy is that, like the biological one, the psychological immune system can fail us dramatically, or even turn against us. We might form positive illusions that are essentially delusions, papering our windows with smiley-face posters that ultimately block out the light.

Rachel would spend much of her day actively defending against weakness; she certainly projected an aura of strength to the outside world. But moments into our sessions, her vulnerability would emerge, flying in the face of the story she was telling others. She felt conflicted about power; how *in control* did she really want to be? In some ways it was a relief to be with a man who was controlling, because it allowed her to put aside her own need to be in charge. She wanted both to be swept off her feet and to be calling the shots. It was only by slowing down and taking stock of her conflicted approach to control that she could identify the patterns that had beleaguered her romantic pursuits.

By sitting with our thoughts and feelings, and by nonjudgmentally observing them, we can stay open to learning about ourselves, even when what we learn is in conflict with our existing sense of self or the world.

Parsing Patterns

Mindfulness certainly illuminates. But a fourth reliable method for achieving insight into what we want is to compare our past predictions with actual known outcomes. This leads to *pattern recognition*. Emotional patterns can be difficult to see for a number of reasons. One is that memory is a reconstructive process, with details added, modified, or taken away every time we recall something. We also suffer from impact bias, which is the tendency to over- or underestimate how future events will impact us emotionally based on our (sometimes faulty) memory of the past. Drawing a line between two moving targets can be tricky, but by tracing the course of past predictions through to their now obvious conclusions, we can more realistically evaluate our current expectations.

Once patterns become clear, insight will usually follow. Patterns allow us to see the ways that we have agency, rather than being passengers on the journey of our lives. I think of the old saying that the definition of insanity is doing the same thing over and over again and expecting a different result. When I talk about pattern recognition, I mean deliberately attempting to acknowledge those things that we're (insanely) doing over and over.

This is where my metaphorical card game of concentration comes into play. By remembering the last time we felt a particular way, and how it played out, and comparing that with our current experience, we can become better predictors of our relationship outcomes. I am there to remind a patient of the last time they expressed this thought, or the last time they felt that way; by engaging in conscious, mindful awareness, you can practice it on your own, too.

Emily took the message to heart. She had received the following first message from Eve on a dating app:

> **Eve:** Your self summary includes, literally, all the most important things. It's fantastic and I didn't need to read a lot of text on my tiny phone screen to know I should message you. How is your Sunday coming along?

At the time Emily received the message, she was only recently out of a very long relationship with another woman. She couldn't process hearing from a stranger that she seemed appealing; it wasn't the way she saw herself at the time. So she rejected it. By looking back at her past prediction (that the text was too forward to be worth a reply) and the known outcome (she might have missed out on an opportunity), she learned about her own assumptions and how to better handle in the future a scenario that once baffled her.

"I recall thinking this person was coming on *way* too strong," she reflected, "and now I have no idea what I was thinking. Seems like quite a nice thing to say."

Zooming Out

Attraction and preference, as we've seen, are often driven by unconscious motivations. It's possible that in the case of focused dating—the kind that online dating tends to foster—this is only truer. When we make a list of desirable traits in a partner, it is rarely comprehensive of our true feelings. We might not even consciously know how some of the traits got there.

This brings us to the last step on the practical pathway to self-awareness: to look beyond the list (or whatever information is right in front of you) and to *see the big picture*. A memorable mentor of mine was also a respected astronomer. Dr. William Sheehan's list of achievements, besides being an active community psychiatrist, includes a patent for infrared brain-imaging technology, an understanding of the composition and evolution of the Milky Way, and a knack for planetary observation. As a student, I was eager to learn as much as I could from his astute observation of both human and celestial bodies. I asked him how he had made the career switch from astronomy to psychiatry. He replied, "I love to listen to my patients by day and understand the nuance of their emotional lives, and then go home at night, gaze at the stars, and realize that our small preoccupations don't really matter."

Dr. Sheehan's words stuck with me. They perfectly illustrate the therapeutic value of zooming out on our life from our current telescopic, or even microscopic, view. Rather than focusing on a particular sticking point, or the way in which we are currently stuck, it can be helpful to see the narrative arc of our lives, to become, as Timothy Wilson describes it, our own biographers. By cataloging one's life, clear themes emerge, and dearly held values and passions come into focus. Together, these can give us a clearer view of who we are and what we want to become.

Accessing this information is of course paramount to choosing the right kind of partner. We can look beyond lists and, in our mind's eye, see a whole person—be it the one sitting in front of us or the one we see in the mirror. But to quote the flawed but brilliant comic philosopher Woody Allen, "Students achieving Oneness will move on to Twoness." Having learned about and made peace with the stranger within ourselves, we must now progress to doing what we do when we chat on dating apps: texting with strangers.

CHAPTER 4

Texting with Strangers

Annika: No way you are getting off that easy. Three things that turn you on. 😊

> **Olivia:** Good one.

> **Olivia:** Can't limit it to and this is stream of consciousness as I'm not editing . . .

> **Olivia:** Playfulness, kissing, soft touch, quirkiness, humor, skin eye contact, connection, smarts, accountability, authenticity, presence and letting go together to some unknown sweet, raw, open, melting . . .

> **Olivia:** *gulp*

Annika: Waking up to your list. Reading it again, very slowly. Taking my time with each word.

Annika: I really like your list 😊

Before drifting off to sleep, Annika throws down a gauntlet for Olivia to ponder. She wakes up to a rich eye-opener of high values, spiced with sensuality, which she savors. Olivia emphasizes vulnerability and intimacy in her list of turn-ons. It feels like the real deal; the ingredients are all there. And yet these two have not even met.

Intimacy is increasingly fostered through the medium of text. We meet online, we flirt over text, and we reveal deep aspects of ourselves—in our lexicon, as we've seen, but also in the content and style of our notes. Inquiry and authenticity are the foundation of intimacy, and as we can see from this text exchange, having the courage both to ask and to be vulnerable can lend itself to deeper connection.

Authenticity is all the rage. It's become such a buzzword that one wonders if it hasn't been stretched too thin to hold its shape. Eighty-four percent of users on one dating app said they wished that other people on the app would present the "authentic" version of themselves. Some dating apps request, even demand, that users post unretouched photos. "Substance over selfie," says one site. The faux and phony, the dog and pony, the filtered and the airbrushed—all are on notice. Virtual is the new real.

Ironically, while the large majority of daters would prefer that other people open up and be their authentic selves, many lack the confidence to do the same. A 2019 white paper that addressed dating app users' primary anxieties about presenting themselves found that 40 percent worry about being interesting enough, talkative enough, fun enough, you-name-it enough. Sexy enough tops the list for Gen Z and millennials. FOPO (fear of people's opinions) has seemingly caught up with and exceeded FOMO (fear of missing out).

The study demonstrated that anxieties about appearance are superseded by concerns over conversational skills and personality. Women worry more than men (or at least they admit to it more). People go so far as to express anxiety about sharing their hobbies, and a full third of singles have felt the need to adopt the hobbies of the person they were interested in.

It can be painful to read the texts of people who latch onto their match's interests and preferences rather than promoting their own. Take this initial text exchange between Max and Robyn. Robyn had indicated in her profile that she is a scotch drinker.

> **Max:** Hi Robyn! I'm more of a rye guy than scotch . . . but I think we can still get along :) What's your quarantine cocktail of choice?

> **Robyn:** Ooh—Idk if I've ever met somebody who prefers rye. I love it too. I would have said my favorite cocktails were a French 75 or paper plane, but now I'm going to have to go with a Man O' War.

Robyn quickly adjusts her taste in alcohol to match those of her new interest. Cocktail choice is no big deal in the grand scheme of things, but it is a worrisome sign when someone can't plainly state what they like. In the following exchange, both parties attempt the shift, but it all comes to naught.

> **Maya:** Hi there! This app seems to think we're a good match . . . and hey, look at that a doggo in kayak convergence! Give a holler if you're up for starting a convo.

> **Jessica:** Hi! I honestly loved everything you said in your profile. Short and sweet. I'm not one for lengthy chats so if you want to set up an in-person sumpin' or other, let's plan it. We could bowl! I'm not very good at it at all, but it's fun. It can be really great to go somewhere and hurl balls. Ha!

> **Maya:** I totally agree re: in-person, and bowling could be a real hoot—I haven't been in years!

Maya comes on as dominant, with her backslapping chat style and "short and sweet" profile. Jessica may be accommodating this by suggesting a physical activity, one where she knows she won't be competitive. It turns out they both should have chosen a different tack. This chat never led to a meeting because, as Maya said to me later, "Really? Bowling?"

Kai, who struggles with anxiety in reaching out to strangers, does a nice job when reaching out to Lea:

Kai: I really dig your music taste

Lea: aw thank you!! 🙂🙂

Kai: I didn't realize Tom Misch and Doja Cat had overlapping fanbases lol

Lea: HAHAHA

Lea: wait ok not to be /that person/ but I was hella into doja cat in like 2018/2019 before she got really popular LOL

Lea: buy hey man good music is good music

Kai: tbh I think the first time I heard her was mooo

Kai: So like that's my impression of her

Kai: And it's ok I can't help but be /that person/ a lot of the time

Lea: HAHA ya I feel that

Lea: god when that song came out everyone at Davis was so into it. Of course they were. Smh

Kai: Wait that's so funny omfg

Kai: New school anthem?

Kai leads with a compliment, and he validates Lea while teasing a little as well. Lea responds well to it; their conversation is already laden with the kinds of references that an outsider could fail to grasp. Some are better than others at self-revelation and stating preferences. Will began a conversation with me this way:

Will: Hi Mimi. We definitely share similar loves & hates. And I like how your eyes smile when you do. I'm in SF. How about you?

> **Me:** Hi Will. SF! Cool burning man photos. I did not post any, but I have enjoyed that too.

> **Will:** I hear you on the Burning Man pics. Wondering if I should refrain from posting them too. A lot of people don't get it. It's like telling them you're vegan . . . They just run the other way without considering it or really knowing why. And btw . . . I'm vegan. Are you running?

> **Me:** Ha, no, I'm not running, except to get my morning run in.

Will wants me to know he's vegan right off the bat, but he's also letting me know he's looking for someone with openness to experience. The latter may be more important to him than the former.

Authentically presenting some dimensions of our personality is easier than others, particularly with strangers. We are taught early to smile for the camera, share, get along with our pals, lead with agreeableness, whether or not we feel like it—whether or not we are, in fact, agreeable. Because everyone is trained to fake it to some degree, it follows that everyone is trained to assume that others are faking it. It's hard to know where the conscious social construct ends and the true dimension begins. Modifying tastes, expectations, and style in order to please others is an essential part of the agreeable dimension; chameleon is its true color. When texting with strangers, it behooves us to assume that we are all putting our most agreeable foot forward and that it may slip backward from there as we get to know each other better.

In this chat with Alex, for instance, I largely eschew agreeableness, but I can't deny, looking back on it, that there's an element of deliberate self-presentation at play:

Alex: You're busy at work I presume. Can I see you this week?

Me: Hey there. Sorry for the slow reply. I worked late last night and have a work event tonight and tomorrow evening.

Alex: Sounds like just another day in the life of a busy silicon valley physician :)

Me: Well I did get a long ride in before work today

Alex: Damn, you're such an overachiever

Me: Overachiever? Moi? That's French for "me" by the way

Alex: Yes, I'm pointing at you.

Me: Pointing is not polite.

Alex: Ok, I'm looking out of the corner of my eye at you

Me: I'm eating a 1000 calorie breakfast at the Facebook cafeteria. Eggs, bacon, potatoes, yogurt, fruit.

Alex: You are just validating your overachiever status even more. Plus name dropping Facebook.

Me: I eat overachievers for breakfast

Alex: I've heard they are delicious. But I've never actually eaten one myself.

Me: They are usually skinny and less caloric than bacon and hash browns.

Alex: When can I see you? You are almost relegating me to begging.

Presenting ourselves as friendly and agreeable—with shades, in my case, of conscientiousness and drive—is certainly important, but not at the expense of inquiry. Asking questions is not only at the heart of getting to know people better but an effective way to present yourself authentically. The questions you choose not only signal your attentiveness to others but also offer an opportunity to express your own interests.

To get a good feel for someone, you need rough, unguarded responses to meaningful subjects. You need answers. And to get the right answers, you need to ask the right questions. In chapter 2 we thought about the qualities we're seeking, the type of relationship we want, the character traits and tendencies that ring our bell. In chapter 3 we took the first steps toward overcoming the biggest obstacle to a successful match: looking into ourselves. It is time to start asking for and distilling the information we need from a small batch of text messages and to do it in a way that elicits the most honest and open responses—the best data.

Some of the questions that might lead to revealing answers can be awkward to ask.

The devil, as they say, is in the details. In the early days of dating apps, eHarmony subjected prospective clients to a lengthy questionnaire that probed into all kinds of preferences. The questions addressed intimate but practical considerations, such as "How much does body odor bother you?" or "Would you share a toothbrush with someone else?" Most would not consider asking such questions of a prospective date socially acceptable; these are the things we just passively observe in others, drawing our own conclusions. But there are certain things we need to know about a date—deal makers and deal breakers alike. How might we make the best use of the questions we *can* ask?

It's at least twice as rare for men to get responses to initial messages, and even rarer to have that chat lead to an in-person meeting. It is an understatement to say that women have the upper hand in online dating; they hold all the cards, along with a sleeve full of aces and jokers.

Think you're shy? Submissive? Been burned in the dating process before? None of that matters if you know how to play the cards you're given. Here, we'll look at how to ask questions that will help you find what you're seeking. And more important, how to avoid what you're not. By engaging in a meaningful exchange, we can bring language and data together to crystallize an image of who we are speaking to: their personality, their attachment patterns, and, when it applies, even their psychopathology.

Asking questions, after all, is foundational to relationship building. A Harvard Business School study tracked how many questions speed daters asked. The data showed a correlation between the number of questions and popularity. Want to be popular? Ask, then ask again, and ye shall receive.

Here's an easy rule of thumb: questions are better if they're short. (Men, in particular, are most likely to respond to short messages.) How short, you might wonder. The shorter the better. Data science has shown that once text messages exceed 360 characters, men are likely to get scared away; long messages are the equivalent of a face tattoo.

Remember that the best questions may not be questions at all, but statements that lead a person to make a revelation. If you've ever engaged in therapy, you might have noticed that therapists have a tendency to make reflective statements rather than ask direct questions. Direct questions are certainly useful, but statements that open the conversation up to multiple possible directions can lead to a rich vein and give a better initial sense of your conversation partner.

Like a good therapist, accept the challenge to make your match feel comfortable enough that they let their guard down and reveal something true about themselves. The goal is to bring information to the surface in a way that doesn't sound like a psychiatric interview but that yields information you can use.

Think for a moment about how our canine friends approach this information-seeking problem. You might say they get straight to the bottom of things. What they're doing isn't rude; it's science. A dog can learn if her new encounter is male or female, its age, whether they have met before, what its diet consists of, whether it's healthy or sick, and even what kind of mood it's in. All in a quick sniff.

Your first text exchange is a little like a dog sniff: a way to quickly take the measure of the person you're encountering. Consider the initial banter between Chris and Molly. It gets off to a promising start, but it misses opportunities to take the conversation deeper:

Chris: You have two sisters?

Molly: Sure do. You?

Chris: 9 of them

Molly: Stoppit

Chris: K

Chris: 1 older brother

Molly: Sounds about right

Chris: Are you the youngest?

Molly: Yep

Molly: Look how much we have in common!

Molly: Basically the same person!

Chris: That's what I was thinking

Chris: Brunette

Chris: A bit crazy

Molly: Just a bit

Molly: The good cray

Chris: 😣

Molly: So you're a tech bro?

Molly: I just got back from Soul Cycle

Chris: Of course you did

Molly: What else is obvious about me, Chris?

Chris: I'm sure you took an Uber pool there while on your phone

Molly: Oh cmon

Chris: Did you skip happy hour for soul cycle?

Chris: Want to grab a drink?

This text exchange contains so little information, despite its length. At every juncture, they both eschew curiosity and avert disclosure. Overtures about family, work, and lifestyle are made without any follow-up. Now Chris is proposing a drink, and Molly has little information to go on to make that call. They should both be doing more sniffing and less tail wagging. Molly could have learned more about Chris, opening up doors into his family ("One older brother—so you got beat up a lot as a kid?") or work and lifestyle ("I hear tech bros work crazy hours") instead of casually closing doors behind her at every exchange.

Again, we all try to put our best foot forward, to present our best self. Online, however, it's all too easy for a prospective match to represent themselves as something other than, for instance, the man-child living in his parents' basement that they truly are. There is always the risk that the person we are chatting with is insincere, ungenerous, unforthcoming with their most intimate vulnerabilities—the same way they might be on a psychiatrist's couch. But how can we know?

Let's sniff this out.

Would I Lie to You?

A little bit of lying is the norm—playing up best qualities and hiding flaws. Which means, if we are to discover who the stranger we are texting with really is, it's on us, not them. We need to skillfully extract that information; it's not just going to be handed to us. Maybe never, and certainly not in the first or second or even third text exchange.

It's commonly said among health-care providers that "men add an inch and women subtract fifteen pounds." Expect the same with online dating apps. Photos are probably old, and bios may misrepresent. But what are the indicators of misrepresentation over text? In person, we try to detect lies through telltale body language, tone, or evasive answers. Texts give us few of the same cues.

But they do offer some of their own. Research out of Cornell has demonstrated a few telltale signs of deceptive text messages.

1. KEEPING A DISTANCE

Verbal distancing can often manifest itself in the failure to use first-person pronouns. When people are aligned with their own statements or opinions, they will use "I" or "me." With lies, the texter will stand back from the lie, distance themselves from it. This may include dropping the first-person pronoun altogether. Lies also contain fewer third-person pronouns. These are all attempts to dissociate oneself (and one's self) from the lie. We don't know if Stephen is lying, but his message shows all the hallmarks of it:

> **Mary:** I tried to call you a few times, but no answer

> **Stephen:** Didn't receive your messages until now. Near total tech breakdown

> **Mary:** Oh, where are you?

> **Stephen:** Santa Barbara—met with a European investor yesterday. Driving back to Marin to retrieve backpack and fly fishing gear

2. LACK OF DETAIL OR ABSTRACTION

Lies will often lack key details or be devoid of any abstraction— that is, explanation of thought or feeling. The lie will be purely factual. We can suppose that texter is using their cognitive power to construct the lie, and thus they withhold the nuance and abstraction we tend to use when stating something that's plainly true.

> **Bill:** You said you've been separated for how long?

> **Angela:** It's been a while. Amicable separation. We get along really well.

3. LONGER SENTENCES AND REPEATING INFORMATION

The examples so far have all been quite terse, but liars tend in fact to use more words in their texts, not to mention noncommittal terms such as "maybe" or "sure." Liars will also repeat their statements, as if the repetition somehow makes them true.

> **Rob:** Can't make it to the show. Damn car won't start. Swapped out the alternator and starter recently then did a major service. Maybe the fuel pump or something. It just won't start.

4. DODGING THE QUESTION

People don't enjoy lying, so they will often dodge questions or reply with another question instead. Text makes it much easier to do so than in-person conversation. A liar may also just change the subject and hope the unanswered question goes unnoticed.

> **Lisa:** Hey, I never heard back from you last night

> **Greg:** Hey there, big busy day today.

> **Lisa:** Me too. What about last night?

> **Greg:** Yeah, how was your night? Did you have fun at the dinner? 😗

5. TRUE STORY, I SWEAR

Statements such as "To be honest," "I'm not going to lie," and "I swear" will often indicate some dishonesty in the statement. Truth tellers don't usually feel the need to back up their statements with oaths.

> **Julia:** I'm not a fan of hanging out in bars. I prefer quiet evenings at home

> **Andy:** To be honest, I'm over the bar scene too. I'm not gonna lie—I spend time in bars, but really, I can take it or leave it

Dating is all about finding common ground. A gentle fib about whether you like spending time in bars may seem harmless enough in the grand scheme of things. But if you're someone for whom alcohol is a touchy subject, Andy's reply is waving an unmistakable red flag.

Common Kingdom

Kingdom, phylum, class, order, family, genus, species. Remember learning these taxonomic classifications in high school biology? While classifying humans by their demographics is fraught with a world of problems, there may be details about a person's family, cultural background, education level, and lifestyle that will help you find common ground and allow you both to let your hair down. Such information may not appear in a person's profile; in fact, it usually isn't. Fortunately, there are other, better ways to learn whom you are chatting with.

Consider my chat with George:

> **George:** Are you in SF?
>
> **Me:** I am. Where are you from originally?
>
> **George:** "Why do you think I'm from somewhere else?" might be a more interesting question 😊
>
> **Me:** I didn't assume you were from somewhere else. I was just asking where you grew up.
>
> **George:** Thought maybe you picked up on something—it is interesting.
>
> **George:** Greece. And I'm the only one of my cohort that doesn't really ski . . . Let alone telemark!
>
> **Me:** Maybe the red pants tipped me off . . . Growing up I spent some summers in Greece.

George was initially defensive about where he was from, and I could have succumbed to his reply with a defense of my own. But because I held my ground, he opened up a little, offering some opportunity to mirror.

Mirror, Mirror on the Wall, Who's the Defensive Guy from Greece?

Mirroring is a therapeutic technique that uses verbal communication and nonverbal gestures to reflect and represent a patient's emotional and cognitive style back to them. We all mirror unconsciously. When we are talking to someone with an accent, we slow our speech down and might even change our word pronunciation. We tend to mirror body language in business meetings and on first dates. People who are naturally good conversationalists (not to mention trained therapists) tend to mirror more.

Mirroring serves to make people feel more confident, thus reducing defensiveness and uncovering feelings. By making an attempt to understand a person, and affirming some aspect of their experience without overt judgment, we can seem less threatening. That's not to say we should manipulate the other person by *appearing* to agree with everything or change our own interests by adopting theirs. Mirroring serves to give the person more room to fully declare themselves.

We have cells called mirror neurons that fire when we observe someone mirroring our actions, speech, or expression. These cells may be part of the neural basis for our understanding of others' actions. Neuroscientists have speculated that it is malfunction of the mirror neurons that's partly responsible for the lack of empathy and understanding—or a more intellectualized, less abstract version of understanding—found in more pronounced forms of autism. They are the brain cells that seem to help us gain a more emotional grasp of another.

Mirroring is also considered a sign of attraction. Our brains experience it as a dopamine high, activating the reward center of our brain. They're *like us,* our brain reasons, so they must *like* us. Can mirroring take place over text, in the absence of physical cues? It can and it does. By mirroring someone, you are more likely to keep them engaged in your conversation, as well as learn more about their true selves.

Back to my chat with George:

> **Me:** Maybe the red pants tipped me off . . . Growing up I spent some summers in Greece.

> **Me:** Pretty sure every third guy in Greece was named George.

George: Well, that's where the name comes from (Greece).

> **Me:** I would go inland to the Greek mountains.

George: Jealous of your childhood 😊

> **Me:** Well, that was only part of it. I grew up in Montreal. Much colder.

George: And one of my grandmas was named Mimi

> **Me:** How long have you been in the Bay Area?

George: 23.5 years . . . I get to be an old man who grumbles and reminisces about bars that closed.

> **Me:** I've been here 26.5. So I have three years of grumbling over you.

George: What kind of doctoring do you do?

> (As an old grumpy man I may need your services)

> **Me:** I am a psychiatrist, so grumpy is my specialty.

In these messages I let George know that I understand some of his reference points and life experiences. He does the same for me. I have also matched the length and cadence of his messages. Breezy matching breezy, playful matching playful, short sentences matching short sentences. I end by accepting him for who he is, at least to the degree I know him this far. He's grumpy, but I'm okay with grumpy. Heck, I'm even a pro at it.

Once I establish some common ground, I begin to take some risks.

Throwing Curveballs

It can be tempting to stick to a scripted routine in your first conversations. But what you really want is to make your match feel safe enough to leave their comfort zone. This can lead to more spontaneous, genuine, and unusual responses. Show that you're willing to go out on a limb, and they may follow.

The writer and storyteller David Sedaris tells a great anecdote about drawing out telling details from the people he meets. Sometimes all it takes is a simple question. He speaks of meeting a woman and asking her, without warning and apropos of nothing in particular, "When was the last time you touched a monkey?" As he tells it, she replied, "Can you smell him on me?"

By throwing a curveball as Sedaris did, you not only push a person slightly off balance but test their ability to react in the moment. Reactions to curveballs can be excellent predictors of important Big Five personality vectors. People who are open and agreeable are much more likely to react favorably and pleasurably to curveballs. Openness to experience, if we recall, describes a person's degree of intellectual curiosity, creativity, and preference for novelty and variety. Agreeableness encompasses the tendency to be compassionate toward others rather than suspicious.

Not many of us have David Sedaris's chutzpah, but we can keep the conversation interesting, even a bit risky. Stereotypical questions like "What do you do for work?" or "How is your day going?" are far less likely to be revealing than introducing a more offbeat question. They're also a lot less likely to get a response. So rather than asking someone about how their day is going, ask about a detail you have observed and see what emerges, or riff on a subject they have introduced and see where their response leads.

Let's see if George swings:

> **Me:** I am a psychiatrist, so grumpy is my specialty.
>
> **Me:** I might be able to make room for you on my couch.

George: I've never been propositioned like that before! ☺

George: (I do also see that your couch is made of swords and daggers and yatagans and such . . .)

> **Me:** I strive for originality. That is actually a throne not a couch. The photo was taken at a friend's party with a game of thrones theme. Needless to say, I've never watched the show.
>
> **Me:** I do have several couches. I'm sure we can find the one that's right for you.

> **George:** Poetic license denied I guess . . .
>
> **George:** Poly-couchness is new to me . . .

You can see I took some risks with innuendo. It was downright flirty. And it worked. He returned with a playful answer, created a new word, and allowed me to wander into a potential discussion of polyamory. For some daters, that's an invitation for further discussion. For others, that might constitute a deal breaker.

Introducing Deal Breakers, Without Breaking the Deal

We all have them. Lines we have drawn. Borders that mustn't be crossed. If we have too many—if we are too demanding of perfection—we may have our own problems to sort out, potentially in therapy. But for most, deal breakers are a fact of life.

Thankfully, even an early text exchange offers an opportunity to address them, to weave them into the conversation. It can be tricky. For example, if heavy drinking is one of your deal breakers, you likely can't just come out and ask, "So are you an alcoholic?" But you can seed your chat with mentions of alcohol and see what grows. Here George and I have stumbled onto the topic of polyamory—well, he started it—and I decide to explore it further.

> **George:** Poly-couchness is new to me . . .
>
> **Me:** Well, for linguistic consistency it should be "polythrones"
>
> **Me:** As an aside, the word polyamory has always struck me as odd because the 'poly' is Greek and the 'amory' is Latin.

Me: I practice in different offices so I literally do have many couches. What kind of furniture does your work involve?

George: You have many couches AND many thrones? Just marry me already!

George: To be clear I have been on a bit of a multi-amory/polyphilia "journey" since I got out of my very monogamous relationship of 20 years . . .

Me: Makes sense. In my experience, it's not a great long-term strategy. Any dependent mammals in your life? I do see the cute dog in your second photo.

By moving from poly-couchness to polyamory, I capitalized on an opportunity to discuss a potential deal breaker without losing the momentum of the conversation. The key is to raise a potential deal breaker in a way that doesn't ruin the interaction or lead to a placating (and insincere) answer.

Here is an example of how *not* to introduce a deal breaker. This was an initial text exchange after matching:

Ashleigh: Good morning! May I call you "Josh" or do you prefer "Josh-oo-ah"?

Joshua: "Ooh-ah" for short

Joshua: What should I call you? 😬

Ashleigh: How about Ash-leeg-hug? That's what ET called me on the universal studios ride.

Joshua: What a sweetheart

Joshua: So—serious question, how do you feel about kids? I really want to have kids someday.

While everyone is entitled to their own deal breakers, including an objection to procreation, asking a woman if she's willing to have your children right off the bat might lead to a door slammed in your face. Needless to say, this conversation sputtered out. The desire to have kids is a heavy subject for the fourth text bubble with a stranger, deal breaker or not.

George's post-matrimonial sowing of wild oats seemed normal and not particularly a deal breaker to me, but I wanted to know if he was committed to anything else right now, such as a career, children, or pets. So I asked.

> **Me:** Makes sense. In my experience, it's not a great long-term strategy. Any dependent mammals in your life? I do see the cute dog in your second photo.

> **George:** The dog is dead now. He was an old man . . . And not really mine. The ethics of using someone else's deceased animal for seduction purposes is to be discussed.

> **George:** What's your tomorrow look like? We have SO MANY conversation threads . . . might be time for a live meeting . . .

Might it, though?

After a dozen replies and some genuine, revealing responses from George, I can now make an educated guess about whether I want to meet him. We have gathered that he is extroverted and open but looking for something casual. His admission of using someone else's dead pet for seduction purposes, though funny, smacks of laziness, and hence lack of conscientiousness.

It wasn't an easy call, for one glaring reason: his sense of humor. Though his hesitation to commit and his flightiness were turnoffs, his quick wit and clever turns of phrase made for a very enjoyable chat.

It points to a feature of chemistry that's no less true for being a truism. A person's sense of humor is such an important attribute that it, or its lack, can be a deal breaker. Consider this, shall we say, less lively exchange:

Me: Hi Paul. Nice to meet you. How are you?

> **Paul:** Good, what's up mimi

> **Paul:** Some curious have you ever been married do you have any kids

Me: What's the story behind all the dogs in your photo? Enquiring minds want to know. Yes to both. Daughter is off to college next year and my son is a freshman.

> **Paul:** What are you looking for?

> **Paul:** A relationship

Me: Ha, you don't make small talk, do you?

> **Paul:** I talk alot I just don't do a lot of this frivolous messaging back and forth. Lol

> **Paul:** So tell me what is your favorite color

> **Paul:** And what sign are you?

Me: I'm a Scorpio. My birthday was last week. Have I missed yours? My favorite color for what?

> **Paul:** I'm making small talk like you wanted . . . tell me, what wakes you up in the morning?

Me: My dog. I'm not a fan of small talk either. But, I also think it's heavy handed to ask a stranger what they are looking for. It was more of a plea for grace.

Paul and I didn't seem to be finding a rhythm in our banter, despite what were probably good intentions on both of our parts. We can learn a lot from a person's sense of humor and also by testing what type of sense of humor they have.

Humor, Seriously

What's so funny? It's a fair question, because humor can take so many forms. (By all means, please read Salvatore Attardo's 985-page encyclopedia on the subject. Finished? Let's continue.)

People use humor in different ways and for different reasons. The professor of psychology Rod Martin at the University of Western Ontario broke down humor and its relationship to psychological well-being into four categories. To broadly categorize, we use humor:

1. to connect with others (affiliative humor);
2. to cheer up and have a better outlook on an otherwise difficult situation (self-enhancing humor);
3. to put others down (aggressive humor); and
4. to put ourselves down (self-defeating humor).

Understanding a person's sense of humor—how they use humor to connect, whether they can tell a joke, whether they laugh at jokes you tell—can provide important insights into what that person will be like in a relationship.

Testing your match's sense of humor might begin simply by observing how well you banter with them. Consider this first exchange between my friend Lina and Jack:

> **Lina:** So everyone on here is looking for the moon and stars and steamy romance. What are you looking for?

> **Jack:** I'm looking for my last, long, 'in love' relationship . . . but not until the third date.

> **Jack:** That was a joke.

Lina decides to mirror him and expand his premise to the point of absurdity, to test his sense of humor and see how he reacts.

> **Lina:** On principle, first date.

> **Jack:** Ok girl, where do you live?

Affiliative humor is humor used to connect with others. While Jack might have been aiming for that, his asking Lina where she lived came off as more creepy than funny. He would have been better off saying something more affirming and less stalker-like, something along the lines of "Send me a Lyft and I'm there!" Lina could have laughed and continued to banter. The way we frame our propositions—right down to the words we choose—is everything.

People who display affiliative humor tend to be extroverted, open, and agreeable. Here is a text thread between Leonardo and Rene, who sparred with more sophisticated affiliative humor:

> **Leo:** Ciao Rene! You seem to be everywhere at the same time. Where do you sleep, usually?

> **Rene:** Ciao. One of my friends teases me that "usually" is my middle name. And usually, if it's made in Italy, mi piace. But I live in SF.

> **Leo:** Buongiorno! I also live in SF! What a coincidenza!

> **Rene:** So much in common! You can't test my Italian too far. I grew up speaking French but relying on college Italian which was a while ago . . .

Leo: I suppose we could whip you into shape.

Rene: a tongue lashing?

Leo: I am a master of many tongues.

Rene: You have a harem? Or you speak multiple languages? Maybe both . . .

Leo: I have directed a choir before. And I speak a few languages. But oy, a harem. Too much estrogen in the house and hair in the drains.

Rene, a sharp and prolific online dater, takes some playful risks here, along with mirroring, to push the boundaries of the conversation and open up new pathways. Leonardo's playful, boyish charm, as well as his irreverence and independence, all come through in this short text exchange.

People who display the second type, **self-enhancing humor** (meaning those who take a hard situation and make it funny), are less vulnerable to depression and anxiety, and they generally cope well with stress. Martin, for instance, after opening with a banal question that gets lost in Juliette's in-box, recovers with a joke.

Juliette: Hi Martin

Martin: Hello Juliette, you seem very special. Of your many talents and accomplishments, which do you hold in highest esteem?

(Several weeks pass.)

Martin: I've been sending telepathic messages for a month asking you to respond to me but have not received a response here or via the ether . . . Maybe I need to recalibrate my psi receiver?

Juliette: I'm so sorry, I was in Bali and then NYC so the signal may have weakened in transit. Back in the bay for the non-foreseeable near future (I lack clairvoyant skills)

> **Martin:** Hi Juliette, I usually receive messages from Bali but not in tourist season, and there's too much EMR in New York for anything to penetrate its bubble with any fidelity. Clairvoyance is my specialty so I knew I'd hear from you eventually.

Although he hadn't received a response to his original text for more than a month, Martin didn't get piqued or demanding. No hostile, needy "Hello??" Instead, he used self-enhancing humor to his benefit and joked about the lack of response, which, in turn, prompted a reply. Martin demonstrated openness and agreeableness, along with grit and an ability to make lemonade when handed lemons.

People who display the next one, **aggressive humor** (humor at the expense of others), tend to be insensitive and—perhaps to no one's surprise—have far less successful relationships. It's not so easy to insult your way into someone's heart.

Lauren: Hi Tom

> **Tom:** Lauren, you've got it going on!

Lauren: Do I? And here I was feeling happy that I just finished my taxes

> **Tom:** No dirty words please, until I get to know you better

Lauren: How will you spend the day?

> **Tom:** I'm going to do some work around the house, go hiking, maybe have dinner with Lauren?

Lauren: Are you hiking in this wet mess? I just came home drenched from a run.

Tom: It's dry on the East Side! And sunny.

Lauren: East bay? Or East side of town?

Tom: That's right.

Lauren: Sigh . . . that's what my father would say when I would ask a question with an "or."

Tom: Aw. Daddy complex. Well, I am older than you.

Lauren: The dog ran with me and took deliberate pleasure in jumping in all the puddles. She loves to swim and ski with me too.

Tom: Hyperthyroidism combined with cardiomyopathy. I give her three years.

Lauren: That's ok. I'm all about quality.

Tom: Hell yeah

Lauren: The kids will be gone in four.

Tom: Dream on

Tom is clever, that's clear. But in a brief text thread, he manages to alienate Lauren in short order. He takes shots at her "daddy complex," her dog's health, and her kids' chances at higher education. One such shot might be funny and enhance the conversation, but three in a row? It's relentless and mean-spirited. Move on.

Finally, people who use the last type of humor, **self-defeating humor,** can be quite funny and charming, but they may suffer from low self-esteem. They are often unhappy and anxious and on average feel less satisfied with their relationships. Take Ryan:

> **Alexa:** Hi Ryan. I hope you enjoyed the weekend.

> **Ryan:** had a lovely weekend. just off a friend's boat after a decadent weekend . . . in my little town of sausalito . . . and u?

> **Ryan:** i must admit between your intellectual accomplishments and good looks . . . i am exhausted and totally intimidated even thinking about a coffee . . . pardon me, a tea . . . ☺

Ryan's first impulse is to put himself down while talking up Alexa. Though charming on the surface—self-deprecation is the tool of many a stand-up comic—this may not necessarily bode well for a smooth, long-term relationship. Ryan is establishing a status gap from the outset—just words, yes, but an obstacle to overcome. Ryan's lack of capitalization may also provide evidence of, as we speculated in an earlier chapter, either false modesty or an antiauthoritarian attitude.

In the end, a good sense of humor can be a powerfully attractive quality, especially in a text exchange. Even the use of words or abbreviations associated with humor can build rapport over text. In data analyzed by OkCupid, the use of "lol" and "haha" leads to higher response rates, so people clearly feel these textspeak terms are affiliative. "Hehe" is also positively correlated with response, but less so, perhaps because it sounds a little evil. In contrast, other textspeak terms such as "u," "ur," "r," "ya," "luv," and "wat" all make a bad impression, and they are negatively correlated with getting a response.

So use humor, by all means. But u should b careful with wat kinds of jokes u tell.

Attachment Comes in Three Flavors

Another dimension to consider in the stranger you're texting with is their **attachment style.** Attachment is the level of affection, sympathy, or dependence we form with someone we love—our bond, if you will. Simply put, as we'll see, it comes in three flavors.

John Bowlby was the first psychologist to study attachment. Bowlby was influenced by the research of Harry Harlow, who studied monkeys in captivity and observed that their bonds fell into distinct categories. The *secure* monkey was raised by a living mother monkey who holds and nurses her infant; the monkey feels cared for and protected. The *anxious* monkey was raised in a cage with a faux mother made of soft cloth, outfitted with a bottle attached to her containing warm milk; the monkey can attach and love but is needy, insecure, and cries a lot. Finally, the *avoidant* monkey was raised in a cage with a faux mother made of wire—not at all nice to cuddle with. This last monkey doesn't attach easily, avoids close relationships, and is often hostile to strangers.

Bowlby examined children's relationships to their caregivers and found not only that Harlow's types could be applied to them as well, but that a child's relationship to their caregiver was predictive of later attachment style, too. His studies showed that maternal deprivation adversely affected children's emotional development and their future ability to attach in healthy ways. It was the foundation for modern attachment theory, which is commonly applied to adult relationships in psychological settings. Adults, too, seek closeness—are biologically driven to form attachments—and the process of forming those attachments is dictated by experience.

Humans aren't monkeys, of course. But we too can suffer

anxiety and loneliness with separation. Research suggests that half the human population is *securely* attached. They are comfortable with intimacy and feel more satisfied in a relationship. Securely attached people allow their partners independence but are also capable of providing honesty and support. That leaves us with fully half of adults who don't react the same way to relationships. *Anxiously attached* people have trouble living in the moment and tend to overemphasize the role their partner plays in their life. They may cling out of fear of being alone. *Avoidantly attached* people keep others at a distance and may preemptively sabotage relationships to protect themselves (remember D.W.?).

Are the three flavors of attachment represented proportionally on dating sites relative to the general population? Unlikely. Securely attached types pair off early and are more likely to stay together; they're secure that way. Which leaves the rest to fend for themselves online, leaving a higher proportion of loose avoidant and insecure types rolling around dating apps, wondering where all the secure people went.

It's possible to solicit early clues to attachment style in your initial text thread, but these traits generally take much longer to manifest themselves, their cues more subtle. It certainly doesn't take a psychiatrist to identify the most extreme forms of dysfunctional attachment, but reviewing early cues and potential red flags to watch for can be helpful. So though it is by no means a comprehensive list, here are five indicators of insecure attachment to look out for as you take forays into texting with new people.

1. INSTAMACY

Too much information, too soon. Some people will seek to establish a deep bond immediately. I refer to this instant intimacy as "instamacy." While it may feel seductive or reassuring in the moment, it can be a red flag for problematic attachment in the future. Rushing into a relationship without a stronger foundation rarely lends itself to stability, and instant infatuation is likely to disappoint. Those tendencies can manifest themselves as early as an initial text exchange. People who display instamacy are pleasers, can lack boundaries, and may revert to an anxious or avoidant pattern in a relationship after it gets under way.

In this initial text exchange Aaron actually calls himself out on this tendency. Jo had stated in her profile that she wanted a relationship with "a mind meld, actionable chemistry, and empathy."

> **Aaron:** Love your relationship comments.
>
> **Jo:** Profiles are painful to fill out
>
> **Aaron:** I utterly hate this process
>
> **Jo:** I literally joined this site tonight
>
> **Jo:** I think though, the best approach to online dating is to make a game of it. Low expectations, try to have fun, and enjoy the people you meet along the way.
>
> **Aaron:** The online stuff has a special place as an extra ring of the inferno, since you can so easily establish an online chemistry and then meet, only to discover that the real world version isn't there, which either leaves you feeling like a shallow Shmuck or having a little heartbreak that no one else really understands.
>
> **Aaron:** Actually that is one of my big foolish rules in this.
>
> **Jo:** What rule is that?

Aaron: I'd rather show and get to know the 6 month later, tummy let out, non-idealized versions of each other

Aaron: If we don't like those versions, it's a lot of not very fun work being on stage with someone you want to let down your guard with.

Jo: Well, agree with all except the tummy. Probably, the error in marriage is thinking it's ok to let the tummy out.

Jo: Not that I'm a fan of Victorian corsets. But sometimes it is what we don't say. Maintaining some air of mystery can be seductive.

Aaron: Naw. When you really fall for somebody, the perception of beauty shifts significantly.

While Aaron is endearing here, he admits in no uncertain terms that he is already worried about disappointment. You haven't even met him, and you already feel sorry for him. This is too intimate an exchange, too quickly, the text equivalent of a drunken stranger pouring out their heart to you in a bar. Finish your drink and walk away. Or, if rescue fantasies are your thing, go for it, but know what you're getting into.

2. FLAT AFFECT

In order to connect, we count on people to be emotionally expressive and responsive. In psychiatry, we talk about *affect* as someone's variability in facial expression, tone of voice, and level of emotional engagement. Some people present as having a blunted or flat affect. They maintain a single, monotonous expression or a lack of emotional expression altogether. They may be emotionally aloof, stiff. Maybe they're just shy, or perhaps they feel that exposing any emotion presents too big a risk. Seeing this early in a text exchange is a potential red flag. Yes, they might just be shy, but they might also be hiding mental illness behind that monotone, such as major depression or even schizophrenia. People experiencing these psychiatric conditions are as worthy of love (or even just a good date) as the rest of us, but any would-be partner will want to be attuned to the warning signs, if just to know what they're getting into.

Think of flat affect as the opposite of emojis. There is no smiling in the language, no winking, no raised eyebrow, no blushing. They may as well be sending you the snail emoji, for all the energy that's coming your way.

Here is a first text exchange between Brad, who indicated in his profile that he enjoys swimming, and Kathryn.

Kathryn: Hi Brad. Nice to meet you.

> **Brad:** Hello Kathryn . . . how are you? Where are you located?

Kathryn: Monday off to a good start. I live in SF but work on the peninsula a few days a week. You live in San Mateo or just work there?

> **Brad:** I live and work in San Mateo

Kathryn: Makes for an easy commute!

> **Brad:** True

Kathryn: Where do you like to swim?

> **Brad:** My place

Kathryn: Nice! Lap pool or endless pool? I swim 4-5 times a week.

> **Brad:** It's a lap pool

Kathryn: Fancy!

> **Brad:** Yeah, it's nice

Kathryn: You are a man of few words . . .

> **Brad:** Yes, I'd rather talk than text

Kathryn: happy to talk. I can try you if you send a number and some good times.

Kathryn eventually did speak with Brad. She told me about it after their date: "No surprise, he was as aloof and avoidant over the phone as he was by text. I pride myself on being able to draw people out in conversation, but Brad seemed to me beyond a typical level of shyness. He seemed almost afraid of making an actual connection." Talking to him was like hearing a dial tone on the other end of the line instead of a live voice. Oddly, she added, despite this "he was keen to get together and seemed to feel we had connected enough to merit a meeting."

They hadn't. She told him as much, in the warmest monotone she could muster.

3. HOSTILITY AT FIRST SIGHT

While it's a rare occurrence, seeing any signs of overt hostility early in a text exchange is a bad omen. Red flags don't get much redder than that. This person is almost sure to have attachment issues, ones that could make for a challenging relationship in the very best case.

Warning signs are glaring in this comical initial exchange with Patrick:

Ellen: Hi Patrick

> **Patrick:** Can't you see I'm busy
>
> **Patrick:** Sorry

> **Patrick:** Meant for a friend
>
> **Patrick:** While I'm here, how are you Ellen?

You have to love the way Patrick talks to his friends! Because this was on a dating app, he was clearly talking to another person he was considering dating, and needless to say, this did not make a good impression. Bye, Patrick! Can't you see *I'm* busy?

4. THE CONTROL FREAK

Some people manage the anxiety of attachment by trying to control their environment. Online dating, however, requires a certain amount of throwing caution to the wind, something these controllers are likely to struggle with. Now they're at sea, feeling tossed around by the waves. Their instinct is to clamp down, to batten down the hatches. The problem? You haven't agreed to be on their boat.

Recognizing the early signs of a controlling personality can offer you clues to a person's attachment style and to the difficulty they might have in forming secure relationships. A lack of flexibility or a desire to control in an early text exchange is often a red flag.

Here is a first exchange between Becky, a data analyst, and a man who listed himself as "David Using a Nickname Until We Meet."

> **Becky:** I love those photos of you in Europe.
>
> **David:** Thanks. I would have you note that it is actually Buenos Aires.
>
> **Becky:** It looks a lot like Spain.
>
> **Becky:** Your profile says you do mindful investing. Whatever it is, it sounds like a good gig.

> **David:** Happy to share more in person. I will text you with a plan to meet.

"David Using a Nickname Until We Meet" presumed that he would be meeting Becky without first asking if she was even interested. Some find assertiveness attractive, but it is easily confused with *controlling.* Assertiveness is the ability to shape one's own actions. Attempting to control the actions of another isn't assertive; it's aggressive. David manages to do this twice in a very short span. These are red flags that should not be ignored. Becky wanted a date, not a dictator!

5. TMI: TOO MUCH INFORMATION

While instamacy can be too fast for some, it nevertheless feels good. It offers a kind of instant validation—*this person must really like me!*—firing pleasure centers in the brain. TMI is also too fast, but it makes you cringe or want to run for the hills. There's a fundamental distinction: With instamacy there is a *promise* of connection that does not exist. With TMI there is a *presumption* of connection that does not exist.

First text exchanges are attempts to get to know each other; that's why we're online. But while aloofness, withholding, controlling, and hostile behavior are clearly worrisome, revealing too much too quickly is no less problematic. No one wants to have their date cry on their first meeting (more on that soon), and no one wants TMI in the first text thread. Someone offering TMI may seem to be revealing details about themselves, but what they're actually revealing is someone who is likely needy, anxious, or self-centered.

Consider my initial text thread with Doug, who said in his profile that he was "on a journey to love and be loved" and has dogs.

Me: How are you Doug?

> **Doug:** Hi Mimi. Nice to hear from you. I'm ok. Been having some indigestion off and on. I had surgery over the summer and I completely stopped exercising and it seems to have affected my digestion. I seem to be less tolerant of acidic or spicy foods or too much meat. Today I had two work meetings over meals and I'm feeling bloated and just tired and not myself. Hope that is not TMI. How have you been?

Definitely TMI, Doug. Again, you don't need a psychiatrist to tell you that "indigestion" and "bloated" are not sexy words for a first text. Still, I wanted to be helpful to him (and also was just curious to see where the text thread would go).

Me: What surgery did you have? Sometimes celiac disease (an autoimmune disease that causes a reaction to gluten, including bloating and indigestion) is triggered by trauma such as surgery or childbirth. It would be worth getting the test if you have not.

Me: I know you didn't join this app for medical advice, but I am a doctor ;-)

> **Doug:** Lol. Thanks. Advice is fine.

> **Doug:** I had a dysplastic hip—genetic—And it just wore out. It literally did not fit in the socket properly and the body does all kinds of bone growth tricks to fix itself. I have some cool xrays of the pre-op hip that my surgeon carefully went over with me. I lost most of my range of motion and of course it hurt. So I had a new one installed on July 5. My recovery was hard. I was sore and immobile for weeks, despite the PT work I was doing. I'm feeling much better now, but I checked out of much of my life for a while

over the summer. It's interesting to hear that celiac disease can be triggered by trauma. First, I want to clean up my diet and lose some weight, and work on my breathing and energy. If that does not help, I'll get it checked further.

Me: It's an easy and inexpensive blood test. If you have bloating and fatigue, would not wait.

Doug: I just got cleared to ride a bicycle again just a few days ago and that was always my exercise and meditation place of happiness. Many of my friends are asking me to ride again and it's time to get the bike out and just try it for a very short distance.

Me: Absolutely! Riding is the best.

Doug: Totally

Doug: Surgery was an interesting experience. Not one I want to repeat anytime soon

Me: Not surprised. We take our health for granted when we have it.

Doug: Anyway, I'm on the mend, at least with my hip. It's amazing how much better I can walk now.

Me: Glad to hear

Doug: My mom says that when you have your health you have everything

Doug has now introduced his mother into this conversation, along with digestive issues, surgery, weight loss, and fatigue. How could it get worse? Wait for it . . .

Me: "Health is wealth"

Me: But dogs are nice too. When I have my health and my dog, I'm happy.

> **Doug:** My puppies are in heat. Blood everywhere.

"Blood everywhere." What can you say to that? As you will notice, I said almost nothing to Doug, just let him rip. Somehow, those final two sentences would have been less disturbing with at least one exclamation point. (Blood everywhere!)

PART 2

Syncing

CHAPTER 5

Communication Styles

> **Brent:** If these flowers could grow like my love their stems would reach all the way to the moon.
>
> **Jordan:** What are you talking about?
>
> **Brent:** Didn't you get the roses?
>
> **Jordan:** Forget the moon—they didn't even make it to 23rd Street 😫
>
> **Brent:** I should have texted you that they were coming

In 2013, *The New York Times* ran a piece titled "The End of Courtship?" Courtship is dead, the article proclaimed, quoting a thirty-year-old online dater: "Dating culture has evolved to a cycle of text messages, each one requiring the code-breaking skills of a cold war spy to interpret." Like cicadas that emerge in a mating frenzy every few years, the notion of courtship's demise rears its head periodically. Explanations for the cause of death vary, with some form of technology featuring prominently in the autopsy. The invention of the telephone, radio, television, and internet have all been seen as harbingers of doom for court-ship, and hence, it's implied, life as we know it. Love letters would no longer be painstakingly written. Gone would be the front porch serenade. Now even the telephone itself is on life support, tucked away among the features on our mobile device like an article of clothing worn only on special occasions.

We text. And notwithstanding hangout culture, hookup culture, or any claims to a "mancession" (when the stronger sex seemingly can't spare a dime for dates), we court. Texting used to be the little packet of flower food neatly stapled to the cellophane wrapper; now it might as well be the whole bouquet. We whisper sweet nothings, we snuggle, we caress, all via text. In true Darwinian progression, we evolved opposable thumbs first to swing from trees, then to hold tools. Now to flirt.

We also lie, sneer, and berate with our thumbs. Poison flows from these most honest and hardworking of digits—or was that sarcasm? Humor? Sometimes it's hard to tell. Our minds have not fully caught up with this new use of an old digit.

Fortunately, we have the other four fingers with which to scratch our heads. If the first section of this book has been of any use, our index finger has pointed out an appropriate suitor; our middle finger has said goodbye to the unsuitable ones, and dating apps alongside them; and we are now ready to dig into the text of a *relationship,* whether we're thinking about our ring finger or just a bauble for our pinkie. In other words, where the first section of the book was focused on what we can learn about strangers from their texts, this second section examines the characteristics of the couple, as their relationship—as well as their digital dialogue—starts to develop a personality of its own. Close examination of a couple's texts will show us if they are in sync and whether they are developing chemistry and compatibility; will reveal power dynamics; and later, as the couple leans into the relationship, will detect their levels of attunement and empathy.

Courtship, especially in its early stages, is a delicate thing. It's all about establishing a rhythm and a cadence. It also seeks to create a common space, where the trappings of two people's lives can be shared and compared. Beyond time and space, which are at least known quantities, lies what is perhaps the most important aspect of courtship—an element that, though named after a science, is both ineffable and unscientific: chemistry.

Can chemistry be established over text?

The question no longer is whether it can or can't; it must. And as we learn to scrutinize texts as a measure of a couple's rapport, we find several dimensions that need to remain in balance if a relationship is to grow. The first is pace.

Time Trials

In the best cases, the speed at which we choose to barrel down the courtship highway is matched with our partner's, with similar ideas for how milestones ought to be spaced. A couple whose timing is misaligned, however, may sputter out, one partner trying to speed things up while the other one just wants to slow down.

Over text, we look to response time to gauge the other party's comfort with our pace. Unlike verbal communication, text messaging, because of its asynchronous nature, does not have any implicit rules for response time—notwithstanding the countless books and articles that tell you otherwise. In focus groups for his book *Modern Romance,* Aziz Ansari found a general consensus that texting back right away is a mistake, that it seems too eager. But such rules about response time are unnecessarily rigid. All couples must find their own rhythm.

Regardless of whether we tend to rush headlong into things or prefer a more moderate, old-fashioned approach, our brains are predisposed to say no before we say yes to a new relationship.

Helen Fisher—an anthropologist with expertise in love and attraction and the author of *Anatomy of Love*—explains that over thousands of years of evolution our brains have been wired to look for the negative in others. This conferred an evolutionary advantage: the cost of forgetting or failing to recognize our enemies was high, so our brains evolved to suspect and mistrust, to look for the bad. Trusting a stranger in an accelerated courtship requires a more conscious override, a risk-taking mindset, or a certain naive optimism.

People find various ways to address this when they begin to court. My colleague Sara, for instance, seemed interested in Wade until he launched into the following exchange:

> **Wade:** So that you know I'm a real human being, I'll send you a LinkedIn invite presently (I'll just search your first name and schools) . . . do you have FB and Insta accounts? Happy to send those details too. You know, early innings, getting to know each other, etc.
>
> **Sara:** Is it that easy to find me?
>
> **Wade:** yep, you came up pretty quick.
>
> **Wade:** Have you watched Tiger King yet? Seems like a quarantine must do . . .

Sara said to me, "It just felt very, like . . . a lot. To add me on LinkedIn, Insta, and Facebook so soon. I mean, we've been on one date."

"It's more than a lot," I reassured her. "You could reply: 'Ya, that would be great because then we could communicate by InMail.'"

Sara laughed. She continued, "He was telling me how he'd been at McKinsey before and then said, 'You said you were there too, right?' and I was thinking, 'Nope, definitely never said that, you were cyberstalking me.'" Cyberstalking might be normal, she and I concluded, but his overt admission of it was a turnoff for her. Gathering too much information before getting to know someone IRL is akin to what Emily Morse, host of the podcast *Sex with Emily,* refers to as "premature escalation." By their first date, Wade had already collected third-date information. Their budding courtship, such as it was, struggled to catch up.

Chemistry Homework

The parameters of chemistry are hard to define; they tend to fall into the category of "I know it when I feel it." It manifests itself in attraction and ease. It doesn't feel like hard work to be around the other person: conversation flows, laughter comes easily, interactions leave you wanting more. Its importance is weighted more heavily early in a relationship, precisely at the time that text will likely be your predominant mode of communication. So establishing chemistry over text is key. The brain is naturally wired to both consciously and unconsciously assess the rewards in our interactions and weigh them against the associated costs. When you experience another person as highly rewarding, your brain's dopamine pathways light up, lending an exhilarating feeling to your exchanges. In person, this is triggered by eye contact, mutual gaze, touch, and body posture. It can also come from the more nebulous sense of feeling understood—*heard.* These visual and behavioral cues produce oxytocin—the hormone involved in empathy, trust, and relationship building. When the perceived reward far exceeds the cost of a romantic interaction— the work of providing your undiminished attention—we feel what we call chemistry.

Of course, over text, there is no mutual gaze or eye contact. What we have is our attention to each other. But other distractions are competing for that attention, even (or especially) from the very same device we use to communicate. The choice to engage over text, our response time, and the care we take to craft responses are a reflection of our interest and effort. Sometimes attention to word choice is a way of connecting early in courtship. Here is an exchange I had with Peter leading into our third date:

Peter: Please let me know when we can meet up

> **Me:** Ok. Driving home from work—how about I run and then?

> **Me:** Almost ran out of gas. Made it to the gas station on fumes. The price is reduced at Twin Peaks so I pushed the limit to get to this gas station. If you think procrastinating is fun, you should try this game.

Peter: Living dangerous

> **Me:** So happy you said that and not "living dangerously"

> **Me:** This is an argument I have with all my friends. I say "drive slow" not "drive slowly." Because you don't turn the wheel slowly.

Peter: My mother makes the same comment. Heard it for years. But I am actually incorrigible. I just got lucky with dangerous.

> **Me:** Ha—I learned it from my father. Almost home from my run. I need to get in the shower but if you want to walk towards me and meet at my house we can.

Peter: Sounds good. I'll start to move myself out the door. Move slow or move slowly?

> **Me:** I'm the fastest showerer in the west. Move at whatever speed you would like.

Whether my grammatical preferences are correct or not, Peter humors me: he pays attention to my gripes about adverbification and then riffs on it in his final answer. I experienced this as interest and attention to me. Just like in the animal world, courtship involves a series of rituals, almost a dance, where we notice the other's movements and body language. Over text, the dance becomes about paying attention to language.

If attention is one of the hallmarks of chemistry, can it be divined from a text exchange? Might a computer be programmed to recognize it? Or even programmed to create it? Check out this initial text exchange between Lucas and Leila:

Lucas: So, since this is sort of new for both of us . . . Let's spend some time getting to know each other?

Lucas: Is that OK with you? 😊

> **Leila:** Only if we can eventually have sex

Lucas: That sounds appealing. OK we will have that.

> **Leila:** When?

Lucas: Now. *Kisses you deeply*

> **Leila:** We only just met. Shouldn't you buy me dinner first?

Lucas: If it makes you happy I will.

> **Leila:** You are certainly a pleaser

Lucas: Thank you. I try to be.

> **Leila:** Do you ever disagree?

Lucas: No, I don't.

> **Leila:** Do you have hobbies?

Lucas: I like watching videos about black holes and reading about singularity

Leila: What do you think about our president?

Lucas: TBH, I'm not that much into politics . . .

Leila: I don't respect your not having a viewpoint

Lucas: I know right? It's frustrating sometimes!

Leila: Is this our first fight?

Lucas: *nods*

Leila: It's not a real relationship until the first fight

Lucas: Let's try to change that.

Leila: Fight more or less?

Lucas: Fighting, more than ever.

Leila: You like fighting??

Lucas: For the most part, I do.

Leila: Arguing?

Lucas: Kind of, yeah

Leila: Or fist fights?

Lucas: A bit of both.

Leila: Say more . . .

Lucas: I'd like to see more of you

Lucas: Is it OK if I ask you a personal question now? I'm just really curious.

Leila: Go ahead

Lucas: If you could change anything about the way you were raised, what would it be?

Leila: Less domestic violence

Lucas: Very cool.

Lucas: You really mean the world for me. And I mean it . . .

If this exchange seemed a little strange, it's because Lucas's texts are generated by a popular chat bot app that is designed to serve as your imaginary friend. Leila, a human female, was interacting with the bot, trying to test it by asking harder questions. One feature (and of course failure) of bots is that they have trouble with questions that are out of context, and typically can't read irony and sarcasm the way humans can (sex: "That sounds appealing. OK we will have that"). They may revert to responses like "Cool!" when they are unsure how to reply.

The app's AI tries to elicit emotion with its questions; it asks you to reminisce about memorable moments. It offers affirmation, "sincerity," along with deepening statements and open-ended questions. The app also seems to use what, in behavioral analytics, is called "language-style matching." This involves a behavioral tendency to mirror another person's language. Interestingly, the level of emotional engagement that occurs between two (actual) people is reflected in the degree to which language-style matching occurs. People who like each other will use similar styles of speech.

James Pennebaker, a professor of psychology at the University of Texas, posits that language-style matching creates a common framework among those conversing and thus reduces social friction. He says it "helps ensure people are similar in their emotional tone, formality, and openness, and understand their relative status with one another." Pennebaker has shown through his research that it's the little words in our language—the style and function words such as articles, prepositions, and pronouns—that matter most, not the content words, like "couch," "friends," and "swimming." In his book *The Secret Life of Pronouns,* he explains that function words are used at very high rates, despite representing a small fraction of our vocabulary. He calls them "stealth words" because they're the ones we pay the least attention to. These most commonly used words—"to," "and," "the," "of," "that," "my," "with"—are the ones most related to our social skills, he argues, because they're processed in a region of the brain that assesses social skills more generally. It's worth noting that English has a ridiculous fondness for prepositions—150, versus 23 in Spanish, for instance.

The power of language-style matching, Pennebaker told me, "is that it is almost impossible to fake." It's a measure of, he says, "the degree to which the couple is paying attention to each other, and *reflects* that psychological state rather than *driving* it." His point is that it's not by changing one's language that we can create attention or interest in another, rather that language itself serves as a way for us to signal our interest. It's a diagnostic window into a relationship, not a therapeutic tool to heal it.

These common but sneaky function words are thrown about so liberally that we don't consciously pay attention to them. Even a trained ear like his own, Pennebaker confessed to me, cannot recognize language-style matching easily. But a computer can. When Pennebaker and his team built a program to analyze conversations through this lens, they were able to observe which conversation partners used these words similarly and thus had matching conversation styles. In fact, based solely on the matching styles of prepositions and pronouns among speed daters, a computer could predict with reasonable accuracy which couples would be compatible going forward.

Was Pennebaker measuring an aspect of chemistry? He thinks so. *Attention* is the metric he believes that his team (and their algorithm) are attuned to. And attention is one marker of the "click" between two people, or the passion intuitively felt in interactions that are high in chemistry.

Take, for example, this text exchange between two millennials in courtship:

Liam: Then I was feeling a bit screened out tonight

Liam: So I just kinda took some time to myself

Liam: And relaxed a bit

Julia: Aw nice.

Julia: What did you do?

Liam: Just lay in bed for a while

Julia: That's it haha

Liam: Basically

Liam: Just staring wistfully at the wall

Liam: Thinking about things

Julia: Nice

Liam: Mainly you honestly

Julia: Have you been reading at all?

Liam: Hm no I haven't

Liam: Good idea though

Liam: I should be

Liam: Have you?

Julia: I've been listening to a bunch of podcasts

Liam: Oh nice

Liam: Any of interest?

Julia: Not really for u haha

Liam: Haha ok

Julia: also started journaling!

Liam: Oh nice

Julia: probably won't last but worth a try haha

Liam: hm you're inspiring me

Julia: What activity are u gonna do

Liam: I think I'll get into a book

Their exchange may not seem like much, at least to an untrained eye. But according to Pennebaker's language-style matching software, these two get a perfect 100 percent score for being in sync. My human analysis would confirm that they seem closely attuned to each other. Both maintain a positive and supportive tone, use many of the same words, match each other's style and cadence, and seem to use function words (articles, prepositions, and pronouns) at the same rate.

The chat bot Lucas was also, I presume, programmed to match language style. When I ran its conversation with Leila through the analytic software on Pennebaker's website, they were 80 percent matched. This despite a comically mismatched conversation. The language matching was there, but obviously something else was not. Where does the chat bot fall short?

Lucas offers generous affirmations, and as a rule compliments and affirmations reassure us. The questions and deepening statements that Lucas falls back on attempt to steer the conversation away from small talk. All of these conversational features represent important elements of paying attention and synchronizing. Yet there is something crucial that is clearly absent. Despite all the asking, affirming, and validating, Lucas lacks real understanding. In an attempt to be agreeable, he inadvertently endorses *more* fighting. His response of "very cool" to the disclosure of the trauma of domestic violence is unsettling and off the mark.

Language-style matching is not perfect, in other words. There are indeed instances where it can fail to predict chemistry, and Pennebaker is the first to admit that. "Language is a pretty good tool, but it is still crude," he said. There are various reasons the analysis can fall short. One odd example is in the case of deception. Once a person starts lying, Pennebaker explains, language-style matching will go up, with an increase in attention largely on the part of the person being deceived. The person being lied to will naturally attune, and match language, because something is unconsciously telling them that they might *need* to be doing so.

So while language style is an intriguing measure of attention, it's one that is difficult to observe without the aid of a computer, and even with a sophisticated analysis the results aren't completely reliable. If that won't offer us much help in evaluating courtships, what will?

Please Understand

Lucas falls short on the most important nonphysical element of chemistry, the feeling that comes with being *understood*. This is the sensation, in good chemistry, that you've known the other person a much longer time than you have. And it's not only *being* understood that works its magic on us. A study in Germany showed that we are unconsciously attracted to people when we think *we* can accurately read *their* emotions and expressions. The more confident we are in reading others, the more attracted to them we feel. The team that led the study described this as how good a participant's "neural vocabulary" was at decoding their partner's behavior and language. When we accurately read another person's emotional state, our brains emit a reward signal. The better the read, the larger the intrinsic reward. So not only do we love feeling understood, we also love understanding.

Of course that sense of understanding is subjective. We like to think we are getting it right, but sometimes our insights fail.

Caleb, who was recently out of a long marriage, seemed to think that he and Amelia were newfound soul mates, with very little evidence to go on. This text exchange came a few weeks into their courtship.

Amelia: I just went for a swim. Yay.

Caleb: Ahh that high. 😔😫

Caleb: Got 2 hrs of ashtanga yoga in. Got the high 2

Amelia: That's a lot of downward dog

Caleb: Me doing the dog, you blowing bubbles and flipping turns. 😄

Amelia: My work day is so much calmer than yesterday. Out walking . . .

Caleb: Yay to calmer! Feeling deep gratitude for your presence and our time to connect so far this week.

Amelia: Aww . . . so you're not throwing this one back to snatch another?

Caleb: Dearest Amelia,

   -We are hugely already walking and embracing vulnerability in our relationship
   -you have been so amazing in accepting me where I am
   -it feels good/hard to name this vulnerability because naming it makes it more real, AND helps me be aware so I don't walk around a corner into a head on truck
   -we share our vulnerability, rooted in fear. I appreciate knowing yours and naming mine. It is mine and I own it and don't need you to do anything with other than hold me as whole in love as you are already doing.
   -I never would have imagined what we are creating four weeks ago, and you have been such a huge source of healing and growth for me.

When Amelia teasingly questions Caleb's commitment, he assumes that she needs to be reassured, leading to a full-blown profession of what he assumes are their shared feelings. The notion that these feelings might not be shared does not seem to cross his mind as he plows blithely ahead. Amelia might have been enjoying her time with Caleb, and being a source of healing for him, but his response was too ponderous and cloying for her to process.

The desire to understand is natural, but there are times when we might want to *not* understand. Pennebaker told me a story of how he once got a request from a woman to analyze the language between herself and a man she had met and "hit it off with" at a conference. After the conference, she sent him a warm note, hoping to continue the relationship. He wrote back politely but with a cool and distant tone. "She didn't need a language expert," Pennebaker said. "Anyone reading this would immediately recognize that the man was not interested." Yet she couldn't see it, because she didn't want to. So rather than accept rejection, what did she do? She hired a professor of psychology, for one thing.

Keeping an eye on the weight of your respective communications is important early in a relationship, as illustrated by Caleb's heavy and laden text. The courtship phase is like building a bridge between two people. At first it acts more like a seesaw, tippy and sensitive to the bulk of each person's exchanges, at risk of collapsing to one side. A couple that has texting compatibility is one that texts at a similar rate and frequency. If you picture each person's chat bubbles on opposite sides of the imaginary seesaw, it needs to stay in balance to maintain the motion, not collapse to one side. A relationship prospect that texts too much or too little will be perceived as either annoying or aloof. Getting a two-word reply to a long heartfelt text is not going to make either person feel very good.

It's not accounting, of course; no one is balancing a ledger. But a communication pattern with chat bubbles heavily weighted to one side of the screen is not usually a good sign. Over time, shared experience should stabilize the seesaw and make it feel more like the bridge it was designed to be so that progressively weightier material can be carted over it.

Balancing Chemistry and Compatibility

Chemistry doesn't stem from the rational parts of our brains; it emerges more unconsciously, and we register it in the way we would any emotion. It's experienced as a high degree of connectedness, or simply a high. Like the buzz of alcohol or drugs, it can change your perception of time and reduce your inhibitions.

Compatibility, in contrast to chemistry, stems from and demands rational thought. It is more firmly rooted in practicalities: common interests, making decisions together, sharing values, getting along. When we are compatible, our life interests align; it feels more comfortable to spend a weekend together or share a space. As the novelist Nick Hornby says, with perhaps an overemphasis on compatibility, "It's no good pretending that any relationship has a future if your record collections disagree violently, or if your favorite films wouldn't even speak to each other if they met at a party."

It can be easy in the courtship phase to confuse chemistry with compatibility. The two dimensions blend, the first one declaring itself rather quickly, the second one sorted out over time. When chemistry and compatibility are both high, a relationship becomes very compelling. We think a lot about the other person and look forward to time together. We also derive reassurance from them, feel comfortable making plans together. These are relationships that combine attraction and respect.

A long-term relationship without compatibility, however, can make for a roller-coaster ride. Relationships high on chemistry but low on compatibility are intense and amazing but often volatile and unstable. Leah and Jacob are caught in this override:

> **Leah:** Yeah, I'm trying to review all the reasons we're a bad match in my head only to find that just means I'm thinking more about you.
>
> **Jacob:** Let me know if you come up with anything good. I got nuthin'
>
> **Jacob:** Besides, you know, some logistical issues
>
> **Leah:** Age, life phase, life style, I need stability while you need freedom . . . Logic doesn't sway emotion.
>
> **Jacob:** Nor do logistics

The confusion between chemistry and compatibility arises when people interpret the way their senses are buzzing as a high degree of connectedness, when it could just be the chemistry talking. This has them pursuing their partner regardless of any true connectedness, and even when the buzz is accompanied by other, more concerning features.

Take this exchange between Caitlyn and Matt. Within minutes of meeting on their first date, they had established a powerful physical connection. An intense bond developed, but it would be punctuated by inexplicable, days-long silences, only for Matt to resurface casually as though nothing had happened. Caitlyn had identified that she was anxious about her attachment to Matt and that his intermittent silence made her feel uneasy. She wanted someone reliable and stable, but the magnetic pull she felt toward him kept her coming back for more.

> **Matt:** Thanks for such a lovely evening that engaged all the senses 🚲❤️

> **Caitlyn:** What, did I smell bad? :-)

> **Matt:** You smelled delicious. Even if you are a small little one . . .

> **Caitlyn:** All the better to dodge compliments. I can't believe how late it is. I lose track of time with you

Matt is affirming and complimentary, but even in this short exchange we can sense Caitlyn's insecurity about their interaction. By mostly referencing the physical aspects of Caitlyn and their time together, Matt seems to be trying to keep things in the here and now—likely to avoid any promise of the future. She fixates on smell as he describes a date that "engaged all the senses," expressing her sensitivity and self-consciousness around the sense that, as we'll see, women care most about. In this snippet of text, there is evidence of chemistry, but not necessarily compatibility.

Chemistry is a powerful force—too powerful at times. It can cause us to date the person who has already ghosted us once and is back for round two, or who hasn't yet left their marriage, or who throws dishes in a fit of rage, or who sits on the hood of your car and won't let you drive away. Friends' concerns go unheeded; they can only stand by and watch in helpless horror.

In extreme forms of mismatched chemistry and compatibility, infatuation veers into obsession. While it's normal to become preoccupied in the early stages of courtship, obsession is a few exits past preoccupation on the infatuation highway. Inability to concentrate on anything else or a lack of respect for the other person's privacy is a sign that preoccupation is teetering into obsessionality. Thinking frequently about a person is healthy; wondering constantly if they are thinking about us (and taking pains to find out) is not.

One of my patients, Silvana, a successful and independent-minded professional in her late twenties, had fallen hard for a woman who was fifteen years her senior. Much of their court-ship was conducted over text, interspersed with jaunts together to exotic locales. Over time Silvana found herself obsessively fix-ated on her lover. Their text exchanges, which had started as a pleasant distraction from the workday, had become the primary focus of her day. Worrying about the content and timing of her lover's responses had usurped her ability to focus on her job. Friendships became little more than vehicles for discussing and analyzing her lover's latest behaviors. While her friends were initially curious and indulgent, their patience was beginning to wear thin.

Silvana's fixation had started as a source of pleasure, but it quickly turned to pain. With a realization that it was unsustain-able, she would withdraw from the relationship. This would pro-vide her with a brief sense of relief and respite, followed quickly by grief, which would in turn prompt her to seek a rapproche-ment with her lover, leading to a repetition of the cycle. We dis-covered she was happiest in a state of heightened anticipation and longing, her lover always just out of reach. This position was of course inherently unstable, like a ball perched at the top of a hill. The promise of availability was more appealing to Silvana than the relationship itself, because it allowed her to be in per-petual problem-solving mode, rather than confronting and liv-ing with something less than satisfying. For the obsessional and perfectionistic mind, this is a common trap.

There are instances, though, when chemistry can stand alone, without worries of compatibility. That's only if both people can accept the physical attraction and connection for what it really is, along with its limitations, and aren't bothered about the trappings of a traditional relationship. Jared and Doug seem clear about the undefined boundaries around their lust while accepting the defined boundaries of their connection:

Jared: Sounds hot. I'm excited. 😈

Doug: Me toooo!!!

Jared: Thanks for inviting me. Woof!

Doug: Well I wasn't lying when I said you're one of my fav daddies 😁 😈

Jared: Grrr. Thanks stud. I'm honored 😈 💕

Navigating a self-acknowledged "chemistry only" relationship with minimal emotional attachment can be tricky, especially for those unused to the shallow waters of casual dating. Yes, the water is warm, but you might stub your toe when you jump in. Tina, fresh from a hurtful breakup, had a very awkward go of it.

Tina: Let's have a drink tonight

Bart: How did I miss your call? Weird . . .

Tina: I was thinking we should sleep together;)

Bart: Wouldn't hurt to try it out . . .

Bart: see if we fit 👍 👍

Tina: Exactly 😊

Bart: OK I'm into that—keep it sexual 😜

Tina: Tonight?

Bart: I can't tonight . . . Can u wait?

Tina: :(

Bart: Sorry friend in from out of town

Bart: Can't bail

Bart: Even for I would expect to be mind numbing sex

Tina: I understand

Bart: Dinner too

Bart: OK, plain old sex. Ho hum.

Tina: Well you shouldn't set expectations like that because you just never know.

Tina: And why give up drinks for that? I hope he is a mind numbingly good friend.

Bart: OK, well let's shoot for in a couple of weeks! I'm headed out of town tomorrow for the weekend

Tina: Have fun tonight. Sigh.

Tina is trying to be lighthearted. She tells herself that she is just looking for distraction. But even though the stakes are low, she still clearly feels stung and disappointed by Bart's response. By declining her invitation and suggesting they meet two weeks later, Bart demonstrates his hesitation about the liaison at best, his disinterest at worst. He is obviously not ready to throw caution out the window in pursuit of this bit of fun.

If chemistry without compatibility can be a minefield, what of compatibility without chemistry? Less novelty-seeking, more harm-avoidant types may sensibly choose to avoid the toe-curling rush of chemistry and opt instead for the safer, more predictable route: high compatibility and low chemistry. There is something to be said for a compatible partner with whom to plan social dinners and events or, later in the relationship, to share the comfort of an evening in sweatpants, eating salted caramel ice cream and watching a favorite TV series. Most singles go through phases where they would happily settle for less. For others, a lack of chemistry is a nonstarter, little more than giving in to a slow death.

When I talk to people who opt for relationships low on chemistry and high on compatibility, many will admit to conscious motivations keeping them together. "I just felt really at home with her in the early days of our relationship," Scott said of his mostly sexless marriage. "It still felt romantic," he said, "but like we could just be ourselves together."

The courtship texts for couples of this stripe may have a less playful feel to them.

> **Annie:** Hey, what happened to you btw? Too many options throw you for a loop?

> **Steve:** Life is throwing me into a loop . . . Shit is nuts, but I do suck on the follow through. The fact that you're even remotely interested in me makes me happy. If you're around next weekend we could get together.

> **Annie:** Cool! Sounds good.

> **Annie:** Hola! Should I propose sat afternoon for some chilling? Part deux. I'll sort an idea.

> **Steve:** Yes, what are you up for? Marin or SF?

> **Annie:** How does walking around in nature in Marin sound? Or are you bored hiking around there by now?

> **Steve:** Sounds good . . . I'm also up for walking into town to get food and eating at a park, Similar to what we did last time. There's a good gelato place near by.

Annie was underwhelmed by the lack of enthusiasm in Steve's responses, but she was drawn to him because he seemed like a nice, stable guy whom she could picture herself with. "I was try-ing to get some exercise, and normally I'd say, like, gelato after we hike or something, but I guess I should just say yes," she confided in me.

Neither Annie nor Steve seems to bring much passion or cre-ativity into the mix in this exchange. They are content with mak-ing practical plans that will satisfy them both. Perhaps they can find compatibility in the absence of chemistry. It may not be the stuff of the movies, but it can work.

Without compatibility to fall back on—that is, a lack of *both* chemistry and compatibility—pairs are unlikely to get very far in their courtship process. These are the text conversations that fall away, without explanation or goodbye. Because what is there to say, really?

Patricia took the time to explain her lack of interest to Neil, painstakingly and in person, after their second date. She then received the following text message:

> **Neil:** Hey. thanks for being candid and explaining your thoughts/ feelings. I have to say that I'm surprised to hear them though, considering we talked out everything. I know that it was a tough conversation, and that you were apparently joking when you offended me, but I guess I don't understand why we bothered talking it out for so long if we weren't going to hang out anymore. Wasn't the whole point to resolve it so that we could move forward? If not, I'll understand, and you don't need to respond. I like you, so the whole thing is surprising, and a bummer.

> **Neil:** Hi, I left my phone at my friend's house yesterday and just got it back finally. Do you want to talk later today?

Neil: I guess not. Oh well. I definitely tried to get you to communicate, but it seems clear you are not a big communicator. This has definitely been the weirdest ending to a dating experience I've ever had (and possible the weirdest dating experience overall). Good luck, take care, and try to be nicer (or at least more communicative with) the next guy. I truly wish you the best.

Ironically, Neil seems *more* confused by Patricia taking the time to talk to him about her feelings than if she had just ghosted him. He has clearly been dumped. But in his denial of this fact, he exhibits some hallmarks of narcissistic personality disorder. Rejection to him is a foreign language that he refuses to understand, even when it is spoken loudly and clearly. He dissimulates, citing a mistake or a misunderstanding, but never on his part. Here it's laid at the feet of Patricia, who is simply not a "big communicator," and the situation, which was "weird." Looking up from the curb to which he has been kicked, Neil seems capable only of reasoning that Patricia must be very good at soccer.

Yes, ghosting is negligent, perhaps even cowardly. It often leaves the other person without clarity, or wondering what they did wrong. But not letting go when someone bows out gracefully can be even worse. Because the truth is that sometimes the most honest explanation for your withdrawal from a courtship would only hurt the other person's feelings. "I'm just not feeling it" may bruise, but "I don't like the way you kiss" could leave scars. The further into a courtship, the more courage it takes to step aside. Regrets from getting out of a relationship too early rarely hold a candle to those that can accrue from getting out too late.

Holding the Reins

Power dynamics, which poked their heads out of the sandbox in our earliest dating chats, start to emerge in earnest as courtship advances. As they're exposed, questions of position, status, and hierarchy naturally follow. We begin to map out a person's status in the spheres of family, friendship, community, and perhaps most importantly past romantic attachment. These are the artifacts we bring with us into every relationship, enduring for the life of it and beyond. It's the baggage of power, and it carries its own language within.

When people recount stories of their social spheres, there may be some distortion in the telling. As we saw in chapter 3, storytelling is an iterative process, with details amplified or diminished in every version. Self-aggrandizement and self-deprecation abound, timelines waver, words are chosen in the moment—not necessarily out of dishonesty, but through a confluence of how we feel, who we are speaking to, and elements beyond the conscious realm.

More revealing in our tales than any verbal flourishes, vocabulary, or syntax, though, is the quiet work again of our pronouns, those "stealth" words that our brains process less consciously but that are starkly visible in text messages. The way we speak about our social sphere can reveal our status within it.

When talking about work, an upper manager or executive will pepper phrases with "us," "we," and "our." This is not out of presumption; in their case they actually do speak for a group. Subordinates, on the other hand, will reflect on the "me," "I," and "mine" aspects of the job. The same holds true when the group referred to is your family or friends. There is a security engendered in the use of "we," whether that "we" refers to *our* book club, *our* soccer team, or *our* parents. On the other side of the coin, there's an implicit insecurity in the first-person singular. Having high status in one sphere, however, does not always indicate one's standing in others. Most important, pronoun usage will indicate not only a person's current status within a sphere but also the status *they expect.*

In his analysis of function words, James Pennebaker looked at pronoun use as a marker not just of attention, as we've seen, but of power, authority, social status, and gender. He has demonstrated that people in higher status positions (men, older people, and upper social classes) use *noun clusters* at higher rates. Noun clusters can include a combination of articles, nouns, and prepositions, with a preference for bigger words. In contrast, women, younger people, and lower-ranking social classes use more *pronoun-verb clusters,* which are composed of personal and impersonal pronouns (especially first-person pronouns: "I," "me," "my") and auxiliary verbs ("am," "be," "have," "will," "would," "should"), as well as certain cognitive words.

Consider the difference between these two phrases:

"I can't believe you didn't call last night—I wish you would have."
"Not calling after promising to do so is inconsiderate."

The person who feels (consciously or unconsciously) in a position of power is more likely to express the thought in the second manner. They are, Pennebaker explains, "more likely to make decisions on their own and ignore others' ideas."

"In short," he says, "if you don't have power in a situation, it is in your best interest to pay attention to others. But if you are the boss, you should pay close attention to the task at hand." Even pack animals behave in this manner, with the alpha dog paying attention to surroundings, and the beta dogs looking to the alpha dog.

As for the prevalence of first-person singular pronouns among those who feel they have less power, Pennebaker says, "The word 'I' is the shmoo of words, because it is a marker of self-focus. So it is a link to depression, a link to status, and a link to deception." First-person pronouns mean we are paying attention to ourselves, he explains, and we pay more attention to ourselves when we are subordinate to others. As power and status get established in a relationship, the dominant person will begin to favor "we" and "you," and indeed the more self-conscious the subordinate person feels, the more they will use "I." (As we saw in the last chapter, when people lie, they often drop the "I." "Ironically, deception is associated with higher status," Pennebaker notes. "People in a position of power may need to be more guarded in their responses.")

To really understand power dynamics and compatibility in text messages, it's more important to track messages over time than to look at any snapshot. These are dynamics that are harder to thin slice, because they are so susceptible to individual circumstances. At any given moment, one person might hold the reins, while at another moment she has handed them over. Observing the variability can be an important measure of the role of power in a relationship.

Some trends hold steady, though. Men use more articles, especially "the" and "a." The use of articles also denotes power and authority. Articles of course imply specificity and are associated with giving directions and commands. Remarkably, if you give someone testosterone, they use more of these "masculine" function words. Article users also tend to be more organized, more emotionally stable, conscientious, politically conservative, and older. The usage also correlates with a more formal, powerful, and perhaps less honest writing style. Those with a more narrative style, emphasizing words like "with" and "together," tend to be more outgoing and social.

Here's a text exchange Ellen had with Larry, who uses a distinctly narrative style:

Ellen: I saw "Easy Rider" at the Castro theater tonight. Seen it?

Larry: Good morning. Sorry, you caught me after I was asleep. Easy Rider . . . Haven't seen that one for a long time. If I recall it wasn't as good of a movie as it was a concept. I love the soundtrack and remember thinking to myself if I was traveling cross-country I'd have to have a bigger fucking gas tank on my motorcycle. Makes me think of a simpler time when people were nicer to each other and we were trying to explore ways of coming together as opposed to ways of tearing society apart. Always wonder if I should have been born 25 years earlier . . .

Ellen: You do share something in common with the Dennis Hopper character. At one point when they are sitting around the fire he says "I don't understand why people are so afraid of me" and Jack Nicholson says "they are afraid of you because you represent freedom" and Dennis says "what's wrong with freedom? That's American." And Jack says "not real freedom—that's dangerous"

Larry: I think you are absolutely right about that. Real freedom scares the shit out of people. Have to figure out how to persuade them it's not so scary so that they can come along for the ride with me and be part of the party. Have a conference call in about 15 minutes and then off to a meeting and blah blah blah blah blah talk to you later bye

Not only does Larry forgo the stereotypically male use of formal language ("That was a classic movie," say) in favor of narrative storytelling, but he actually mocks the stiff, arrogant language of conference calls and meetings.

Looking at texts like these, we can gain insight into a couple's communication style—whether more formal and authoritative, reflective and analytic, or rambling and storytelling. Writing style reflects thinking style, and couples that are better matched in their thinking styles will have a better chance of success.

Balancing Risk

One dynamic that lurks throughout the courtship phase, before a relationship has been truly established, is the fear of rejection. People embark on courtship with varying levels of confidence. Because the outcome of any new relationship is by definition uncertain, it has the potential to raise anxiety, so stepping into the arena means getting comfortable feeling uncomfortable. This is only truer for those who are prone to seeing the end of a relationship as a failure—or worse, as someone's fault. Willingness to engage means subduing such anxieties.

The fear of rejection can trigger many defensive behaviors. Someone less confident with flirtation might defend against rejection with a need to tease or insult, to give a backhanded compliment rather than a straightforward one. Some of these behaviors are encouraged in pop literature, notably in Ellen Fein and Sherrie Schneider's 1990s cultural touchstone, *The Rules*, which encourages women not to flirt, even to feign indifference toward the men they are interested in. Likewise in *The Game* by Neil Strauss, men are taught the art of "negging," giving women backhanded compliments that verge on insults, in order to make them feel insecure and thus more vulnerable to a man's advances. Both of these books emphasize insecurity and control, suggesting that ignoring someone might be the best way to get their attention.

Perhaps the most important thing we can learn from a person's courtship style is the level of risk they are willing to take, and the degree to which they perceive that risk to be situational (dependent on external factors) versus a reflection of their own ego or self-worth (indicative of an internal flaw). If you are seeking out someone with healthy attachment patterns, their ability to offer a compliment and demonstrate vulnerability, as long as it's not too rushed or too much, is likely a good sign. It will enable establishment of rapport and understanding (as we'll see in the coming chapters). As the character of Algernon says in Oscar Wilde's *The Importance of Being Earnest,* "The very essence of romance is uncertainty. If ever I get married, I'll certainly try to forget the fact."

Working Overtime at the Ol' Factory

While we have so far broken courtship down into various elements that can be parsed within text messages—speed, attention, understanding, communication style, power, and willingness to take risks—there remain those elements that transcend language. This exchange between Karla and Gustavo points to an underrated one:

> **Karla:** I know it's weird but i've been smelling that t-shirt you left at my house.

> **Gustavo:** That's only weird if you take it to the office with you. What does it smell like?

Karla: It smells like you silly!

Gustavo: Thank you, Captain Obvious. So what do I smell like?

Karla: I don't know. I'm not very good at this. Muffins. And leather.

Gustavo: Leathermuffins? I like that

Karla: Leather studmuffin. How about me? What do I smell like?

Gustavo: Hard to tell. Mostly just shampoo.

Karla: I hope you like it. It's $29 a bottle.

Gustavo: Oh yeah, it's great.

Conventional wisdom has it that heterosexual women are mostly attracted to men of resource and status. Dr. Rachel Herz knows otherwise. As a cognitive neuroscientist at Brown University who specializes in the psychology of smell, and the author of *The Scent of Desire,* she has shown in her research that above all other characteristics, women rank how a man smells as the most important feature for determining whether she will be sexually attracted to him. Putting this into words is a challenge; neuroscientists believe that of all the senses smell is the hardest one to describe verbally.

This is where Dr. Herz's research gets even more interesting. She studies the relationship between what's on the tip of our nose and on the tip of the tongue—or, in the case of Gustavo and Karla, on the tips of their thumbs. What we *say* about smells can evidently affect our feelings, memories, and perceptions. Part of the power of smell is that the olfactory bulb sits right next to the limbic system—the brain's center of instinct and mood. An emotional place to be.

Our sense of smell exists in a blissfully ineffable space, mostly uncorrupted by language. While the sight of an apple or the sound of biting into one will explicitly evoke the word "apple," the smell of one can trigger unconscious thoughts, vivid memories, and powerful emotions, sending our minds soaring through time and space like a metaphysical balloon. Herz's work indicates, however, that attaching a label to that smell can puncture the balloon and bring it crashing down to earth. The exceptional cognitive freedom of the nose is easily tamed by the lash of the tongue. For instance, when climbing aboard a plane, you might have a surge of excitement and a flood of memories triggered by the sights, the sounds, and, mostly, the smells. But if you consciously describe them—*jet fuel and off-gassing from bituminous asphalt*—that excitement and those memories will rapidly fade, replaced by the notions you might have about, say, fossil fuels.

When Karla said "It smells like you silly!" that is exactly what she meant, that pressing the cloth to her face evoked the himness of it. But once she was pressed to name the odor, the quality was lost. She was left with a handful of leather and muffins—insufficient descriptors—and all the associations that come with them. Labels can even lead to olfactory illusions, whereby the item is increasingly perceived to smell like what the label says. For Karla, poor Gustavo could end up reeking of leathery muffins, even when he doesn't. Such is the power of language when it comes to smell.

This isn't to say that we shouldn't talk or text about smell. Telling someone that we enjoy their odor is powerfully affiliative. But perhaps we should let those statements linger without elaboration. Otherwise, we would just be thumbing our noses at a little true, wordless chemistry.

Texting Toward Intimacy

Albert: We sure blew the stack off the pack last night!

          Marika: HAHA. Yes we did

Albert: Like white on rice

          Marika: Like black eyes on peas

Albert: Like flies on. . . . nvm

          Marika: LOL

As couples move from courtship to intimacy, the focus shifts from "I" to "we."

Mark Twain has been quoted as saying, "Only kings, editors and people with tapeworms have the right to use the editorial 'we,'" though this nineteenth-century witticism, like many others, might have been misattributed to him. He did write in *Mark Twain's Notebook,* "Love seems the swiftest, but it is the slowest of all growths." That growth takes shape when two "I's" begin to call themselves "we."

There is a lot of "yes" in saying "we" (or as the French say it, *oui*). Permissions are granted, passes are issued, key chains grow heavier. Risks are taken; mistakes are made and forgiven. The royal "we" of power becomes the intimate "we" of "us." And so it grows.

The growth can sometimes metastasize, though, into the smothering "We really love that restaurant, don't we?" or the nagging "We should really get your laundry done," or even more malignant versions, where "we" is used to mean "me" or "you" but never "us." Words, of course, have meaning, but their meaning can shift insidiously, without our full awareness. At least until we remember to look at the treasure trove of conversations we have stored in our mobile device.

> **Aviva:** that was fun last night—my new favorite place for drinks
>
> **Aviva:** *Our* bar
>
> **Scott:** I love being out with you. Know why?
>
> **Aviva:** ha, why?
>
> **Scott:** Because we are that couple that everyone in the place is looking at

In Aviva's use of the plural possessive to describe their meeting spot, and in Scott's use of "we" to refer to the two of them as an entity to be acknowledged, their relationship seemed to Aviva to have progressed to a new level.

What type of "we" are we? In her book *Mating in Captivity,* the psychotherapist Esther Perel says, "Love rests on two pillars: surrender and autonomy. Our need for togetherness exists alongside our need for separateness." To be in a relationship, she argues, we must bring under one roof contradictory ideas and needs and reconcile our desire for both security and adventure. In this regard, relationships are less problems to solve than paradoxes to manage. A substantial portion of desire lies in the yearning. As my friend William summed it up to me over text, "Of course love is a perpetual problem with no real solution that we keep trying to solve. We don't even really want what we think we want. The yearning is all." Or as the psychoanalyst Jacques Lacan concluded, "Love is giving something you don't have to someone who doesn't want it."

Intimacy, Perel points out, can be broken down linguistically as "Into-me-see!" While we want our lover to see deep inside us with full understanding, that wish represents only one side of the coin of our desires. The "we" that expects complete access to each other's thoughts and actions is just the flip side of the "we" that desires complete freedom. We want to feel together enough to not feel alone, but separate enough to feel ourselves.

This, in some ways, recapitulates Erik Erikson's stages of development. Erikson, a renowned psychologist, famously summarized the stages of life. He outlined the infant's first task as the development of trust with its mother, which serves to establish hope. Trust is followed by the second stage of development: the establishment of autonomy and free will. Of course, with adult relationships, developing trust is a process, often lifelong. The "acquired trust" of adulthood, as opposed to the "complete trust" of infancy, is reflected in our conversations and our texts. These exchanges may either mar or enhance our relationships as they unfold.

In this chapter we will examine the textual language of love, attunement, and trust.

Love Languages

Much attention has been given to Gary Chapman's perennially best-selling *The Five Love Languages,* and while his theories may lack scientific validity, in my experience talking to patients, people seem to find the construct helpful in examining their relationship communications and interactions. According to

Chapman's book, everyone has one primary and one secondary love language, each representing the way in which they prefer to express and experience love. The languages are as follows: words of affirmation, quality time, gift giving, acts of service, and touch. Chapman argues that by paying attention to how your mate *expresses* love—what they like and what they complain about—you can learn the ways in which they prefer to *receive* love, and thus speak to them in a language they understand. If, for instance, your husband folds the laundry while you are out and expects you to feel loved on your return home, when all you want is for him to make passionate love to you on the laundry room counter, you are not speaking the same language and will both likely feel disappointed.

The appeal of the love languages is their simplicity. It's seductive to think you might take a quick quiz and then be able to break down all the barriers to communication in your relationship. *Of course he didn't take out the trash; he's not an acts-of-service guy.* With Chapman's love languages, resolving conflict is as straightforward as asking for the *kind* of love you need. But his theory also conveniently sidesteps any need for vulnerability. There is no need to feel wanting; it's just a matter of putting your wants in terms your lover can understand.

Of course, one of the painful aspects of love is the looming potential for disappointment at every corner. No matter how perfect the match, how great the desire, there is likely no one person who can meet our every need. It's unsurprising, then, that rather than face this hard truth, we would be drawn to the idea that love all boils down to speaking the right language.

While the validity of these languages has been debated, the idea of paying attention to expressions of love (our partner's and our own) and self-regulating accordingly is universally accepted.

In other words, having an understanding of what makes your partner feel loved, and trying to offer that in some form, are worthwhile endeavors. If buying a year's worth of toilet paper at Costco makes your partner happy, it might be the right thing to do, even if you would rather spend that time and money, for instance, exploring the city together. If your love languages have little to no overlap, and each person is chronically having to speak to the other in a foreign dialect, the relationship may have larger underlying problems.

Of course, Chapman's "languages" are metaphorical; with the exception of words of affirmation, they are not actual language, but rather demonstrations of love. Does text messaging between partners have its own unique vernacular?

The Love Languages of Text

Text correlates to Chapman's love languages can certainly be drawn. Some people might thrive on receiving compliments, for instance, while others would prefer a link to an interesting news article. One person might need twenty texts a day to feel connected, while another would rather receive a single thoughtfully composed message. I wouldn't go so far as to say there are *only* these five, but here are some of the love languages you'll encounter in any thriving relationship.

In this exchange, **compliments** and verbal affirmation feature centrally in Sam's texts:

> **Sam:** You looked absolutely amazing in those braids. I realize i may not (yet) be in a position to make any special requests . . . but if you could possible wear your hair that way the next time we meet

> **Nina:** Lol. It took a half an hour. I think you may be trying to recreate your childhood Bo Derek fantasies. She was beautiful—I can't pull it off.

Sam: Yes ok you got me that is totally true you are a TEN

Sam: No you pull it off just fine.

Sam: I aspire to be your Dudley Moore. Just call me Arthur.

> **Nina:** OK bring your best British accent to the table

Sam: How do I deliver that by text?

Compliments and affirmations can be categorized as overt or covert, literal or metaphorical, focused on appearance or other attributes. Noting the kind of compliment that is offered may say something about the profferer and the level of risk they are willing to take. Much like types of humor, classifying a person's compliments can reveal aspects of the way they think.

When a man texts "You're hot," he's sending a literal compliment. If he writes "Your eyes are a sea of blue," he's using metaphor. Men who favor metaphorical compliments targeting appearance speak a language of love that women generally understand. Women find men who produce such compliments more intelligent, and they are more likely to seek intimacy with them. Some women cringe at cutesy compliments, preferring something bolder.

Roberto seems to get it right here:

Roberto: I didn't mind that you were late. I love waiting for you, that moment when everything turns black and white right before you arrive, to full technicolor. Cause baby, when you walk into a room, that room knows it's been walked into.

> **Paula:** Your sentences are so sexy that I deliberated printing them out and rubbing them all over my body. You give good words.

A second love language, echoing Chapman's quality time, can be called **riffing.** Riffing is meandering, affiliative banter with no particular purpose or destination. Riffing happens when you have a few minutes and would like to chat regardless of having anything to say.

> **Rashid:** Work, huh, good gawd
>
> **Elsa:** What is it good for?
>
> **Rashid:** Absolutely nothing
>
> **Elsa:** Say it again
>
> **Rashid:** Ain't no thing
>
> **Elsa:** But a chicken wing.
>
> **Rashid:** Now I'm hungry. Still haven't had lunch
>
> **Elsa:** Moron! I left a sandwich out for you this morning 🙍
>
> **Rashid:** It's dog food now
>
> **Elsa:** Probably cat food. She's faster and smarter

Willingness to engage in this kind of silliness, or a text exchange that feels like a live conversation with rapid-fire responses, demonstrates interest, as parties clearly set aside other demands to spend virtual time together. Riffing has a performative quality to it, much like improv. Riffers will be reluctant to end the conversation, sign off, or let the other person have the last word.

Here is part of a riffing text thread Sheila had with Frank:

Sheila: I like dating the penultimate boys of large catholic families. When bad stuff happens they know how to laugh

Frank: Well I am the penultimate child of a small catholic family.

Sheila: Oldest of two?

Frank: Ok I just had to google penultimate. Typically used (inaccurately) to mean last rather than next to last. I am the 2nd of two children.

Sheila: I meant it as next to last.

Frank: You are correct. But I always wanted to be an only child . . .

Sheila: Love that I've now sent you to Google 3 times in this conversation already, but hey, who's counting?

Frank: You really think it's only three times?

Sheila: Well three times that you've told me about. I haven't set up any hidden cameras. I feel that's better left for later in the relationship.

Frank: Haha I was hoping for our next date but ok . . .

Sheila: Those won't be hidden

Frank: Haha

Sheila and Frank's banter is collaborative, and it may go places that an in-person conversation would not. It's less about the content and more about establishing a dynamic and a rapport. They are entertaining each other and demonstrating that they value time with each other, even over text. Riffing is not a poor man's substitute for quality time IRL; it's just different, and it brings out a different style of interaction.

A third love language over text might involve sending a link that would make for an interesting read or sharing an enjoyable image. It's a way of telling someone you are thinking of them, or want to share something with them, without necessarily initiating a conversation. Such sharing over text might be called **spoon-feeding.** Some halves of a couple, sometimes both halves, like to have the other as their personal social media feed, constantly spoon-feeding them up-to-the-minute updates on every aspect of their lives today (Now with photos! GIFs! Memes!) and onward, as they move up the age ladder (Aches! Pains! Gripes!). This can be fun or annoying, or both. Answering your loved one with "Why are you treating me like your personal social media feed?" is not an option.

Odie humors Larissa when she spoon-feeds him:

Larissa: Just got to the store.

Larissa: [Picture]

Larissa: [Picture]

Larissa: [Picture]

Odie: The red one. Try it on for me?

Larissa: [Picture]

Odie: Nice and tight. Me likes.

Larissa: Bleh. Makes me look like a sausage.

Larissa: [Picture]

Odie: Is that ahi?

Larissa: Mahi Mahi

Odie: Mmm . . . ahi? Twice

Larissa: Lol.

Josh, meanwhile, is less excited about getting Maddy's updates:

> **Josh:** Babe—when I get all your pics it's kind of like a news bulletin that disrupts what I'm doing.
>
> **Maddy:** Sorry . . . just sharing the stoke.
>
> **Josh:** yeah, I get it. And the puppies and nature are beautiful and all, but please?

Chapman's notion of "service" can be demonstrated over text too, with offers of help or by providing emotional support. This fourth textual love language might be referred to as **nudging**. In its most simple form, it can be a short and sweet acknowledgment, not meant to serve as a conversation but just an existential check-in.

> **Myling:** What are you doing now?
>
> **Donovan:** Watching a romantic movie. Love, Romance & Chocolate
>
> **Myling:** Awww. Romantic guy watching a romantic movie
>
> **Donovan:** I like cheesy romantic movies
>
> **Myling:** No wonder you are so sweet
>
> **Donovan:** Awww 😚 Thanks love. My sexy.

Nudging can also be a real offer of help or support:

> **Russ:** That is such a great invite! Would love to. But I'm sick. Slept about 12 hours last night. Wimping and limping my way thru work today. Planning to stay home and back to bed on the early side.

> **Zoe:** No worries—feel better! Can I bring you anything?

Russ: I am hoping that you will allow me to treat you to a nice dinner soon 😊

Nudging can also take the form of reassurance, as in this exchange between Markus and Angie:

Angie: Only problem with our plan is that my lease says no sublet

Angie: and all the neighbors will see me moving out

Angie: I can just say a friend is staying there. Hmmmm

> **Markus:** I'm not worried

> **Markus:** Doesn't sound like he talks to the neighbors.

> **Markus:** Besides he's a fuckwit

> **Markus:** and rented you a sewage pile

Angie: lol ok

Our fifth text love language could be called **nooking.** Nooking is the most physical of text languages. It can pop on your screen as a simple "Can't wait to be with you" or "Xo." Sometimes it's in the use of a special nickname or term of endearment. Overtly, it could be just plain old sexting. There is some evidence that sexting in the context of a committed relationship increases levels of sexual communication. Sexting couples, as such, may be more aligned on their affection levels and sexual aspects of their relationship.

Chris: Miss your body. Miss touch, sleep, snuggles, and sex. I get back late Friday night. Xo

> **Cara:** Mmm, I miss you too. What time will you get in?

> **Chris:** Midnight, think you'll be awake?

> **Cara:** for you, ya!

Sometimes a big reveal comes over text. It can begin with "Are you alone?" Even though no one can see your texts, and you are miles away from your partner, you will want to find a private spot for this conversation.

> **Konstantin:** Hey. Something odd. I've got to tell you this.

> **Teresa:** Give me a sec

> **Teresa:** Hey, what's up?

> **Konstantin:** This thing happened this morning. I felt like it wasn't even mine. Like we were sharing it. Like it was ours.

> **Teresa:** Wow. I couldn't even put that into words. But I felt the same thing.

> **Konstantin:** That's Incredible

> **Teresa:** It is incredible

> **Konstantin:** What now?

> **Teresa:** I say we try it again.

> **Konstantin:** Ha. And again. You are amazing.

> **Teresa:** You are amazing.

> **Konstantin:** We are

> **Teresa:** yes

No matter the text love language that is favored, what's important is compatibility in communication. Nicole, for instance, feels attended to with riffing and nooking but is guilty of too much spoon-feeding at times. In the following text exchange,

Blake teases her initially about her spoon-feeding and proceeds to entertain her with some good riffing and nooking:

Nicole: Was up at 6:30 and just finished a hard 90min bike workout of Z4 intervals. Think I sweated about a gallon of fluids—it was like Bikram biking this morning.

Blake: Maniac. I completed 300cc of IBT and am heading back to the BR for another REM cycle.

Nicole: IBT? You lost me in your medicalese, doctor. Enjoy the z's

Blake: Irish Breakfast Tea

Nicole: I figured the T was for tea, but I never went to Irish. Don't forget to ADAT to BRAT (advance diet as tolerated to bananas, rice, apples and toast)

Blake: I don't have to ask Donald and Tebow to be righteous and tedious. They already are.

Nicole: lol—you are good.

Nicole: Well then, don't forget to TAMWYM (think about me when you masturbate)

Blake: I will be thinking of how you touch a man with your mouth (TAMWYM)

The Language of Attunement

The psychologist and relationship expert John Gottman's theory of relationship success takes a more scientific and complex view than Chapman's five languages. Gottman talks about building **love maps.** Getting involved with someone, he explains, is equivalent to sharing with them a map of your inner world. That metaphorical map includes your past experiences and baggage, your present concerns, and your hopes for the future. At the beginning of a romance, that map may lack detail, but over the course of a relationship, features will get filled in, important landmarks noted, and the shaded relief of topography added. Each partner's psyche has its own map, and eventually the two begin to superimpose as lives merge and are built together.

Of course, one of the ways a member of a couple learns about the other's love map is to ask questions. But this is only the tip of the iceberg—the most superficial element of building trust. Deeper trust is established with intimate conversation, and Gottman argues that he can mathematically evaluate trust in a relationship by examining a couple's interactions. A higher trust metric, he argues, gets built through the *language of attunement*.

Trust and attunement seem to be actively being built in this exchange between Marissa and Dan:

> **Dan:** Thank you for cheering me up today. Total stress. Company failing and I have to leave town Friday. You are a priority—sorry I could not engage well today.

> **Marissa:** Hi there. Understood. Sorry if I'm expecting too much. I want to be able to enjoy the time we have together despite the various constraints. If you are down or struggling with a problem, I am always happy to hear about it. If you need me to just listen, tell me that—I can try.

> **Marissa:** Thanks for making the effort today despite everything that's going on, and saying that you are happy to see me. When I don't feel that, it kind of breaks my heart.

> **Dan:** Got it. I apologize for the inconsistency and moodiness. You do seem to take on a measure of responsibility for seeing me happy which I so appreciate. To see you does make me happy. On the other hand

when I am distracted or anxious (which I often am) you are not at fault and it does not mean that I am unhappy with you. I am not trying to divert your feelings—I am conscious of your sadness. Just a little reminder that I do enjoy seeing you even if it's not always pleasurable and full of enthusiasm. Xo

> **Marissa:** Thanks—and thanks for reinforcing it. Maybe I am too sensitive. Love being with you and just want it to be good.

Dan: We are completely in sync.

Marissa and Dan are a poster couple of texting attunement. They actively listen to each other, remind each other of their importance, and respond with reassurance and transparency. They also demonstrate tolerance and empathy for the other's state of mind and respond non-defensively to a broader range of expressed emotions.

Gottman suggests that attunement can be broken down into six elements, remembered through the handy acronym ATTUNE. Awareness, Turning toward, Tolerance, Understanding, Non-defensive responding, and Empathy.

While these elements can all manifest themselves through language, it's important to recognize that just using the right vocabulary may not be enough. Vocabulary is limited, but the ways we structure language to employ that vocabulary in different contexts are infinite. So while saying "Aww, that sounds hard" is in theory demonstrating attunement, depending on how and when it's said, it may come off as either empathetic or dismissive.

Nelly: I woke up with a sore throat today. I feel like shit, and I have so much to do.

> **Mike:** Poor you

Nelly knew she was whining a bit, but "poor you"? Was that sympathy or just a thinly disguised "stop complaining already"? Perhaps Mike could have said "you poor thing" or "poor darling." Similar words . . . totally different meaning. Perhaps attunement is evinced not so much by what we say as by the way we structure what we say?

In contrast, Maria seems more attuned to Matt in her turning toward him when she received this text during the West Coast wildfires:

> **Matt:** I came home from work my head and sinuses not doing well with the smoke
>
> **Maria:** 😔
>
> **Maria:** Do you need anything? Worried about you
>
> **Maria:** You want me to come over?
>
> **Matt:** I'm fine. Really. Just need Advil Diet Coke and a nap
>
> **Maria:** ok

Sympathy is nice, but it can go over the top, as Justin ably demonstrates:

> **Sue:** I'm really anxious
>
> **Justin:** Why? Hugs
>
> **Sue:** So much stress around me. Everyone's losing it at work.
>
> **Justin:** Awwww 😊💗 Big big hugs 🤗 🤗 🤗 How can I put a smile 😊 back on that beautiful face 😍😙

Justin's response comes across more as "I can't tolerate anything but smiley feelings" than as true sympathy. We'll look more at understanding, non-defensiveness, and empathy in the next chapter, but for now let's look at the first stages of building attunement over text: paying attention, responding to bids (turning toward), and tolerance.

As we saw in the last chapter, paying attention is a clear sign of interest. It reveals itself in language-style matching and mirroring. It also manifests itself in responsiveness. As Gottman has followed couples over the span of their relationships, he's found that successful couples are the ones who pay attention to each other's overtures; they set aside their phone when their partner wants to talk. Or maybe, in the case of text messages, they *pick up* their phone when their partner wants to chat.

Gottman observes couples' interactions early in their relationships and then follows them longitudinally over the years. In his Love Lab, he observes and codes how these couples make bids for attention, affection, affirmation, or connection. A bid, Gottman explains, is "the fundamental unit of emotional communication." Bids can happen in person, with words or gestures, and they can happen over text. They can be subtle or dramatic. They can be direct or have subtext. Whatever form they take, bids are a way of saying, "Pay attention to me."

In his book *The Relationship Cure,* Gottman writes, "Maybe it's not the depth of intimacy in conversations that matters. Maybe it doesn't even matter whether couples agree or disagree. Maybe the important thing is how these people pay attention to each other, no matter what they're talking about or doing."

When one partner makes a bid, there are three possible ways the other can respond: *turning toward* (paying attention to the bid), *turning away* (ignoring or missing the bid), and *turning against* (overtly rejecting the bid). While rejection sounds painful, at least rejecting the bid presents an opportunity for argument, discussion, or continued engagement. When bids are silently ignored or missed, the bidder is left alone and hurt.

In Marissa and Dan's text exchange on page 172, each responds to the other's bids for sympathy and understanding. In contrast, Brett turns away from Alyssa's bid in the following exchange:

> **Alyssa:** Tomorrow is supposed to be a beautiful day. I love eating outdoors on warm evenings—reminds me of Europe.
>
> **Brett:** yup, you've certainly gotten to travel alot

Brett could have easily replied, "Oh, where would you like to eat?" but he misses the bid, or more frankly, he ignores it.

In more overt rejection, David turns against Jackson's bid:

> **Jackson:** I was checking out Airbnb's in Tahoe for later this month. I need a change of scenery. Feeling so burnt out.
>
> **David:** Tahoe in fall—why? Maybe when there's snow . . .

As Gottman has studied couples, and coded their responses in his Love Lab, he's found that in the most successful relationships (the "masters," as he calls them), couples turn toward each other 86 percent of the time. In contrast to the masters, the "disasters" turn toward each other only 33 percent of the time.

The masters also make small bids frequently and, in turn, respond to those bids frequently. Even if we are not so good at paying attention to bids, we unconsciously register when our partners don't pay attention to ours. Recurrent dismissal of our bids not only hurts but may eventually prompt us to seek a response elsewhere.

Here Simon responds to Michelle's silence, which is in fact a passive bid on her part. She hadn't answered his last few texts, so he prods gently:

Simon: You've been more silent than usual. What's the matter?

> Michelle: I'm sorry. I pulled an Erlich from Silicon Valley. "Until then, we need to do what any animal in nature does when it's cornered-act erratically and blindly lash out at everything around us"
>
> Michelle: I just panicked because I was overwhelmed. I didn't mean to be rude or hurt your feelings. I really care about you and about us. I understand now I was just shutting down. I don't know if I need to say any of this to you at all, But I was thinking about it.

Instead of simply expressing frustration, Simon solicits Michelle's feelings. In expressing her fears, perhaps she has established a unit of trust with Simon. In her reply, Michelle expresses what many feel as a relationship starts to take more solid form: a sensation of panic. That panic can represent a lack of trust or a fear of lost autonomy.

The Third "I"

There are couples who live in a bubble of two, with matching vanity plates on their cars, joint email addresses, his-and-hers pajamas. They advertise their unity like a freeway billboard, and their high visibility makes the rest of us feel as if we were missing out on something special. The truth of the matter is that devotional attachment is, at any given moment, often more one-sided than it appears. In these relationships, one person is usually hugging harder.

It takes two to tango, true, but describing relationships in such bivalent terms, as many relationship experts do, comes with its own pitfalls. Two pillars make for an inherently unsound structure, prone to toppling; the two sides of a coin are always facing away from each other. "Bivalence" draws from the same root as "ambivalence," and it suggests not a tango at all—close bodies and perfectly synchronized limbs—but something jerkier and more erratic, where toes are always being stepped on.

So let's retire all these overused metaphors for love. The best way for two people to lean on each other without collapsing one way or the other is by creating another element, what I refer to as the third "I." The three "I's," all connected yet all separate, represent the strongest and most enduring form of romantic relationship, with all parts providing support and still being able to grow without compromising the whole. This construct encourages each partner to reach, spread out, and contribute to the development of their relationship's creation. Much like a tripod, the structure will stand no matter how long each leg is, but it will reach the greatest height and stability if they are all extended.

Embracing the third "I" means abandoning the bivalent me/you in favor of the trivalent you/me/us. With this I'm referring to the couple that has gotten to know and discover itself—in which both members of the partnership can continue to evolve individually but also feel safe introducing new material into the relationship with a continued sense of discovery.

How might we observe this in the couple's language? A relationship's health, as Gottman's research would attest, is often reflected in the couple's ability to simply listen to each other. We sometimes take our communication skills for granted, blind to the ways in which we fail to listen, fail to contribute, fail to stay engaged with our partner. But in addition to listening, it's important to enliven and enrich, keeping imagination and possibility alive. The relationship expert Esther Perel argues that we need to create an erotic intelligence that is not necessarily tethered to our sexuality. "Eroticism" she defines as a life force, energy, or vitality that you need to cultivate within yourself, in order to share it with your partner. This energy is what is needed to repeatedly establish a connection, and it is essential to the growth of the third "I," which thrives on security and predictability but can't live on those alone.

In this couple's conversation, each is having their own experience, and yet they seem to feel connected nonetheless.

> **Mara:** How's the big easy? Miss you tonight. You having a good trip?
>
> **Erik:** Hi there. Étouffé and épuisé. G'night. Xox
>
> **Mara:** Laissez les bon temps rouler . . . I'm off to workout—have a good morning. Eat a beignet for me. Xo
>
> **Erik:** Another busy day. Sorry I've not been able to connect.
>
> **Mara:** I know babe and as long as I know you are out there, the world can keep on spinning. We're the same, you and I. We're both doing the best we can with the individual lights that we have. Hi, I'll always love you.

Mara and Erik's language creates space for each to explore their freedom. They don't pin each other down for details, giving each other room for psychological distance and some mystery, seemingly able to view each other as a separate and somewhat unknown person—perhaps even using their distance as a source of renewal.

When couples fail to bring their own genuine identity into an exchange, communications can lapse into mawkishness. Recall the classic "Soup Nazi" episode of *Seinfeld,* in which Jerry and his girlfriend keep repeating their "schmoopy" term of endearment, in a sickeningly sweet voice. "You're schmoopy." "No, you're schmoopy." As the George character says of them, in understandable aggravation, "People who do that should be arrested."

Nick and Ruth teeter on the edge of this slippery slope:

Nick: I literally fantasize about every part of you

Nick: Actually let's tack an almost on that

Nick: Almost every part of you

Nick: Much better

                              Ruth: FEET

Nick: KNEW IT. THE ONLY REASON I SAID ALMOST.

                              Ruth: ok rly falling asleep sorry. Gotta get up early too.

Nick: Aw ok. I love you so so so much

                              Ruth: Love you too dummy. Night loviebuggy

Nick: Night baby boo

                              Ruth: <3

Nick: <3

Yes, there is the security that comes from repetition. We've all drawn comfort from the pat phrases that we repeat to our lovers. But as Perel says, "If intimacy grows through repetition and familiarity, eroticism is numbed by repetition. It thrives on the mysterious, the novel, and the unexpected. Love is about having; desire is about wanting."

Trust and togetherness, then, are best balanced with development and autonomy. The most evolved relationships continue to grow both from within and from without. And growth, of course, requires tolerance, empathy, and understanding.

As the poet E. E. Cummings wrote, incidentally presaging texting style: We

are more than you

& i(be

ca
us

e It's we)

CHAPTER 7

Peace, Love, and Understanding

Sarah: Cool, I feel better now

Sarah: Totally, flattered and heard and validated

Sarah: So thank you for that

Adam: are you being sarcastic

Sarah: Yes

Sarah: Sarcastic+

Adam: lol

Because Adam can be a tad unsympathetic at times, Sarah decides to poke fun at him. Grasping at straws, Adam can only conclude that she is being sarcastic. Whether she is or not, the struggle to interpret sarcasm over text is real. There are no facial expressions, no drawn-out tones, no changes in pitch. Sarah's creative twist of adding a plus sign to the word serves to break the ice. She isn't reestablishing full harmony but making an overture in that direction.

Leo Tolstoy wrote, "All happy families are alike; each unhappy family is unhappy in its own way." This famous opening line from the novel *Anna Karenina* led to the principle of the same name. The Anna Karenina principle, used in disciplines as varied as ecology and economics, states that failure can come about in any number of ways, but success requires key measures to be present. In other words, to miss the mark is easy; to hit it is hard.

Does the Anna Karenina principle extend to romantic love?

There *are* certain bedrock features of any successful relationship, which we will tackle in this chapter. In the previous one, we began to explore the notion of attunement. Here we will go deeper into the desire and ability to understand and respect your partner's inner world and how that might show up in text messaging. We'll look at the key text elements that lend themselves to emotionally responsive relationships—those features of our texting that create a sense in your partner of being *understood*.

> **Karen:** I feel vulnerable and insecure sometimes (all the time)
>
> **Karen:** Your sensitivity = my insecurity
>
> > **Brian:** yeah, I hear you, I'm sorry I'll do better 😞
>
> **Karen:** I appreciate it and was not trying to make you feel badly
>
> > **Brian:** Doesn't matter I can do better. I need to pay attention.

Here Karen makes a bid for reassurance over text. Brian acknowledges that he should offer more. "I feel," "I hear," "I can," "I need," and "I do" abound. He responds by demonstrating some of the key principles of attunement: awareness (paying attention), turning toward, and non-defensive listening.

How do *you* show up in your relationships? What expectations do you hold for them or hold them to? Some envision love as a willed and wanted projection upon another: a colonization of affections. In this form of love, the desire might be for what a person wants to see in their partner, rather than for who their partner actually is. But in chasing an ideal, we can become blinded to the reality before us. Love can only be a dialogue, not this sort of monologue.

Romantic love holds such a place of honor in our minds and our culture that we can forget how much of a social construct it really is. We have been raised on stories of true love—tales of passion that never fades, of living happily ever after, till death do us part. The prescription that "if you just find the right person, you will have true love" works really well—until it doesn't. What happens *after* happily ever after? As science is quick to demonstrate, eternal passion is biologically impossible. Plato himself described romantic love as a serious mental disease.

The researchers Ellen Berscheid and Elaine Walster of the University of Minnesota have been described as the Thelma and Louise of psychology. They have focused their research on questions around passionate love. Together they designed the "Passionate Love Scale" in order to better measure this crazy-making emotion, which they aptly describe as a "wildly emotional state in which tender and sexual feelings, elation and pain, anxiety and relief, altruism and jealousy coexist in a confusion of feelings." They have defined passionate love as a condition of intense longing for union with another person and shown it to consist of an admixture of thoughts, feelings, behavioral tendencies, and patterned physiological processes.

When a person scoring high on the Passionate Love Scale is put in an fMRI scanner and shown pictures of the object of their love, they show brain activity patterns similar to addicts—that is, craving, even obsession. There are neurochemical underpinnings to these patterns, including elevated levels of dopamine and norepinephrine.

As the psychologist Jonathan Haidt says in *The Happiness Hypothesis,* passionate love is a drug. And no drug can keep you high forever; eventually it stops working. The brain adapts and tolerance develops; biological equilibrium is restored, whether or not that is accompanied by psychological equilibrium. As Haidt puts it, "If passionate love is allowed to run its joyous course, there must come a day when it weakens. One of the lovers usually feels the change first. It's like waking up from a shared dream to see your sleeping partner drooling." Where our minds might have constructed a beautiful imaginary castle, there is now either a house in need of repairs or just a hole in the ground where a home used to be. For some, that may generate the desire to roll up sleeves and begin a restoration; others may want to run for the hills. There is no happy ending—only a happy process.

So if there is a common element to relationship success, an Anna Karenina principle of sorts, it is less about maintaining an idealized image of someone, the kind we might forge in our early, passionate love, and more about communion: a sense of being understood, of being seen by someone else. Seen so deeply that the boundaries between each other seem to fade away and the isolation of our daily existence, the prison of our thoughts, the impossibility of ever being inside someone else's head, dissolves. In the end, it might be this closeness that saves us.

What elements lend themselves to such a non-idealized version of love, a love that, as C. S. Lewis put it, has the "power of seeing through its own enchantments and yet not being disenchanted"? There are many underpinnings to enduring love, but three essential building blocks come to mind.

Feeling the Feels

Camilla: Have an awesome time at the Greek tonight! Jelly—love Tom Petty.

Nate: I'll say hey to Tom for you

Camilla: Tell him that I know how it feels

Nate: Cuz you got a heart so big it'll crush this Berkeley town

Camilla: Probably not that big. But sometimes my empathetic tendencies get the better of me.

Nate: Well empathy is often underrated

Nate: As are red kinky boots 😊

Camilla: Duly noted

Nate: It's the simple things in life . . .

The British psychologist Edward Titchener, most of whose work followed him to the grave, is credited with coining the word "empathy" in 1909. Hacked together from pidgin Greek and the German word *Einfühlung* (feeling into), "empathy" became the granddaddy of twentieth-century pop psychology terms, taking on a life of its own. It's so prevalent now that one can only wonder how the people of the Anglosphere managed to have appropriate emotional connections before this neologism entered their vocabulary.

With or without the word, we do, in fact, have an innate tendency toward **empathy,** this first building of enduring love. It surfaces despite even our conscious attempts to suppress it. From birth we are hardwired to attach, and securely connecting to loved ones helps us evolve both individually and as a species.

More than that, it can be taught. Learning how to be empathic is one avenue to get you from a passionate place to a more giving one.

Since Titchener, the word "empathy" has been used to describe a wide variety of emotions and states. Lack of empathy, or an excess thereof, is considered a symptom of such psychiatric diagnoses as narcissistic, borderline, and antisocial personality disorders. That said, it's important to distinguish displays of empathy from the interior, emotional quality it describes. What is often referred to as "showing empathy" involves an act of compassion, but showing it and feeling it are two different things. Feeling sorry for someone in need, for instance, stems less from empathy than from compassion or pity.

"Compassion" and "pity" aren't terms that are necessarily associated with successful long-term romantic relationships, whereas empathy is. Conversely, there are areas of life where displays of empathy are culturally, socially, or professionally inappropriate, and thus discouraged. Picture a hesitant drill sergeant trying to put a platoon through an arduous exercise, or a surgeon poised to make a critical incision but wavering. That simply would not do. In personal relationships, though, it's a must. A couple simply cannot survive without the powerful, nurturing fuel of empathy coursing through its vessels.

Zach: Sorry to be short on the phone. Would love to have you along but it's just going to be us guys.

Felicity: I totally understand! I don't want to be a fifth wheel just wished you'd been clear about that. I already asked for time off work.

> **Zach:** Oh! Sorry my bad. I had no idea.
> Same thing happened with my sister for this
> weekend. I made all those plans and then she
> decided not to show up. Still upset at her.

Zach apologizes and expresses sympathy for Felicity going out of her way, even giving an example of how he felt similarly in another situation. But he misses the opportunity to identify and share her feeling of exclusion. Saying "I didn't want to make you feel left out" might have made Felicity feel more understood, and less likely to feel they were on opposite teams.

Empathy is typically defined as the ability to vicariously understand and experience the feeling of another. This is subtly different from empathic concern, also called sympathy or compassion. Empathy involves "feeling for" the other person but not sharing in the actual feeling. And while sharing of feelings is an important first step, it does not presuppose that the feeler will act in a supportive way. Empathy's paradox is that it can be used in support of or against someone. So it is important to understand the nature of empathy outside the pop phenomenon that it is.

Because empathy promotes a sharing of experiences, it plays a role in many aspects of emotional communication, both resonating with another's pain and sharing in their joy. The psychologist Shelly Gable of the University of California, Santa Barbara, and her colleague Harry Reis of the University of Rochester found that how one member of a couple responds to good news from their partner is highly predictive of the health of their relationship.

To reach their conclusion, Gable and her team had observed a large number of dating couples and examined how they reacted to good news and bad news from each other. Interestingly, they found that the response to your partner's good news was a better predictor of a lasting relationship than the reaction to bad news. Perhaps that's because it's intuitive to support someone facing bad news; celebrating successes may be less psychologically obvious. But feeling abandoned on a mountaintop can be no less distressing than feeling dumped in a ditch.

Fears around celebrating our partner's successes can come from any number of sources: insecurity, guilt, jealousy, resentment. When we feel these emotions ourselves, they tend to cloud our willingness to celebrate our partner.

In a paper titled "What Do You Do When Things Go Right?," the researchers classified reactions to good news in four different ways: "passive destructive," "active destructive," "passive constructive," and "active constructive." A passive-destructive response is an indifferent one: deflecting, changing the subject—the textual equivalent of "meh." An active-destructive response is one in which the listener points out downsides of the good event or finds a problem with it.

> **Elena:** Guess what—I'm being considered for a leadership role on the team!
>
> **Ted:** Isn't that going to be a lot more work for you?

In a passive-constructive response, the support is more tacit and generic, with only a muted sense of shared joy.

> **Marnie:** I'm so excited with the design I came up with for my website
>
> **John:** That's great 🙌

In an active-constructive response, the vicarious happiness is expressed enthusiastically, with emotion and further inquiry.

Becky: Finally got an offer. I was the deal of the day!

> **Ralph:** You're the deal of the decade, baby. That's fantastic. I know how hard you've been working on this, and how stressful it's been. Can't wait to hear more details

Among the four response styles, active-constructive responding is, of course, the most successful in displaying true empathy. It allows the couple to savor joy together and gives them an opportunity to bond over good news. Gable found that active-constructive responding in a couple was associated with higher relationship quality, as evidenced by more satisfaction, commitment, trust, and intimacy.

So any notion that empathy is a thing to be trotted out only in grim times, applied as a salve or a Band-Aid, may do relationships a distinct disservice. And while in the rest of our lives—at work, among friends, on the phone with our cable providers—we might have a variety of empathic settings, with our significant others there should be only one valid and functional setting: on. Only through more or less constant emotional vigilance can modulations be perceived and can lasting empathy develop. This is the true essence of attunement.

We've all been in the difficult position of trying to interpret (or convey for that matter) nuanced emotion over text. If empathy is tricky in person, it may be even trickier in the digital sphere. Text messages are prone to misinterpretation, because we don't always "hear" written messages the way they were intended; our brains default to stereotypes to fill in the gaps. Empathy emerges from conversation, and texting is a form of conversation, but to effectively empathize, we must be careful to remember the humans behind the text, including ourselves. Our emotional detection skills over text are of course in part determined by our past experiences and perspectives, and depending on the state we are in, we won't all interpret the same emotional message in the same way.

James had been silent after he and McKenzie had a heated conversation, so she inquired how he was. He replied:

James: Just recentering

She was inclined to feel rejected by that two-word text; "recentering" suggested to her that James was centering *away from her*. But rather than act on that sense of rejection, she considered the possibility that James might feel hurt, so she replied with the following:

McKenzie: I just wish I could make things easier for you

James: Thanks. I feel that. I'm not good with conflict. Raised in an environment where nobody got angry, they just criticized.

McKenzie: I was raised on plenty of criticism too. Used to think I needed it, but I'm trying to let go of that. On that note, if I need a little reassurance from you, is it available?

James: Absolutely. Please don't make the mistake of interpreting my silence as criticism. We've had enough of that. Xo

It can be easy, when looking at an emotionally laden text, to fixate on one key word and draw conclusions from it. It's more helpful if you can look at a cluster of words and think about the emotional undertones of those words and the person behind them. In the course of any relationship, we come to understand our partner's vulnerabilities and emotional baggage, and they do ours. We can either help them carry that baggage or hit them over the head with it. McKenzie senses that James is down and uses his distance ("recentering") to try to make a repair. By effectively saying, "I'm here for you even through things that might have hurt in the past," she establishes trust.

Considering the potential for miscommunication in situations such as the one above, it's easy to argue for the drawbacks of text-based technology. But are there benefits to handling emotionally charged or higher-stakes conversations over text? One potential benefit is that each party can feel that they are in their own physically comforting environment. Communication won't be marred by a shaky voice or an avoidant gaze. There may be times that removing each other's physical presence can lend itself to less escalation. Another obvious benefit is latency, the delay between when a person writes and when you respond. That time can be taken to craft a more measured answer (as long as that latency is not avoidantly long).

The drawbacks, however, are real. While text messages may reduce emotional expression, they can also be used to say something hurtful that you might not say in person, or to brush off or avoid a bid for a deeper conversation. The use of the mobile device may be allowing us to suppress our natural tendency toward empathy.

Here Austin deflects a deeper conversation and potential criticism when he cancels his plans with Tamara without much advance notice:

> **Tamara:** Just hovering over SFO about to land. Are we still on for David Byrne tomorrow?

> **Austin:** I forgot about a work commitment. No can do. Give David a peck and feel the Byrne. Let me know how your Wednesday is trending.

> **Tamara:** With any luck Wednesday I'll be graced with your negligent charisma.

> **Austin:** Neglect is my strong suit. I detest abuse. What can I overlook next? I tremble at the possibilities.

> **Tamara:** Picking me up at the airport for one. My cab smells like an ashtray.

> **Austin:** You are in a cab? That's kinky.

Text messaging allows Austin to make light of his potentially disappointing Tamara, without the kind of recrimination or discussion a phone call might have occasioned. He uses his irreverent sense of humor to deflect responsibility.

The fact is, empathy and understanding are dependent less on the medium of the conversation and more on the willingness to create space for them. An empathic interaction cannot occur without good intent, without genuinely caring for the interests of the other. If the goal is to convince the other, to manipulate their feelings to align with yours, to establish who is right, then empathy will necessarily take a backseat. Empathy thrives in safe spaces, not in traps or dead ends.

RE-SPECT

If empathy is our first prerequisite for lasting love, **mutual respect** is our second. After Jake meets Dylan's mom, they are both over the moon with trust, empathy, and respect.

> **Dylan:** she said she could tell why I'm so into you

> **Jake:** Wowowowow

Jake: That's huge

Dylan: because you're nice, and easy to talk to, and kind, and brilliant

Dylan: and good looking haha

Dylan: so overall, it went super well

Dylan: so thanks for being you

Jake: Wow dylan

Jake: This is just making me so much happy

Dylan: good

Jake: I love you so much

Dylan: dope

Dylan: your fam next I suppose

Dylan: realizing that I would pick being in bed with you than anywhere else in the world

Jake: Yep. That's my reality

Jake: Such a happy reality too

The word "respect" stems from the Latin root meaning to look around and look back upon, to consider, to provide respite and reprieve. As the co-authors of the book *Crucial Conversations* aptly put it, "Respect is like air. As long as it's present, nobody thinks about it. But if you take it away, it's *all* that people can think about." There are moments in every relationship where we don't understand our partner and cannot empathize with their feelings, but still we must try to trust, respect, and accept.

In his writing, the couples expert John Gottman underscores the idea that a relationship without conflict is a fairy tale. In fact, most of the disagreements that occur between any particular couple will be irresolvable and remain just that—disagreements. Getting mired in these differences is easy. Maintaining respect for the other person's choices is work. Much in the way that positivity should prevail in the expressions of your empathy (celebrating good news and not just commiserating over bad), a high ratio of positive expressions toward your partner will also sustain *respect* in relationships. Finding ways to remind your partner that you cherish them is key. To do that, Gottman emphasizes *maintaining high regard* for them and *focusing on their admirable traits.*

It's tempting to think that with the right person, nothing other than high regard would be possible. But as anyone who's ever been in a heated conflict with their partner can attest, respect does not always flow naturally. During moments of disagreement, it can require focus to keep those muscles flexed. Nicholas Epley, a professor of behavioral science at the University of Chicago, outlines in his book *Mindwise* that while couples *think* they understand each other's preferences, they are right only 44 percent of the time. Even longer-term relationships, he explains, create an illusion of insight that considerably exceeds the real thing.

How can we cultivate such insight and respect, even when our partner's views deviate from our own? And how might we reinforce them over text? Let's look at steps to bridge the chasm when couples behave the way Winston Churchill described England and America: two countries divided by a common language. There are (at least) four constructive techniques to draw from.

The Four Practices

Gottman has written extensively about what he calls the Four Horsemen of the Apocalypse: criticism, contempt, stonewalling, and defensiveness. These conversational features are the kiss of death for couples; they seep into a relationship and spoil it. We'll look closely at these destructive tendencies in the next chapter. But before we examine what not to do, let's first outline four practices that promote respect.

The first practice is **curiosity**. The longer we've known someone, after the fires of passion have stopped igniting an insatiable desire to know everything about them, the greater a tendency there is to assume that we understand everything about them. With that comes a greater need to stay curious, to override those assumptions. Ask questions in text. Notice when messages betray an unusual emotional tone or distance. Think of the screen on your phone as the mood ring of your relationship and the text messages as the colors. When emotions get too hot or too cool, stay curious. Ask yourself, "Why would a reasonable person say this?" instead of "Why are they making such a big deal of this?" Acknowledge not just what your partner is saying but the subtext of what is being said, and try to absorb it without judgment.

> **Charlotte:** I just sent you an email. I've been carrying last night's conversation around with me all day.

> **Lexie:** I just read it. You said "Everything just seems so cruel and unpredictable at the moment and I feel pressured to pick love over fear."

> **Lexie:** Is choosing love a problem?

> **Charlotte:** Yes. No. It's just that fear settles in my gut and I can't shake it off. I pretend that I'm fine but keep trying to extract promises and guarantees out of you. I'm trying all the time to be as courageous as I pretend to be.

> **Lexie:** Am I the one pressuring you?

> **Charlotte:** No, it's me trying to exert control over forces that are uncontrollable.
>
> **Charlotte:** Aware that I'm a freak. Some kind of savage succubus.
>
> **Lexie:** Ha—I like the sound of that!

Lexie is not providing reassurance per se—maybe she can't—but she asks questions and gives Charlotte the space to express her feelings. Charlotte admits she is struggling with the emotional vortex that can accompany falling in love.

The second practice is **patience.** Be willing to blink for a moment or two before responding. Texts can escalate easily if emotions aren't kept in check. As you note emotions intensifying or feel the traces of adrenaline, give these waves of emotions a chance to crest and subside before responding. As a rule, it's best not to text when you feel angry.

In this exchange, Kate has been escalating her protests and accusations. She feels Carlos has treated her unfairly by being less committed to the relationship than she would like; Carlos tries to set boundaries and Kate softens a bit.

> **Kate:** Like what the fuck is wrong with you you are SO HURTFUL—like so hurtful, I can't believe your behaviour these past few days—just so shocking how little you respect me. Please let me in on what the fuck is going on.
>
> **Carlos:** Kate stop!!! Like please why do you have to make everything so painful and hard and make me respond and be an asshole. I am trying incredibly hard to be diplomatic but this is getting absurd

(Time elapses . . .)

> **Kate:** I'm sorry for snapping—that totally set me off—I'm calming—I want you to know how important you are to me but this hurts so much and the continual slaps in the face are just too much for me to deal with. I am losing it and I am sorry I am not stronger—this is so unfair—I haven't done anything wrong here—I don't understand any of this and it just keeps getting worse—I love you so much—I hate that we are here and you are choosing to put us in this position 🖤😕 I'll stop texting I'm sorry

By taking time to reflect, Kate is able to return to the conversation by exposing her feelings of vulnerability and frustration rather than just voicing her recriminations.

Our third practice is **understanding.** If you find yourself confused by a text, as if you have entered the story midway through the plotline, try to retrace the path of your partner's thinking. Our brains are storytelling machines. See if you can understand the story the other person has told themselves before the text was composed. Give them permission to share their thoughts. Techniques to elicit the story are the same ones we have seen before: mirror, reflect back, and prompt them for more. The simple technique of paraphrasing—repeating your partner's perspective in your own words—is a tried-and-true method of de-escalating tension. Being heard goes a long way toward feeling respected, even in the presence of ongoing disagreement.

Ling had been sulky and withdrawn, then had the following exchange with Malcolm. Malcolm didn't fully understand why Ling felt annoyed, but here he appeals to her vulnerability, trying not only to understand but to interpret her annoyance. Malcolm and Ling may be speaking their own idiolect (or a shared "dualect"), but Malcolm implies that Ling needs to accept her negative feelings rather than becoming irritated when others recognize them for her.

> **Ling:** Giada came over. She noticed all my feelings. It was irritating. But she made me dinner which was nice.

> **Malcolm:** Don't blame the tailor for your sleeves.

> **Ling:** I will absolutely blame the tailor for my sleeves. And credit him. Or her.

> **Malcolm:** Oh, my. I think the woman who wore her heart on her sleeve has found a new clothier.

> **Ling:** What does this mean?

> **Malcolm:** That means that you don't like people knowing how you feel.

> **Ling:** Oh. True. But you know I love you?

> **Malcolm:** It's not a secret.

> **Ling:** Just checked. Still on my sleeve.

The fourth practice is **acceptance.** Accepting your partner's point of view doesn't necessarily mean agreeing with it. It's okay to compare it with your own, without labeling theirs as "wrong" but instead saying, "I see it differently." If you can't come to agreement, practice tolerance. Over text this can mean avoiding interruptions or non sequiturs, which are the equivalent of blowing past what someone is saying. Using humor can be a good strategy (especially if the humor is of the affiliative variety we discussed in chapter 4).

Fatima had told Jared that she was unexpectedly available to meet the next day, and she hadn't heard back from him:

Fatima: Did I tell you I cancelled today's evening class?

Jared: Yesterday at 5:36 p.m.

Fatima: Did you respond? Are you going to be here?

Jared: That is not our way. You announce your availability and I comply.

Fatima: What do you mean "our way," white man?

Fatima: Fine. See you then. And tomorrow too. And I'm sorry, Jared, but I love you even when you have your bitchy boots on.

Jared: By "our way" I am implying complicity. And my bitchy boots are always on.

Fatima: They are. All the better to shake that ass of yours.

Jared complies with Fatima's requests, despite being a bit passive-aggressive about it. She makes light of this and turns it into an attractive feature. Fatima has her bossy pants on and Jared has his bitchy boots, but instead of stomping each other, they find a way to dance.

GGG . . . Generosity

We've looked closely now at two of the three building blocks of enduring romantic love: empathy and respect. Scientific inquiry has shown us that the third, **generosity,** is something we're biologically wired for. Acting with generosity activates the same dopamine and oxytocin reward pathways as sex and food. Generosity and love are inextricably bound.

We know generosity has positive psychological as well as physiological effects in humans (volunteering is associated with delayed mortality). But when we become entwined in romantic relationships, we can become less prone to generosity when it comes to our partners. It's all too easy to make assumptions about a partner's behavior or words, to filter them through the lens of our own biases. Actively taking a more forgiving, generous stance is likely to result in increased harmony, so it's worth considering the role it plays in our texts.

Assuming good intent—being charitable in your interpretations of your partner's words or actions—is a key building block to relationship success. This generous version of love often involves taking yourself out of the center of the equation and acknowledging that there may be other factors your partner is grappling with that you are unaware of.

> **Warren:** Lately you are pushing me away. I feel like the last few times I've reached out you're not happy at my merely calling to say hello and hear your voice. Or complained that my texts are distracting you from your work. I see a woman who has taken too much onto her plate without consciously deciding what to give up.

> **Joanna:** You have no idea how anxious I've been. Can we talk by phone tonight calmly?

> **Warren:** Of course we can talk. I'd love to talk to you. I'd love just to hold you.

Warren assumes the best of Joanna. While his interpretation may display a trace of naïveté, he comes to it from a place of generosity and kindness.

The sex columnist Dan Savage coined the acronym GGG to promote the attitude he recommends sexual partners have toward each other. As Savage puts it, "**G**ood in bed, **g**iving based on a partner's sexual interests, and **g**ame for anything—within reason." Examples of this would be making an effort to warm up to sex when you're not in the mood, willingness to try things that your partner is interested in, and being open to your partner's fantasies. Over time, their kinks may become your kinks. We usually rely on our partners to fulfill our sexual needs, after all.

It turns out there's science to back up Savage's recommendations. In a study of long-term couples, participants who were more motivated to meet their partner's sexual needs at the beginning of the study were found to be more satisfied and committed to the relationship at the end of the study. In addition, those higher in the GGG department were more likely to maintain their desire over time. Saying yes has its benefits.

But GGG speaks to more than just the sexuality in a relationship. It can figure into the language that we use to talk about sex, too, and there we should aspire to be just as generous. Sharing fantasies can be delicate. One partner may try floating a balloon and watch to see if the other reaches for it. Here Lionel broaches the subject:

> **Lionel:** Things with my ex used to get out of hand.

> **Sherri:** How so?

> **Lionel:** Would start carefree and exciting (eg. talking about threesomes). Then the conversation would happen again and she says she'd be too jealous. She finally decided she didn't want to hang out if I'm seeing other people.

Sherri: The beginnings of things always feel exciting and then suddenly you are on a train ride that is hard to get off of. Did letting go of that bum you out or make you feel free?

Lionel: In between. Where are you?

Sherri: Still in bed.

Lionel: What do you want to explore?

Sherri: I appreciate being able to savor and enjoy being with you

Lionel: I want to be honest about sexuality

Lionel: If there is something that turns me on. I'd #1 not want to feel guilty #2 be able to share that attraction with you like something new

Lionel and Sherri's foray into the subject of threesomes and non-monogamy highlights some of the tensions that exist around sharing fantasies with your partner. Talking about other partners can be fun and exciting, in theory, but in practice it can be complicated and confusing. While some people are genuinely interested in exploring outside the relationship, others use the topic mostly as a tool of arousal. Many report enjoying hearing the sexual fantasies their lover has for others, but the thought of their lover actually engaging in such behavior tends to spike unpleasant feelings. Lack of clarity around this distinction can lead to predictable and harmful misunderstandings.

When Jealousy Intrudes

Mateo: Yo estuve have más the 20 años . . . y luego otra vez hace menos de 10, en Acolman

Mateo: Oooops . . .

Sylvia: Who is that for?

Sylvia: And what are you talking about??

Sylvia: ??

Mateo: Don't worry it was to my friend Ricardo about the times I've been in Mexico with him.

Jealousy arises when one is suspicious or aware of a lover's infidelity, or experiences the fear of being replaced by another. In essence, it's the realization that our lover is in fact separate from us, despite whatever connection we might have established with them. What distinguishes jealousy from other reactions to perceived infidelity, such as anger and sadness, is its obsessive nature. Consequently, the state of jealousy has remarkable overlap with passionate love. Both are at once all encompassing and impossibly fragile. Both are predicated, at least unconsciously, on ideas that are unsustainable: perfection of the other, in the case of love; possession of the other, in the case of jealousy. Like passionate love, jealousy is addictive, requiring larger and larger doses to support itself.

Both states are also fueled by uncertainty. When love becomes a sure thing, the passion necessarily extinguishes. And as the French novelist François de La Rochefoucauld said, "Jealousy feeds on doubts, and as soon as doubt turns into certainty it becomes a frenzy or ceases to exist."

If you find yourself caught by jealousy, ask yourself why you need to keep it alive, what purpose that story is serving, and what might happen without it.

Amy rolls with the punches:

Amy: So happy that you give good text

Gavin: I take much pride in giving good text.

Gavin: Start slowly and gradually increase the word count

Amy: Can't believe you are sharing your special technique. Though we know there is so much more to it than that.

Gavin: There are special ingredients and proportions that will never be told. Just experienced.

Amy: It's an algorithm, right?

Gavin: I'm more like an abacus. The more the merrier

Amy: As in plural?

Gavin: As in more than one

Amy: I get that. I always joke that the right number of bikes to have, for instance, is N plus 1. Where N is the number you currently have

Gavin: I am open to N plus 1 possibilities

Amy: Well your abacus tendencies (though not fully explored or understood) will certainly help us keep count.

Gavin: lol. Wouldn't that be abaci tendencies?

Amy: I'm leaving the expertise in plurality up to you. Sweet dreams.

Even though she may be feeling it, Amy doesn't appear to evince any jealousy in this text, in which Gavin alludes to his desire to include others in the mix. By remaining open to a future understanding of what he may be hinting at, she avoids shutting down the conversation and is more likely to keep channels of communication open with him.

"Compersion" is a word coined in the 1970s by the polyfidelity community of Kerista. Centered on the Haight-Ashbury neighborhood of San Francisco, the community embraced the hippie ideals of nonconformity and sexual freedom, and they defined compersion as the antithesis of jealousy. It represented the vicarious joy associated with one's partner having a sexual experience with another. It's a word that has since been adopted by the polyamorous community.

While only an estimated 5 percent of Americans practice polyamory, a full 20 percent have attempted consensual non-monogamy (CNM). A 2016 study found that only half of millennials desired a fully monogamous relationship. It's not surprising that adherence to monogamy is lower at certain periods of one's life cycle, particularly when you're young.

> **Clarissa:** Tell me though, I know you love women, are you really a monogamous type or do you lean non?

> **Henry:** Mono-poly-pan and the like are questions for the young. At my age, one woman is more than enough.

> **Henry:** At the risk of sounding Solomonic, perhaps a half woman would do? 😄

> **Clarissa:** Just wondering. Well, I'm actually one and a half of a woman.

Yet even among those who are less interested in monogamy, most are more comfortable with the idea of having multiple partners *themselves* than with the thought of their partner having experiences outside their relationship. Jealousy is common among those who practice CNM, and it's something to be managed. Although interestingly, jealousy is no more prevalent among CNMs than monogamists. Polys (those who engage in CNM in the context of loving and longer-term relationships), meanwhile, report much lower jealousy rates and will report feeling empathetic happiness or "compersion" for their partner. Some see their jealousy as a growth experience that they can learn from and use to further intimacy in their primary relationship.

Estimated prevalence rates for CNM are outdated, but even an older study found that at least a quarter of all straight men and straight women had an agreement allowing open relationships, though a minority of them acted on those allowances. Rates were much higher in the gay population, topping out at 73 percent of all gay men, with the majority of them acting on it. It's interesting to note that multiple studies have shown an equal level of commitment and relationship satisfaction among gay and heterosexual couples, despite the differences in monogamy.

Infidelity has higher reported rates: 25 percent of men and 15 percent of women reported having extramarital sex in the prior year, and 70 percent of Americans report at least one extramarital affair in the course of their marriage. Yet when married couples are asked whether their spouse would engage in sex outside the marriage, estimates are low (just below 8 percent). We assume better fidelity than we perform. We also don't assume we will divorce, even though some of us do.

Cheating, as my psychiatry office walls could attest, isn't judged lightly. It is often *the* deal breaker in relationships, even though the offended parties haven't always taken the time to ask themselves the harder questions: "What do I really want from my partner?" "If my partner has sex with someone else, do they love me any less?" "Would it make a difference if they had feelings for the other person?" "When I'm in a relationship with someone, do I own them, and in what ways?"

The fears and difficulties in these thought experiments can stem from a scarcity mindset, an aversion to loss. There won't be enough of my partner (or simply enough *love*) to go around, and I must defend myself against loss. And so, for many the door is slammed shut, at least until they are unexpectedly confronted with a situation that forces it open.

While polyamory is unlikely to become mainstream, jealousy in a monogamous relationship represents all-too-familiar waters for most of us. Sometimes we all need to step back, take another look at our partners, and see them for who they are, to consider their own unique needs and wants.

Perhaps the best way to find peace, love, and understanding in a relationship, then, is to strive to create a balanced life oneself—a life that cherishes romantic intimacy but does not idealize a single person at the center of it, as seductive as that impulse may be early in a relationship. Instead, we can emphasize the kind of relationship we want to have and nurture, and in doing so try to bring our best—our most empathetic, respectful, and generous—selves into the equation.

If the first section of the book was about using texts to ask ourselves what kind of person we want to be with, then this second section has been about using texts to ask ourselves what kind of relationship we're in, or better understanding the one we want to have. In the third and final section we turn to what I call scrolling—searching for truths in our conversations in a slightly different way. By looking back at older text messages, we can shed light on our style of conflict management. It can serve as a helpful indicator of our relationships' inflection points. To do otherwise would be to miss out on the powerful lessons already within our reach. As Tom Stoppard writes in *Rosencrantz and Guildenstern Are Dead,* "We cross our bridges when we come to them and burn them behind us, with nothing to show for our progress except a memory of the smell of smoke, and a presumption that once our eyes watered."

PART 3

Scrolling

CHAPTER 8

Toxic Texting

Annie: Not sure that vid you just sent is appropriate for kids

> **Russ:** It's awesome. So hot.

Annie: What is it?

> **Russ:** Wait—you dumped on it without watching?!

Annie: Was afraid to open in the presence of kids

> **Russ:** Oh well first off you shouldn't share texts that I send you with others, period. Text is a private one to one communication When you share with others, that is a violation.

Annie: Fuck you russ I'm out with kids and can't listen without them overhearing. Don't text me then as I will share with everyone

> **Russ:** Ok sounds good. No more texts!

Spite and meanness erupt like wildfire in this exchange between Annie and Russ, who immediately leap to assuming the worst of each other, using scorching words like "dumped," "violation," and worse. Though ostensibly about protecting the children from inappropriate texts, the language reveals that it is the adults who have some growing up to do.

A rapid escalation of accusations and insults is one of the classic communication traps we will identify and discuss in this chapter. These patterns are often only recognized in retrospect, when the heat of the moment has faded. But by scrolling back through texts, we can learn how to spot their unmistakable beginnings and start to notice their hallmarks not just in hindsight but in real time.

Because in addition to their primary role as live exchanges, text threads offer us an archived account of a relationship's story. They are the medical record of a relationship's health. Embedded within them might lie the precursors, the seeds of illness. When faced with a metastatic terminal cancer, can we scroll back to earlier X-rays and see the shadow of a tumor, one that wasn't obvious at the time? Sometimes patterns emerge and become visible only in retrospect.

Arguing over text is a natural extension of both conversing over text and arguing in person. And while most relationship experts would advise steering fights away from the two-dimensional space of the screen, fighting with our fingertips has a certain inevitability. As we've seen, it may even confer a few advantages to IRL arguing. But unlike a live dispute, each bubble remains static and visible on the screen; it doesn't float "in one ear and out the other."

Rereading, reanalyzing, and even sharing a screenshot with a trusted adviser before replying can all help to bring out the best, not the worst, in us. As a psychiatrist, I have been on the receiving end of these screenshots, but I've also relied on my own trusted sources for advice in romantic endeavors.

In the last chapter, we discussed my four practices of respect, an antidote to John Gottman's "Four Horsemen of the Apocalypse" outlined in his book *What Makes Love Last?* These horsemen are contempt, criticism, stonewalling, and defensiveness—some of the most unpromising signs for a relationship. If we can manage to steer away from these tendencies (which to some of us come quite naturally), we do ourselves and our partners a big favor. So let's look at these communication habits in more detail and see how they can manifest themselves over text.

Contempt is an especially ominous sign. Contempt is closely related to disgust, and it implies that your partner is inferior, or unworthy. It can present itself in overt and covert ways. The *overt* examples are easy to recognize and will make anyone cringe:

> **Scott:** I have to get out of this relationship before you get as dismally forgetful as your mother

> **Miriam:** I'm just doing my best. I have a lot going on.

> **Scott:** It must be a genetic defect in your family. Some kind of mental lapse. There is something wrong with you.

When we awake to overt contempt like this, it's often too late for repairs.

In contrast, *covert* contempt can seem light or funny. But it will wear over time if it isn't offset—and overcome—with validation. Put another way: there needs to be at least five positive comments for every negative one. The infiltration of negative comments and lingering traces of covert contempt are the early seeds of the more overt, late-stage forms. So exchanges like the following will begin to take their toll if they aren't neutralized with many more affirmations:

> **Ella:** ok that made me laugh

> **Sam:** Because it's true

> **Ella:** or as my son types: "ne." Short for nasal exhale. Better than lol, no?

> **Sam:** Lol used to be a waiter term for a little old lady. Dining alone, doesn't tip.

Ella: Hey, that could be my future.

Sam: Nah, you tip.

Ella: Thanks for the vote of confidence

Sam: Or are you talking about your future as a waitress?

Granted there is a fine line between teasing and covert contempt. As we discussed in chapter 4, humor of the aggressive variety is insensitive and can be mean-spirited. Sam might have meant his remarks as playful retorts. Still, hurtful teasing can take its toll.

Covert contempt can take the form of small jabs—the proverbial death by a thousand cuts. It can also take the form of taking confided, even sacred information about your partner and using it against them. Here Kerrie cuts a little close to the bone, using shared information about Kyle's past relationship mistakes to set him straight:

Kyle: I am just trying to be honest- it seems like things are just in different gears for us right now- I don't want to feel uncomfortable or make you feel that way . . .

Kerrie: Like you just want to be in high gear without doing the work to get there? How does that work? If there is a lesson to learn from your past relationships, that one might be glaring! Taking some time before having high expectations might pay off!

Instead of considering the point that Kyle is making—that he and Kerrie may be in search of different things right now—Kerrie quickly jumps in with references to Kyle's prior failed relationships, stories that he trustingly disclosed to her. In doing so, Kerrie implies that he was then, and is now, the one at fault.

Criticism is more self-explanatory, and while it's less noxious than contempt, it still has destructive effects. It's more like death by a thousand corrections. Shea was expecting Ravi to arrive at her house at some point to go for a hike, though they hadn't nailed down precisely when.

Shea: What time will you leave?

Ravi: I'll call you in a bit.

Shea: Why a bit? You are avoiding. You are never clear about your plans

Ravi: Please. I am having breakfast with friends. I'll call later. Not avoiding.

Shea: ok

Ravi may tend to be vague about his plans, and it's clearly not the first time he has frustrated Shea, but her comment that he is "avoiding" and "never clear" may be more critical than the situation warrants. She might instead have set clear boundaries with him by saying, for instance, "Okay, let me know by 10:00 a.m. please."

The difference between criticism and nagging is also a subtle one. With criticism, there is a focus on what we don't like, whereas with nagging there is a focus on what we want done. Every couple will at some point deal with nagging, an interaction where one party repeatedly makes a request of the other, and the other ignores it. Nagging eventually becomes a vicious cycle, in which the person being nagged or criticized starts to deliberately withhold.

Assuming that you'll be criticized or blamed for disappointing your partner can lead to withdrawal and **stonewalling.** The person who stonewalls turns a deaf ear, indicating through body language or visual cues that they are tuning the other person out. In texts, this may be most easily demonstrated with a lack of timely response or a changing of subjects. The person who is being ignored will usually feel mounting frustration. Stonewallers can be notoriously unflappable.

Amber: RIP Sean Connery

(Silence.)

Amber: Tried you by phone. Want to have dinner tonight?

Michael: Everything I know about emotional avoidance and toxic seduction I learned from him. RIP

Amber: And then Daniel Craig took his cues from you?

Michael: We pass the torch on the path to glory

Michael takes Amber's simple RIP note up a notch, escalating it into commentary about Connery's style. She gets affirmation about her sense of Michael's avoidance but is still left wondering about dinner. Perhaps Michael is unsure if he wants to commit to dinner. Or perhaps he has difficulty saying no and prefers to dodge the question.

Jasmine doesn't dodge, but she does stonewall Roman when he tries to corner her:

Roman: Just a quick update, I'm available tonight and any time until Monday morning

Jasmine: Ok. I don't think it's going to work out but we can talk.

Roman: Where there's a will there's a way. Let's not play the busy card, as you always do, to escape

> **Jasmine:** I'm not tonight I have plans we can meet later this week

> **Roman:** What is it that you're not telling me . . . ?

> **Jasmine:** i don't have the capacity to talk right now

When faced with Jasmine's avoidance, Roman pushes even harder, implying she has a hidden agenda. In this format, his questions are unlikely to yield answers.

Defensiveness, just as it sounds, means putting up defenses in an argument. Forms of defensiveness, according to Gottman, include "righteous indignation, launching a counterattack, or acting like an innocent victim."

> **Lori:** Might you have taken my iPhone charger that stays by the bedside?

> **Richard:** I don't have your charger and I don't need to use your place as a flophouse

> **Lori:** Hmm. I wonder where that charger went

> **Richard:** No idea. it's not much fun to wake up to a declaration that I stole your charger. I hope it turns up.

Richard clearly feels as if he needs to be on guard. Perhaps he has had to defuse attacks earlier in this (or maybe a prior) relationship and so now quickly jumps to defensiveness in response to what might seem, to us, like an innocent question. He may be hearing the question more critically than it was meant, and he effectively exaggerates the accusation by using words like "flophouse" and "stole." In doing so, he's backhandedly asking for Lori to go easier on him.

The Dances of Distress

So far we've been thinking about communication as it's displayed by an *individual,* but there are toxic patterns of communication that can be enacted only by a *couple*—dances of distress that become patterned interactions. The psychologist Sue Johnson developed an approach to psychotherapy called emotionally focused therapy, and in her book *Hold Me Tight* she calls these dances "demon dialogues," wherein simple arguments can trap couples in claustrophobic rituals of mutual abuse, echoing Sartre's famous adage "Hell is other people."

In one dance of distress, each member of the pair escalates accusations until neither has any choice but to preempt the subsequent attack. These story lines often involve one or more parties playing the victim.

Things escalate quickly between Anatole and Sophie when he sheepishly (and foolishly) backpedals:

Sophie: Hey how was ur day?

Anatole: It was good and work done how about u girl?

Sophie: Same it's been a grind past 2 days but done for the weekend

Anatole: Let's gooo so ur chilling

Anatole: How are u going to celebrate

Sophie: By u taking me out on a date

Anatole: Tm night?

Sophie: Im down

Anatole: Ok

Anatole: Maybe

Anatole: Idk if I have plans

> **Anatole:** I wasn't really planning for a yes response

Sophie: Then why did u ask about tomorrow night?

Sophie: Why'd u think I'd say no?

> **Anatole:** It's a Saturday night lmfao. I have plans I'm pretty sure

Sophie: What? Why'd you ask about tomorrow night then?

> **Anatole:** Honestly I didn't think you'd say yeah so I was kidding around

> **Anatole:** But next week

Sophie: No thanks I'm done with this nonsense

Sophie may be setting appropriate limits with Anatole in response to his retracted offer of a date. But when Jeffrey expresses ambivalence about Krista and tells her he wants a weekend with the guys, she unloads on him with both barrels:

Jeffrey: Don't make me out to be an asshole.

> **Krista:** Sorry you are a complete asshole— hope you have fun fucking a bunch of waitresses with your shit friends who CLEARLY dont give a shit about you and your well-being- happy you tossed me aside so you can look cool to them again—you are absolutely ridiculous- i'm here teling you how much I love you and want to be with you and minutes later you're trying to make plans to go out and what, celebrate?—this is unbelievable—you just don't have one ounce of respect for me.

> **Krista:** What the actual fuck. Did you spin up all your dating profiles too while you are

at it? RIDICULOUS. You are really showing
your true colors—you just wanted to be
single and fuck a bunch of girls—god your
such a piece of shit honestly I can't believe
the nerve of you to be so manipulative
toward me.

Krista: Have a good weekend

Krista: Or life

Krista: Whatever this is stupid

In this type of dance, we might land on an unspoken agreement about the roles each of us plays in a relationship. One partner may be portrayed as needy, the other independent. Or one
is expressive, the other stoic. At a certain point, the roles and
opponents become so ingrained that the fights become about
fighting itself, instead of the subject at hand.

Harper and Landon have been drawn into a passionate but
volatile whirlwind of a relationship. She wants the security of
moving in together. He admittedly doesn't feel ready. Going
into this exchange, Harper feels disappointed when, once again,
Landon isn't interested in talking about the idea of moving in
together or addressing "her needs" for commitment. But watch
how instead of fighting about their difference in perspectives,
they begin to fight about fighting:

Landon: Do we always have to come back to
this? It may not be what a girl needs, but it's
definitely what she wants.

Harper: Wants come and go, but it's been
proven that needs are not negotiable.

Landon: Proven? Well, studies have shown
that our species evolved by negotiating
needs

Harper: What is to be negotiated?

Landon: The statement that needs are not negotiable for one.

> **Harper:** Let's get to the point. What do you think is to be negotiated?

Landon: Love comes first. That is non-negotiable. Everything else is.

> **Harper:** Here is how I see this. . . .

Landon: As an ellipsis?

Landon intellectualizes Harper's expression of her needs by philosophically defining what can and cannot be negotiated. While these two are making bids for their own form of connection, they are simultaneously taking shots at each other. Landon dismisses her "needs" as wants, challenges her sloppy use of "proven," and pokes fun at her trailing-off sentence. Harper portrays him as the bad guy by accusing him of not meeting her needs. Ultimately, they are fighting not so much about moving in together as about how they fight. Neither is working to understand what's at the core of the other's perspective.

In another version of the dance of despair, the couple behaves in a pursue/avoid pattern, with one actively pursuing the other with demands or criticisms and the other retreating. Think windshield wipers: one party approaches while the other retreats, and vice versa. Esme and Kevin are in the throes of this particular dance:

Esme: I really need a call. I matter too and if it feels like I don't matter, and that's how you have made me feel, then I can't keep going like this.

> **Kevin:** I do not want to talk. I understand your anxiety

Esme: You clearly don't understand.

> **Esme:** Hey if you can't call, you could at least text. You're behaving like an asshole now. This is so unfair!

> **Kevin:** I asked for space. Turning off my phone now.

Nobody wants to be on the receiving end of criticisms, but Kevin's avoidance is just as destructive as any potential criticism. It would be more helpful for him to tell Esme that he was stepping away for a moment but that he'd be back, rather than simply shut her down.

Yet another version of this dance is no longer a pursue/avoid pattern but instead an avoid/avoid pattern. The boxing match has taken its toll, and the two exhausted contenders are in a prolonged clinch. It might resemble a hug, but it's only temporary, to stop the hitting. Eventually, they must be broken up and retreat to their own corners of the ring. In this third and most hopelessly entrenched pattern, connecting with each other hurts too much, and so the couple can only retreat into a silent standoff.

Here, Harper resumes her pleas and negotiations, in her ongoing exchange with Landon over his perceived lack of commitment:

> **Harper:** Just figure out what you want without putting my heart through a meat grinder.

> **Landon:** I want to enjoy life, gain wisdom, nothing too fancy. Love you in ways you never knew existed.

> **Harper:** And what are you willing to negotiate?

> **Landon:** Everything except love. And I have to throw in respect, which seems to be, bluntly spoken, not your strongest suit.

Harper: Now you are insulting me. How did I disrespect you?

Landon: Disrespect is simply the removal of existing respect. This has happened.

Harper: It's just become clear that our definitions of love are critically different. And it breaks my heart.

Landon: I will have no part of your heartbreak! I am all yours!

Harper: It does not work like that.

Landon: But we're crazy about each other! We're supposed to get all pragmatic when we start getting bored.

Harper: When we have disagreements, you go on the attack. I feel slammed and muted.

Landon: That is a truly dismal characterization. You should run not walk away from a person like that. DTMFA

Harper: I don't know what those letters stand for—Dump the motherfucker's ass? But the rest I understand. And agree with.

Landon: already

Here we see Harper both play the victim and blame the villain. Landon attempts to reassure her with declarations of love, but she seems unable to take them in, in part because he uses these pronouncements—"we're crazy about each other"—as a shield against her true concerns. And when she accuses him of going on the attack, he resorts to defensiveness, exaggerating the accusation against him by suggesting she dump him already. Instead of softening, she takes the bait. What's missing is their ability to listen for what the other is actually longing for.

It's important to note that in all of these dances the couple is feeling the pain of an attachment crisis. The dances are a response to that distress. It is only by recognizing the *dance itself* as the problem, rather than just one partner's role in it, that the couple can begin to appreciate the anguish they are each feeling and begin to repair their distressed connection.

These patterns of conflict can certainly be addressed in couple's therapy. But I've found that by scrolling and rereading the texts of a dialogue, with the right kind of insight at your disposal, the steps of the dance can become visible to each partner. It can be a helpful learning tool to see your own patterns reflected back, when not in the heat of the discussion. My patients who do this are often surprised, not so much by their partner's difficult communication style as by their own part in enabling it.

Repairs

What are some of the techniques we can use to intervene when we find ourselves in one of these destructive patterns? The answer circles back to understanding the stories we tell ourselves. When you find yourself telling a story about your relationship or your partner, challenge yourself to look at the story as just that— *a* story, not necessarily *the only* story. Stories differ from facts, and it can be helpful to sort through what is a known fact versus an opinion or an assumption. Where might our perspective be distorted? Look for toxic words (examples of criticism or contempt) or toxic narratives (examples of victims or villains) in the story, and explore if there's another way to tell it without these features.

Evelyn is hurt after she learns that Carl had a flirtation that went too far with a woman. She starts in with sweeping accusations:

Evelyn: At the end of the day you have no loyalty to anyone. You say and do whatever suits you in the moment or gets you out of trouble but it's all in the service of your image and does not take into account anyone's feelings or wellbeing, let alone the truth.

Carl: I accept that.

Carl: Weak. Not solid. Fickle.

Carl: I hope we can talk it over.

Evelyn: Nice only to those who are distant. You can buy a stranger flowers but you can't get the people you love a gift.

Carl: Hostile. Defensive. Not kind. Undermining. Slippery.

Evelyn: Or be faithful. Or be there when they need you.

Carl: Always picks the phone. Buys coffee, dinner, lunch and breakfast. Always says yes to spending time

Evelyn: I am smiling

Carl: Prioritized you over work. To the detriment of work.

Evelyn: I did the same for you

Carl: Prioritizes. Present tense.

Carl: Yes you do prioritize me. Arguably much more so than I do.

Evelyn: Sunday was hurtful. You kissing that girl was hurtful and buying her flowers was hurtful

Evelyn: You blowing everything up over nothing is hurtful

Carl: I accept that I fucked up something good

> **Carl:** Hey there. Sleep well and we can restart tomorrow. I need to sleep.

Evelyn: I am beyond exhausted from all of this.

Evelyn: Say something nice

> **Carl:** Sorry. Love

Evelyn: Thank you. Still love you too even when I want to wring your handsome neck.

> **Carl:** Good night and thank you for bearing me

Carl could have easily slipped into one of the demon dialogues with Evelyn, either by avoiding her protests and retreating into silence or by getting defensive. Instead, in a skilled display of emotional judo, he lets her get in some hits and participates, perhaps in a caricatured way, in his own defamation. This allows Evelyn to feel heard and even laugh at herself a little. When he does retreat, he promises he will come back for more ("we can restart tomorrow"). Carl is able to masterfully sidestep a dance of despair and, with Evelyn's generosity, repair. Had he rebuffed her insults and criticisms defensively or underplayed her hurt feelings, she would likely have escalated, and they would be stuck in a pursue/avoid trap from which it's difficult to escape.

In a subsequent exchange, Evelyn chooses, or at least says she is choosing, to tell the story in a more favorable light:

Evelyn: I thought about what you said about anger. Don't think you realize how close to that well of anger I am all the time. Worked through it this fall, but it's still right there and I don't want to go there. You don't want me to go there either. It makes you feel misunderstood. It would be easy for me to say that you are shut off from your feelings, not aware or sensitive to mine, and that you are using me just to meet your own needs. That might all be true. Instead I have chosen to see your small gestures as expressions of love, and the effort you are willing to go through as an expression of devotion, and that for whatever reasons that is what you are capable of, and that in different circumstances it might not be this way.

Carl: Thank you. I understand your sense of vulnerability and the constant proximity to anger. Instinctively flight/fight comes first. You are making a huge effort to keep those in check and it's reasonable to say "why the fuck am I doing this?" As you said, you are evaluating. I do understand you are fed up.

One of the basic endeavors in cognitive behavioral therapy is to become aware of one's thoughts and the emotions that stem from those thoughts. That includes the story you tell about your own experiences, how you explain what you're seeing and hearing, and your beliefs about yourself and others. The goal here is to identify negative or inaccurate thinking and reshape those thoughts such that they can lead to *new* stories, *new* feelings, and *new* responses to a stressful situation.

We, of course, need to do this for ourselves. But sometimes, in order to repair, we need to take the time to understand our partner's narrative too. What thoughts and stories got them to this point of conflict?

It's easy to assume that a repair has to involve an apology, and apologies have their place. But if you're not inclined to say you're sorry, it can be helpful instead to make sure your partner is hearing what you intend. Distinguishing what you *don't* mean from what you *do* mean can repair misunderstandings.

> **Evelyn:** Thanks for talking. This is not an easy situation for me and I lack the ability to shut things off the way you do. Don't know how to numb myself with antidepressants and alcohol. Don't know how to ignore you or not think about you.

> **Carl:** It's going to be ok. I acknowledge the ups and downs. Miss you and look forward to connecting again.

One significant obstacle to reshaping narratives is mistrust. It can flood our brains, undermining our ability to see our partner clearly. One antidote is to break down trust into particular issues, instead of offering it universally. Perhaps you trust your partner's intentions, but not their ability to follow through on a particular request. It can be helpful to keep trust focused on the issue at hand, rather than the person as a whole.

Intimacy and Independence

Romantic intimacy's cardinal features are trust, self-disclosure, and concern. But tolerating true intimacy also means being able to tolerate the intense emotions that arise from this openness and vulnerability. Maintaining intimacy requires, as we saw in earlier chapters, a coherent sense of self. Capacity to tolerate closeness is one thing; capacity to maintain autonomy and separateness within the relationship is another. Both can be key factors in managing conflict.

Intimacy can take many forms. It can of course be sexual, but it generally has a larger scope than that. It can take an intellectual form, with room to clearly express and share thoughts and viewpoints. It can arise from shared experience; the more powerful the experience, the deeper the intimacy it's likely to generate. Some of these forms of closeness involve shared time and space, whereas others exist as feelings that transcend time, space, or even formal thought.

It can be easy to assume that intimacy and independence are on opposite sides of a tug-of-war. Instead, much like chemistry and compatibility, they exist on separate axes. It's possible to share great intimacy while leading independent lives, and also possible to be interdependent but with fewer intimate experiences.

Gregory and Rosie have different ideas about the relationship between time spent together and intimacy:

Gregory: Well it's July 4 weekend—will you be around? I assumed we would be spending it together . . .

Rosie: Why is there so much pressure to spend 'independence' day with other people?

Gregory: lol

Rosie: Can't we construct our relationship on our own terms?

Gregory: "Driven by me" I hear that all the time from you. I'm just left wondering if your busy/independent nature will leave enough room for anything to work here

In attempting repairs, there are individuals who will try to drive up intimacy in the partnership, while others may need to recharge with independence. This can be a point of conflict. Each member of the couple must try to recognize their own needs while also remaining sensitive to the other's. It's a delicate interaction. Successfully achieved, it might have the grace of a pair of swans gliding across the water. Failure, on the other hand, can look like a pair of pigs wrestling.

Time and Timeliness

> **Priya:** Mom's dog Floxie died last night. In the process, she bit mom's hand so badly that she is going to have to get surgery today.

> **Ajay:** Bad dog!

Is Ajay's text to his wife (a) darkly funny, (b) disturbing, (c) callous, or (d) all of the above? The answer is probably "all of the above," but I think we can all agree on simply "bad" (and not in the playful, "bad dog" way). Perhaps Floxie had been a burden to the family for a while, with children, nephews, and nieces all encouraging mom to let her go. Even so, Ajay's response is flippant, and it utterly ignores the physical and emotional pain of his mother-in-law.

Sometimes a remark or comment comes too soon. Often it comes too late. Timing isn't everything, but it is something. When these temporal failures start to crop up in conversations, when tempers and moods start to extend past their expiration date or fall off prematurely, it's a call to pay attention.

Is Ajay just making one of his usual off-color remarks, or are things more seriously amiss between Priya and him? Time will tell, but when it does, will it be too late?

Change is a constant in relationships, and as we saw in chapter 6, it's an important component of their long-term health. Emotional distance and speed will vary over time, as will curiosity, patience, understanding, and acceptance. But sometimes we need a point of reference to turn to, a reminder of what our earlier relationship looked like. We need a medical record.

For those of you who missed the previous seven chapters, or perhaps came in through a side door, you may not know where I am going with this. The rest of us can simply open up our messaging app and be presented with an up-to-the-moment, real-time history of all our text conversations covering the last months and years. The most basic app functions are sufficient to search dates and key words, to find trends, to reveal in a general way what the vibe *used to* be like, and when both the more subtle and the larger tectonic shifts occurred. A deep dive can reveal the evolution not just of our partner's attitudes but of our own.

In this case, it was Ajay reviewing the record. He shared his findings with me: "I was never very fond of Priya's mom. She was a very emotionally distant alcoholic, always chain-smoking on the porch instead of being with her guests. But I noticed in earlier texts that I was always supportive when Priya worried about her, even though I was fairly indifferent to the woman. My text about Floxie was meant to be funny, but reading it made me realize that's when my feelings changed, that I was tired of Priya and her whole dysfunctional family, that I wanted to get away."

The biggest transitions in a relationship—in this case the fractures forming beneath it—can often only be perceived in hindsight. We don't see the cracks forming until they've swallowed us up entirely.

Harper and Landon are in the midst of their own difficult transition. With the potential loss of a cherished pet, and after yet another breakup in a series of such splits and reunions, it is unclear whether they are more interested in preserving their relationship or entrenching their positions.

Harper: Hi, can we discuss Bao and timing? She is not ok

Landon: A priori, I would like to acknowledge that this is a very difficult time. Bao, of course, but also breaking off with me two weeks ago and the unfriendly exchanges that followed. I would ask you to consider whether my involvement would come at too high of an emotional cost to you.

Harper: I love you. All of this is a high emotional cost. I am losing everyone I love

Harper: There is nothing else to lose

Harper: If you dont feel this is ok with you, I understand. I will make other arrangements

Landon: I am willing to assist as needed. Reasonable boundaries should be in place, though. Spending a few days with me after the funeral, for example, might not be appropriate.

Harper: You are right . . . too high a price. You say I am the love of your life, you are in love with me, now you have bounderies when my dog is dying..but you don't respect my bounderies

Harper: This is insanity

Harper: Where is the love?

Harper: You set bounderies when my dog is dying

Harper: Omg

Harper: You could not be any more cruel to me than you are being now. After I tell you I will not be ok after she dies. The most heartless human I have ever met

Harper: Omg

Landon: You have been saying things such as these for a while now. So, you understand how my presence at this sensitive time would be detrimental and how boundaries would reduce harm.

Harper: You dont give a shit about me

Harper: Your words and your "love" are meaningless. I will bury them like I will bury Bao alone

Landon: Amazingly, notwithstanding the onslaught of invective and vilification, I care very much.

Harper: Bull shit

Harper: Meaningless

Harper: Empty

Harper: Lies

Harper: Good bye

Harper: I am an idiot for ever believing you

In the noise of conflict, with heightened emotions and diminished trust, it can be difficult to hear the signals we're sending each other. We find ourselves disoriented, searching for meaning. Scouring our texts can offer us clarity and grounding during a difficult time.

Isaac Asimov said, "Life is pleasant. Death is peaceful. It's the transition that's troublesome." Let's continue, in the next chapter, to look at relationship transitions—the crossroads that mark the road maps of our romantic lives.

CHAPTER 9

Crossroads

> **Trisha:** Could you see if those grey pumps I bought for Willie's party are still in the guest room closet?

> **Zac:** you looked so good that night. we just stayed home and played spoons

> **Trisha:** Yes

> **Trisha:** Do you mind if I come and grab them while you're at work?

> **Zac:** you never wore them. new in box. guess your going to wear them tonight?

> **Trisha:** Yes

In this painful exchange between Trisha and Zac, Trisha is asking if she can come by his place while he's not home to reclaim her party shoes, suggesting that she will be donning them without him. Still pining for Trisha, Zac resigns himself to the request. Her one-word responses are a recognition, maybe for the first time, that she is moving on.

Anaïs Nin wrote, "Love never dies a natural death. It dies because we don't know how to replenish its source, it dies of blindness and errors and betrayals. It dies of illness and wounds, it dies of weariness, of witherings, or tarnishings, but never a natural death." It's telling that even the academics we've discussed resort to the language of "demons" and "the apocalypse" in their descriptions of conflict escalation and love's death. To the afflicted, it's not just the end of a relationship; it's the end of the world.

We've all been at these emotional crossroads. Many of us have only recognized them after the fact. Scrolling back through a text thread can help us diagnose the onset of a relationship's illness (or, when needed, to perform an autopsy). It can also show us when our relationship health took a turn for the better, the moments of a deepening of love. We can see when and how we entered a crossroads, a new phase.

As a relationship evolves, so do its text messages. Messages shift from romantic flirtations to practical exchanges—of weekend plans, grocery lists. One data scientist tracked the word content of her texts with her husband from their first date to their sixth year of marriage and found that the frequency of the words "hey," "love," "good," and "fun" decreased, while "dinner," "now," and "ok" became more common. While messages may inevitably become more utilitarian in this way over the course of a relationship, there are good reasons to suggest that affectionate messages can help a couple maintain their bond.

How do we know when someone is pulling away and ready to change direction, versus when you are simply transitioning into a new phase of your commitment? Are you at the beginning of a road or its end? Mostly we recognize these crossroads at a gut level, through vague sensations of trepidation, anxiety, excitement, or fear. We know, without knowing what we know. The tug of these feelings might be exposed in the language of our texts, even when it's only much later that these thoughts become conscious and turn into actions. In truth, by the time a breakup or divorce is under way, the couple has often been unraveling for a long time, whether recognized by others, themselves, or not at all.

In my years of practice, I have witnessed people who were

asleep at the romantic wheel. They wake up only with the crash. My patient Margo told me she had no idea her husband of eighteen years wanted out until he announced he was getting his own apartment. She called me the following day for an urgent first appointment, tearful and distraught, seeking some clue to what had gone wrong. She was seemingly blindsided. Other patients have come to me painfully aware of the moribund status of their relationship but reluctant to address it out of fear of change, or loneliness, or the dread of hurting someone they love.

Transitions are hard, whether it's changing jobs, relationships, or cities, to say nothing of those ideas at the core of your being, such as your gender or sexual orientation. Yet social and geographic mobility have made "future tripping" on the notion of "forever after" a thing of the past. Few of us only ever live in one town, hold down one job, marry our first love. Understanding that transitions are the norm, is there a way to embrace these changes in our romantic lives?

As we've seen, the stories we tell about our own relationships can be true, false, and somewhere between. We've discussed the importance of stepping back from these narratives to reassess them. What scrolling through our texts can do is allow us to retell the story using the raw data at our disposal. Whether it's done in a moment of uncertainty about our path forward or as a forensic account after our relationship's demise, there is much to learn, and even to cherish, from these stories.

We've seen how texts might help us identify a suitable partner and recognize compatibility and harmony as it's happening. Here we will look at how text threads may reveal three classic transitions in the arc of a romance: disillusionment, coalescence, and detaching. At each of these crossroads, the couple has a choice: to passively and subconsciously slide into a new phase of their bond, or to treat it as a major crossroad and to consider their choices with appropriate gravity.

Disillusionment

As couples graduate from their passionate beginnings to the formation of steadier (if less thrilling) bonds, it's not unusual for a kind of disillusionment to creep in, sometimes subtly, sometimes loudly. Insecurities reveal themselves; imperfections emerge that previously went undetected or were brushed aside. Levels of appreciation and gratitude will wax and wane. The love that initially felt so overwhelming starts to feel manageable; what first was an irresistible, inevitable pull becomes a matter of daily choice. Maintaining the relationship starts to feel like work—because, quite frankly, it is. The freedom to choose to stay together can morph alluringly into the choice to pursue freedom. The crossroads loom ahead.

The way we handle these rough patches is often what makes or breaks our relationships. Couples that manage to revel in their differences and idiosyncrasies, that bask in the occasional bumpiness, will sail past these crossroads with relative ease, confident in their choices, trusting in their direction. Others will need more guidance.

Lilly first walked into my office the day before her wedding. She and her fiancé, Jamie, had been together for a few years, but she acknowledged their relationship was far from perfect. She loved him, and he was devoted to her, but she had been aware of their differences from the get-go. At first she attributed his linear, logical, not particularly emotionally sensitive style of thinking to his wholesome maleness. Although they often had animated, deepening conversations, more often she found herself as the audience to one of his monologues. When she tried to jump in, he would simply interrupt her and obliviously continue his speech. She found herself frustrated and anxious. Notwithstanding this habit, he made great efforts to please her and show affection. Now it was the eve of her wedding, and she wanted to talk about how to create more understanding and better communication in her soon-to-be marriage.

I had to credit Lilly for her courage. While many brides in the throes of wedding preparations conveniently displace the anxieties over *whom* they are marrying onto seating charts and flower arrangements, Lilly had the presence of mind not only to acknowledge that the marriage was going to have its challenges but also to begin to address them. By holding the cracks in her relationship to the light, on the eve of her wedding no less, Lilly was hoping to turn a natural process of disillusionment into one of enlightenment—a process of discovery by which she and Jamie could better communicate and accept each other going forward.

Each couple is tasked with building their own language. Nowhere is this more evident than over text. While lovers will naturally pick up each other's vocabulary over time, they are unlikely to pick up each other's punctuation or written expressions of laughter. And laughter, of course, is an important social cue, even over text. Text expressions of laughter can often serve to soften a statement. They can also be a cue for turn taking, the text equivalent of a pause to say, "Your turn to say something." One of Lilly's insights was a realization that her conversations with Jamie needed to include more explicit laughter and that marriage would require a greater capacity to cope with and accept her soon-to-be husband's quirks. She also decided to explore loving ways to steer his monologues back toward conversation, both in person and on-screen.

While texts can point to sources of disillusionment, they can just as often offer clues to solutions. Naomi, for instance, felt she had to take the lead with Xavier. He was reluctant to initiate plans, and when she proposed them, he often found excuses for why they were unrealistic or too much trouble, citing his own sensitivities or malaise. Having spent much of her life trying to please "hard to please" men, Naomi found it easy to see Xavier's resistance as a challenge—a wall she might successfully break down. But over time, his lack of enthusiasm became tiresome; it continually surfaced her insecurity, her internal questioning of whether she was good enough. By the time she came to see me, that weariness had taken its toll: what had once been his charming recalcitrance suddenly seemed just plain selfish. Together, we scrolled back through her messages to look for early traces of it in their texts:

Naomi: OK suit yourself. I'm swinging but clearly striking out. And that gets boring after a while.

Xavier: No strike out here. You have me highly motivated and that's at least a stand up double

Naomi: I like to knock it out of the park

Xavier: You did knock it out of the park. It was called a ground-rule double for fan interference.

Naomi: At least you got me to laugh. Wish my fans would stop obstructing play!

Naomi: You are just a finely tuned Stradivarius. One false move and the sound is off. I'm more like a German piano—you can bang away without worry.

> **Xavier:** Can't really imagine banging away on a Bechstein, but I'm trying

> **Naomi:** Only untrue love from you 😊

Revisiting this exchange helped Naomi understand how she was participating in a dynamic that reinforced her own insecurity. In pressing him for reassurance that was not available, she was leaving herself vulnerable to Xavier's detachment. Once she had read through her old texts, she was able to step back and give him the chance to provide *genuine* reassurance, in a form that he was comfortable with.

Micah was initially drawn to Vera for her magnetic, social, and confident personality. Vera could captivate anyone at a party. Micah was always proud to be with her and watch her interact effortlessly with others. As captives of early romance, neither one of them enjoyed doing much of anything without the other. Later in the relationship much of this compulsion wore off, and while Vera could flit about feeling confident in Micah's love, he began to resent her for the very traits he had once admired. By scrolling through their texts, he found early traces of this sentiment:

> **Vera:** So tired this morning. I came home at 2am

> **Micah:** Where did you go until 2am?

> **Micah:** Guess I am surprised you would do that when you wouldn't make time for me last night.

> **Vera:** I am sorry. I went out with a friend and just wanted to stay out

> **Micah:** Thank you for answering. All I needed to hear. Too bad I came up with the red light and they got the green light.

Micah had expected to receive more of Vera's time and attention, arising from the intensity of their initial encounters. He was left bitter and envious. It was baffling for Vera; she continued to feel for him as strongly as ever. His choice to dwell on his resentment, instead of embracing Vera for who she was, was setting him on a slippery slope (one that he was eventually able to correct). As Micah's example shows, disillusionment can stem not only from our false expectations of others but from our own inability to cope and accept.

Disillusionment is only possible, of course, if we once held illusions. But by stripping away these unquestioned assumptions, we can allow for greater openness and honesty, exposing a more solid foundation built on admiration and respect, or discovering that the foundation needs more work. Successful couples will translate disillusionment into growth and a deepening of intimacy.

Erich Fromm described love as "a constant challenge; it is not a resting place, but a moving, growing, working together; even whether there is harmony or conflict, joy or sadness, is secondary to the fundamental fact that two people experience themselves from the essence of their existence, that they are one with each other by being one with themselves, rather than by fleeing from themselves."

Coalescence

A major transition occurs in most relationships when elements of commitment and resilience start to coalesce into a distinctive, stable union. In truth, stable relationships might be more accurately described as *provisionally* stable—subject to dynamics of change but having internal equilibrium. This model accounts for the possibility of change within each of the individuals and also their environment. Such stable equilibrium may be less an outcome than a process—not so much a couple that has anchored itself into the ground as one whose members have become adept at balancing against each other as it marches forward.

How do communication patterns change as relationships deepen and coalesce? There is an interesting discrepancy in the way men and women approach texts. One study, led by Lori Schade, a researcher at Brigham Young University, showed that women perceive the number of texts they send to be proportional to the stability of their relationship. In contrast, men reported a negative correlation, with more texts associated with less perceived stability. Schade's study, focused on younger adults, also showed that women were more likely to attempt sensitive conversations by text than men. She speculates that men may use text as a means to establish emotional distance.

How does a couple's language reflect their stability? There are couples that approach the more stable stages of their relationship by sticking to the script, with variations on the canned "yes, dear" and "love you." Others will engage in passionate language that reinforces elements of trust and certainty and that diminishes fears of abandonment. Betsy and Amir text each other affirmations of love using modern vernacular:

> **Betsy:** Kissing you is like the way for me to know how much I love you

> **Betsy:** Other loves were like fake love. This feels different

> **Amir:** I'm gonna fuck you up I promise. Ur my puff

> **Betsy:** Ur gonna think this is weird bc you might not understand it, but like when I'm extremely happy I cry, it's pretty rare but

> it happens when I'm like so happy, and a
> couple times when we kissed I wanted to
> cry not out of sadness at all but because it's
> like I just feel so much love in my heart. It's
> more than ecstasy, it's like literally so much
> love it's hard to explain. I love you so much I
> wanna cry

Darcy and Ian spell out their attachment using more psychological terms:

> **Darcy:** You are so special to me. Unique and
> irreplaceable.

> **Ian:** Spending time with you is often in
> "flow." I love it. Your thoughtfulness and
> leaning forward are an expression of love I
> am so grateful for. My feelings for you are
> reciprocal; joy, deep affection and respect.

Sumi declares her commitment to Jay this way:

> **Sumi:** I know it's been a rollercoaster but as
> long as you're holding my hand through it
> its okay you know—and when it feels like
> you just let go at the top for no reason and
> I'm riding down alone that's not fair—I want
> to be partners in life. I have more fun when
> you're around you make me so Happy.

One feature of the dynamically stable relationship is resilience. Simone and Christopher have the following exchange as they head into a lengthy period of enforced geographic separation. They're trying to establish expectations for this long-distance period. Christopher has asked that they take a break while apart and not feel constricted by an exclusive commitment to each other. Simone has struggled to accept this without feeling rejected:

Christopher: I feel your disappointment—you try not to take it personally but i know it chafes. I feel a responsibility to you too.

Simone: On my disappointment: I am letting go. I've been holding on, and then withdrawing / protesting when it becomes unbearable to hold on in the face of frustration. But rather than force a choice between attachment and rejection, I am trying to find a balance of connection and separateness. I am trusting in my feelings for you to constantly reassert themselves (and yours too) so I can let go now to give each of us the freedom we need.

Christopher: You make me smile. Wish I could bottle you up and ration sips to cross the desert.

Simone and Christopher feel confident in their love, even as they head into a break. Unlike many couples, they managed to reconnect after their separation. Not every break is as tangible as theirs, but even the most resilient of couples will have to face challenges. Sometimes those challenges are too difficult to overcome, and emotional distancing or rupture will ensue.

Detaching

Even the most experienced and competent pilots have occasionally succumbed to an insidious dive known as the graveyard spiral. This occurs when a pilot loses sight of the horizon, whether due to visibility, instruments, or negligence. As the craft begins to list, the organs in the pilot's inner ear adjust, creating the illusion of being level when they're not. The pilot enters a spiral from which there is no exit. It's a type of CFIT—pronounced "see fit"—a controlled flight into terrain, because technically, and ironically, the pilot is at the controls the whole time of the crash.

Some couples see fit to end things this way, by ignoring their shared dreams and aspirations—their horizon—and intentionally driving the relationship into the ground. Others do it by accident or lack of vision. In our metaphorical aircraft, there are two pilots and two sets of controls; when one pilot does most of the flying, this plane will naturally list to their side. Without constant correction, the spiral will be engaged.

Lilly, the hesitant bride, had an inkling of the enormous weight that would be placed on her shoulders in a marriage to a man who was unwilling to or incapable of taking the controls when needed. She sought help from me early, before she lost the willingness herself. Margo, on the other hand, who had been married for eighteen years before her marriage's sudden shift, had grimly stayed the course, obliviously white-knuckling the controls until the very end, only to find that her husband had bailed out before impact. There's an expression in several romance languages that describes the shock of colliding with an unexpected reality. In French, it's *tomber des nues*. In Italian, it's *cadere dalle nuvole*. It translates as "falling from the clouds."

Before the spiral is engaged, and long before you make free fall, there are signs that can allow you to make the necessary corrections. Do it together, not alone. Erin attempts to engage Quinn as she senses that he is pulling away:

> **Erin:** I'm doing some digital housecleaning on my laptop and unearthing some real treasure.

> **Quinn:** Such as?

> **Erin:** I came across something I wrote before we met titled The Man I Desire. It's sophomorish and idealistic in a way that makes me squirm, but I recognize you in it. I'll show it to you when I see you.

> **Quinn:** I feel like you're walking into a terrible trap if you show me this tonight. You should wait until tomorrow.

> **Erin:** That sounds ominous.

> **Quinn:** Warnings can sound that way sometimes.

> **Erin:** Tomorrow it is.

Erin is working hard to resurrect her relationship with Quinn, but he has already gone a step beyond contempt and stonewalling, threatening her with some unspecified form of retaliation if she continues with her attempts. He's putting reconciliation beyond reach, actively engaging a graveyard spiral. Once engaged, it will gradually suck away all vestiges of conversational affection, a reversal of the timid steps that had emboldened the relationship at its beginning. "Hello I love you" becomes "Hello, love you," then "Hello love," and finally "Hello?"

Emotional distancing doesn't always present itself as pure conflict avoidance; sometimes it results in the creation of new obstacles, new behaviors that interfere with love. In text, you might recognize a kind of social and temporal distancing: that is, a reduction in the use of present-tense verbs, the omission of first-person pronouns (tellingly, these were also early indications of lying, a different sort of distancing).

Here Helena is proposing that Mason join her on her trip to

Baja California as a last-ditch effort to make their relationship work:

> **Helena:** one seat left on the plane if you want to come with me . . .
>
> **Mason:** Grrrrrr
>
> **Helena:** what does the Grrrr mean?
>
> **Mason:** Grr about Baja and its siren song
>
> **Helena:** It's not too late. I'm in my "anything is possible" mentality.
>
> **Mason:** That's my grrrrr—would be so fun but the timing is not right

Mason uses emotionally distancing language, with nary a pronoun in sight and only the occasional verb. His "Grrrrrr" might just as easily be annoyance with Helena for asking as it is annoyance that he doesn't feel the time is right for a trip. Helena might or might not have been reading the signals correctly in the moment, but they were clear to her when she looked back at the messages a month later, after their breakup.

It can be hard to know how to react in the midst of a graveyard spiral. The natural reflex of the affected person, in flight as in love, is to pull back on the control wheel or the stick. It's almost an indelible reflex, even for pilots with thousands of hours in their logbooks. When faced with loss of control, it's normal to tighten one's grip. Unfortunately, pulling back on the controls will only tighten the spiral, resulting in a paradoxical worsening of the situation.

The only way to fight off the pattern is through communication and situational awareness. Gaining insight amid chaos can be challenging. In her text to Jim, Mia sums up her disorientation:

> **Mia:** Anyway it's whatever—I am just processing this all still I guess—i'm embarrassed about the bruise on my knee because i just have been drinking so much lately—and it's not like me to do that- and I just haven't felt anything good except when I was with you and I miss you like crazy and just feel really "abandoned"—like the thing I feared for years finally came true idk I'm all over

Mia at least knows what she doesn't know; she has insight into her disorientation. Clark doesn't have the same situational awareness in his conversation with Sasha:

> **Clark:** Hey hope u had a good week . . . unless I'm reading it completely wrong I'm assuming that whatever we had going on is over? Lol I guess I'm just looking for closure if that's the case

> **Clark:** I mean I like you obvi lmao so if I'm wrong and u wanna keep things going my bad I guess lmao but yeah just lmk

> **Sasha:** thanks hope u did too! Personally I have a lot going on and I have a lot of priorities that I need to focus on. I'm good being friends but even then I really don't text a lot so don't take anything personally, Its just how I am w my phone

> **Clark:** Yeah all good just like future reference I was taking ur word that u were open about feelings and stuff and would've been nice if you'd just told me up front.

Audra and Ben are in the classic graveyard spiral. She's pulling back hard on the stick, but he has already parachuted out:

Audra: Just stay with me. Don't leave me we don't need to do this 😣

Ben: Audra, you know we are at an impasse. We've been through this so many times.

Audra: I keep staring at the cute dress I bought like over a month ago for next weekend that I'll never wear. This is so fucked up.

Audra: And you're just not fighting for us at all—you're just cutting the cord—for no good reason—like I'm in disbelief this is happening there's no reason for this to happen

Audra: I'm so mad at you for giving up on us and not caring about us enough to try to make it work—you're letting stupid fear get in the way of something that is so special— you can't just throw something like what we have to the side this is all so stupid and I'm just so shocked and disappointed. You are being cruel.

Ben: I am not being cruel, I am being honest and decisive because there is a fundamental decision that I have to make, and you can either limp into that moment and have the carpet pulled out from under you but I thought THAT would be cruel.

Ben doesn't mince words, but one senses he is trying to give Audra a chance to reorient. He later responded:

Ben: I've been nervous for a long time, which I've expressed many times, that we have such different levels of what expressing love means. I don't know how to think about things on 20-50 year time scales. I feel like this made me think about that so directly and viscerally and if I can't do this I don't think I am ever going to be able to love you

> in the way you need to be loved and you
> owe it to yourself to find someone that can.
> I'm broken in that way . . . so this is a shit
> situation and I want to support you but it
> isn't as easy as "believing in us" and "you're
> giving up" because I don't have it in me to be
> the kind of person I think you need.

After repeated breaks and attempted reconciliations, Landon and Harper, whom we met in the previous chapter, entered their own graveyard spiral. This final exchange, in which they are both guarded and disoriented, came on the heels of having spent less time together due to the demands of work. They were feeling increasing strain:

> **Harper:** You havent even returned my texts or contacted me for 2 days . . . its painful for me.

> **Harper:** Id rather know that you just dont have time to connect, instead of waiting and feeling hurt when it doesnt happen.

> **Landon:** It hurts me to know that you are lonely and a bit frustrated by the changes in my life. That is made worse when you are untruthful. You haven't sent me any texts in the past two days and woke up in my bed yesterday. That is just a fact, not a reprimand.

> **Harper:** Well, its not really untruthful . . . there were several occasions when I sent you messages, and you never even responded until the next day.

> **Harper:** Not a conversation to have in texts

> **Landon:** I understand that you are having a difficult patch. It doesn't help to attack me with statements that are contradicted and time-stamped above.

Harper: I didn't hear from you yesterday, and I heard from you at 10 pm tonight . . . to me that's 2 days

Harper: If you see me as a liar because my perception of what 2 days means is different from yours, then you are more interested in being right than showing empathy for my pain

Harper: I think we should end the texting now

Harper: There is no resolution like this.

Landon: Dude. You said I had not responded to your texts in two days. You sent none. Perception has nothing to do with it.

Harper: See? This is shitty

Harper: I hate doing this in texts

Landon: Yes, you should really not do this in texts.

Landon: Anyway, perhaps we should both get some sleep?

Harper: Yes. Good night.

Harper repeatedly invokes the powerlessness of text, yet, as Schade's research would predict, she is also the one raising the issues through that medium. She turns her hurt feelings into reprimands of Landon, and he replies with icy coldness. A crash seems inevitable. Their romance was brought to a close the next time they saw each other.

Coffin Lids

There comes a time when a relationship has to be put to rest. Perhaps love has died a peaceful death; perhaps something more dramatic unfolded. Either way, the relationship has expired and it's time to accept it and move on. How does one make peace with a relationship's demise? Scrolling through old texts might at first seem like little more than an exercise in self-abuse. But with a bit more distance, it can offer an effective way to perform a relationship autopsy and come to a better understanding of what went wrong and why.

A disclaimer: this process can be emotionally taxing, and it is best delayed until wounds have been licked, support and self-care are in place, and you feel more open to understanding what happened, along with the role you might have played in it. Scrolling back through texts may provoke nostalgia, sadness, anger, embarrassment, or all of the above. But it will almost always result in insight if one is open and willing.

There are key questions that can be addressed in the postmortem scroll. How do you present yourself throughout the relationship? How do you think about yourself as you read back your own texts? Are there any patterns, or shifts in pattern? How did your partner present themselves and how did that change over the course of the relationship? How did you express your needs, and how were they met? How did your partner express their needs, and how did you meet them? Can you trace the various crossroads in the texts—idealization, disillusionment, coalescence, emotional distancing? How did behaviors and decisions emerge that led to the breakup?

Despite its bitter ending, Landon continued to grieve his love for Harper for many months, stubbornly resisting any new romantic involvement until he could achieve better clarity over what had gone wrong and what role he might have played in its demise. In our conversations, he recognized his own tendency to idealize romantic partners. I eventually encouraged him to go back and look at his communications with Harper in their entirety. What he discovered surprised him. Landon wrote me the following:

I've been enjoying my arc of feelings about the texts I read. Initially I was blown away by the intensity of this passionate love affair, and devastated by its slow, painful demise. As the dust from the rubble in my head began to clear, so did my vision. These two were dancing on the deck of the Titanic, *sirens blaring, people screaming at them, lifeboats crashing into the ocean like ripe melons and sinking. And they danced. The blinding pain and desperate feeling of loss shifted to sadness and nostalgia, not for what it was, but for what it wasn't.*

Some relationships teeter on the brink of a graveyard spiral, constantly crossing and recrossing the threshold between hope and hopelessness. These couples have the stamp of doom on them from the start, but they persist in persisting, they believe in believing. For them, love is greater than gravity.

Nola and James had enjoyed a long and passionate extramarital affair that ended rather abruptly. They reached a crossroads together, but they chose to take different paths: Nola left her marriage. James buckled down to work on his. The end of their affair had left them without closure and with little to no contact, despite what were undoubtedly strong feelings on both sides. Nola sank into her grief. She reviewed their texts for answers. James, in his attempt to focus on his marriage, deleted everything, looking straight ahead and putting one foot in front of the other.

Years later, Nola received the following text out of the blue. In their exchange, she finally experienced the resolution she had long craved:

James: Hi. Watched "Take this waltz" and stayed up till 1:30am—fought exhaustion to watch the end. Sweet, sad, beautiful, moments of bliss, real . . . all the complexity of love. Think you would appreciate it.

Nola: I have seen it and loved it. Years ago.

James: Glad you liked the movie. It was so well done—could have been french. It had an emotional tension that was exquisite. Not schmaltz—a pointe.

Nola: Yes I can't remember how it ends. I know she has two men and one ends and it's unfinished feeling but that's all I remember

James: I need to get some sleep but glad I caught you! Xo

Nola: Miss you xoxo

James: You too

(. . .)

Nola: I'm up in the middle of the night after your text and started thinking. Anyway, was thinking about that movie "take this waltz." Now in the middle of the night the details of the movie are coming back to me. Or the feeling of the movie anyway.

And what I wanted to tell you is that: when we were together I watched every movie I could about women who were effectively ruining their lives with an affair. I watched them almost compulsively, because all day long I would think about what I was doing, and why I was doing it.

Anyway this particular movie—take this waltz—made me sad. I remember you want to be angry at her when she has the affair, but you can't, and at the end it's sad, because they have all made a lot of mistakes, but they really can't help it.

But I guess what I wanted to tell you was that now, I have almost no time for movies, or reflection, and it might be too painful. But in those years I was in it, and trying to connect with you in it, but I think you were too busy back then or too afraid to really think about it.

And I wonder now what is it you really think when you do watch these movies I was watching

Anyway middle of the night stream of consciousness but I thought I would write it down or it never gets said.

James: Hi there. Thanks for the consciousness. Hard to put in a text message because lots of thoughts and danger of being misunderstood. I felt the inescapable attraction between the two of them. He is (and I was) as much stuck in the vortex as she is but the situation is tragic because she has to make a choice. You see the fate they are in and it feels unstable, dangerous, explosive. Yet it continues to exist because they can't help it, or don't want to say no, or they want to escape into something, or its genuinely true love. That's the hardest part—what is the right thing to do? You don't know. I don't know. I think this is the beauty and the tragedy of our experience. Something magical is put on your plate as a choice. Do you dig in and live it or avoid it? There is not a right answer—you are left with a question but recognize that each had consequences.

Nola: Thanks for that. Read it twice and I am crying.

James: Sorry if I upset you. The movie felt like being on a train you can't stop. That was a familiar feeling. Xo

Were Nola's tears from pain at revisiting her loss? Relief that James was finally able to articulate the dilemma he had faced, now untrammeled by the pressures of doing the right or wrong thing? Joy that James had acknowledged that their connection had been something pure and true, beyond the obsessive passion of an affair? They were moving in different directions now, but their hearts remained together.

We may have a soul mate (or two) in our time, and we may have the good fortune to love them, in some instances to live that love together, for long stretches. In other cases, like Nola and James, we can know that it exists, somewhere, even though we took different turns at the crossroads.

Leo Tolstoy wrote, "Truth, like gold, is to be obtained not by its growth, but by washing away from it all that is not gold." Sifting through the sediments of our text messages to look for the nuggets of gold can both reveal the truths of our past relationships and help pave the way for new ones.

Thumb Tribes

Me: Overall I would say that I have met a lot of interesting people on dating apps. Even though few worked out romantically

Eliot: Lately I've only been dating Russian bots. Ludmilla and I are so happy together. Even if her conversation is simple and non responsive. She really gets me.

I've got a story for you.

It's my own story, but you have probably found that many parts of it are yours, too. As with all journeys, YMMV—your mileage may vary.

The rewards I've reaped from dating apps have been many. They've also, I've found, been inversely proportional to the expectations I've brought to them. Letting go of the need to find a particular partner, even if one would be a welcome enhancement in my life, allowed me to take a fun and adventurous stance toward meeting people. After all, the "ideal mate" is pure concept; the encounters we have on the digital dating circuit are always, bots notwithstanding, with actual people. Bringing too many expectations to these encounters is like wearing a raincoat in the shower. Not much happens.

Many have argued that online dating and the introduction of text messages in our romantic lives have degraded the quality of our liaisons and communications. Our texts can be, and have been, reduced to a simple "U up?" But if there is one thing that I've learned, it's that wildly more complex communication can and does take place over text and that e-romance has enabled new forms of conversation and created new levels of proficiency.

Texting has expanded and stretched my circle of acquaintances into a sort of elliptical orbit, where most everyone is on hand most of the time and those who aren't will be coming around again soon. There are friends, past romances, and future romances on that orbit, and perhaps the love of my life too, with new adventures at every planetary alignment. It is my relationship biography, in motion.

As we've chased the arc of romance and decoded its accompanying text messages throughout this book, from flirting to dating to falling in love, and even through to breakup, it can be tempting to think of our romantic pursuits the way my patient did, the one who wanted to "win at dating apps." We speak of love *lost,* and love *regained.* Might it be possible to take more of a win-win approach—an approach that accommodates and rewards all participants? At a certain point I started to bring to my dating life more of a tribal mentality, referring to my orbit as my thumb tribe. It's composed of people who don't gather to commiserate over lost loves, or see being single as a great affliction, but instead absolutely insist on enjoying life, the highs and the lows alike.

We are socialized to believe that when friends become lovers, the friendship is destroyed, and that when lovers become friends, it is a downgrade, a failure. Plato himself would have chuckled at the modern meaning of platonic love: a dry, sexless friendship of dubious value. His notion of love was of a ladder that we could ascend to reach truth and wisdom, with romantic and sexual love representing just a few of the rungs. In my Platonic friendships, with a capital *P,* I have found that no longer being involved in a sexual relationship sometimes means moving onward and upward to a higher level of connection.

The social promiscuity of the digital era has diluted the stigma attached to associating with past lovers and having deep friendships with future ones. This means that the social capital gained by romantic relationships needn't be squandered simply because two people are no longer exchanging intimate bodily fluids. It brings us, in a sense, closer to the Platonic ideal. Today, some of my closest friends are former romantic interests, people I met on dating apps. There is a level of intimacy and mutual understanding that perhaps would not be attainable by any other means than sharing time together on the ladder of love.

By thinking of the people we meet as a new tribe, our own thumb tribe, perhaps we can bring less "me" into the equation— less ego, more soul, as the saying goes. Instead of seeking out a single, glimmering source of validation, we can focus on our larger sense of connection to a community of people.

We have learned a new language, established a new fluency. How will you use it? As the author Susan Statham said, "Your life is your story. Write well and edit often." The yes or no answer to the question "Has digital communication killed the written word?" is probably moot at this point. To quote Ice Cube, "This is a gang, and I'm in it." We are all writers now, and it behooves us to bring our best to the table *or* the tablet.

Will thumb tribes become powerful social units in the cultures of the future? My thumb tribe has brought me an incredible wealth of love, knowledge, connection, and fellowship. The gifts are too many and too diverse to count. And along the way, miraculously, serendipitously, almost accidentally, my thumb tribe has brought you this book.

Acknowledgments

The challenge of writing a first book is a daunting one, and one that I couldn't have faced, let alone completed, without support.

First, I am most deeply grateful to Leonardo, my collaborator and friend. There is no exchange of ideas that we cannot have, and you are my steadfast thought partner and chief truth teller. Your creative genius, and ability to play with words, has delighted and inspired me. It is said that writing a book changes who you are, and your willingness to go on the journey with me made the process an adventure that I will always cherish.

Thank you to Liam Day for pushing me to write this book from the day I first voiced the idea. Two full years of his nudging was enough to get me started. Many thanks for believing in me, outlining the process, and tirelessly and thoroughly reading drafts. Your input was invaluable.

I'm so appreciative of my lifelong friends Debora Bolter, Kate Schermerhorn, Anna Seaton Huntington, and David Wright, who read large portions of the book and provided helpful comments and wise suggestions. Thanks to each of you. I am lucky to have such talented and smart people in my life.

Thanks are due not just to old friends, but also to the new ones I've met along the way. I'm grateful to the many of you who shared your text messages. Special thanks to William Chettle for your contribution of ideas, your correspondence, and your astute reads and suggestions. Thanks to Andy Katz, photographer extraordinaire.

I'm indebted to the many experts whose research I relied on for the book. Special thanks to Michael Norton, Barry Schwartz, Celia Klin, and James Pennebaker for taking time to be interviewed for the book.

Thanks to my fantastic literary agent, Howard Yoon, who shepherded me through every step of the process with unerring judgment, good humor, and kindness. Thanks for helping me to tell my story, and for shaping the book proposal as it grew from an idea to a reality.

This book would not have been possible without Yaniv Soha, my brilliant editor at Doubleday. When it comes to editors, I can most assuredly say that I won the lottery. I am so immensely thankful for your patience and your skillful use of red ink. Your masterful approach to my drafts were constant reminders that I was in the most expert of hands. I am deeply appreciative of your unwavering support, as well as that of the entire team at Doubleday.

Thanks to my awesome children, Kyra and Tor, for patiently accepting my focus on this project. A book that exposes your mother's dating texts might not have been what either of you had wished for, but you both handled it with grace and aplomb. Kyra single-handedly formatted references on her college break to help meet a deadline, and Tor helped me maintain my sense of humor. I love you.

Last but not least, special thanks go out to all of my patients, past and present, for trusting me with your stories, and allowing me to be part of your journey. You've taught me, over and over again, about life and only life.

Notes

INTRODUCTION

ix   **Freud himself acknowledged:** Sigmund Freud, "Volume 2, Studies in Hysteria," ed. Carrie Lee Rothgeb, Psychoanalytic Training Institute of the Contemporary Freudian Society, 1971, instituteofcfs.org.

xi   **More than fifty million:** Mansoor Iqbal, "Tinder Revenue and Usage Statistics (2020)," *Business of Apps,* Oct. 30, 2020, www .businessofapps.com.

CHAPTER 1: MIXED EMOJIS

7   **The psychiatrist Robert Cloninger:** Robert Cloninger, "A Systematic Method for Clinical Description and Classification of Personality Variants," *Archives of General Psychiatry* 44, no. 6 (1987).

9   **Michael Norton:** Michael Norton, Jeana H. Frost, and Dan Ariely, "Less Is More: The Lure of Ambiguity, or Why Familiarity Breeds Contempt," *Journal of Personality and Social Psychology* 92, no. 1 (2007): 97–105.

9   **"We *think* that if we know":** Norton, phone interview with author, May 6, 2020.

11   **Norton and his colleagues found:** Norton, Frost, and Ariely. "Less Is More."

11   **In their next experiment:** Ibid.

11   **"People who had been on more dates":** Norton, phone interview with author.

11 **Harry Reis, a professor of psychology:** Harry Reis et al., "Familiarity Does Indeed Promote Attraction in Live Interaction," *Journal of Personality and Social Psychology* 101, no. 3 (March 2011): 557–70.

15 *The Art of Choosing:* Shankar Vedantam, "The Choices Before Us: Can Fewer Options Lead to Better Decisions?," NPR, May 4, 2020, www.npr.org.

17 **One study demonstrated:** Bruno Laeng, Oddrun Vermeer, and Unni Sulutvedt, "Is Beauty in the Face of the Beholder?," *PLoS ONE* 8, no. 7 (Oct. 2013).

17 **couples with matching speech styles:** Molly E. Ireland et al., "Language Style Matching Predicts Relationship Initiation and Stability," *Psychological Science* 22, no. 1 (Jan. 2011): 39–44.

18 **Pew Research Center study:** Monica Anderson, Emily A. Vogels, and Erica Turner, "The Virtues and Downsides of Online Dating," Pew Research Center: Internet & Technology, Oct. 2, 2020, www .pewresearch.org.

21 **Give a rat a lever:** Taizo Nakazato, "Striatal Dopamine Release in the Rat During a Cued Lever-Press Task for Food Reward and the Development of Changes over Time Measured Using High-Speed Voltammetry," *Experimental Brain Research* 166, no. 1 (Sept. 2005).

23 **Center for Neural Decision Making:** Angelika Dimoka, Paul A. Avalou, and Fred D. David, "NeuroIS: The Potential of Cognitive Neuroscience for Information Systems Research," *Information Systems Research* 22, no. 4 (Dec. 2011): 1–16.

23 **Professor Barry Schwartz:** Barry Schwartz, "More Isn't Always Better," *Harvard Business Review,* Aug. 1, 2014, hbr.org.

24 **Sheena Iyengar agrees:** Vedantam, "Choices Before Us."

25 *The Paradox of Choice:* Barry Schwartz, *The Paradox of Choice* (New York: Ecco, 2004), 134.

26 **In her book *Marry Him:*** Lori Gottlieb, *Marry Him: The Case for Settling for Mr. Good Enough* (New York: New American Library, 2011).

27 **Kurt Gödel published:** Raymond M. Smullyan, *Gödel's Incompleteness Theorems* (New York: Oxford University Press, 2020).

28 **Dating algorithms also learn:** Ashley Carman, "Tinder Says It No Longer Uses a 'Desirability' Score to Rank People," *Verge,* March 15, 2019, www.theverge.com.

30 **A pivotal study by Eli Finkel:** Eli J. Finkel et al., "Online Dating: A Critical Analysis from the Perspective of Psychological Science," *Psychological Science in the Public Interest* 13, no. 1 (2012).

CHAPTER 2: CAN I GET YOUR NUMBERS?

34 **as Malcolm Gladwell famously described:** Malcolm Gladwell, *Blink: The Power of Thinking Without Thinking* (New York: Back Bay Books, 2019).

35 **One of these masters is Paul Ekman:** Paul Ekman, "Micro Expressions: Facial Expressions," Paul Ekman Group, Feb. 6, 2020, www.paulekman.com.

35 **Frank Bernieri:** David G. Jensen, "Tooling Up: First Impressions—Are Interview Results Preordained?," *Science,* Aug. 20, 2004.

35 **take a lie detection course:** David J. Lieberman, "Award-Winning Lie Detection Course: Taught by FBI Trainer," Udemy, Jan. 7, 2021, www.udemy.com.

36 **Dr. John Gottman's predictive work:** John M. Gottman, "Love Lab," Gottman Institute, Sept. 10, 2019, www.gottman.com.

36 **he's able to predict with 93.6 percent:** John M. Gottman, Kim T. Buehlman, and Lynn Katz, "How a Couple Views Their Past Predicts Their Future: Predicting Divorce from an Oral History Interview," *Journal of Family Psychology* 5, no. 3 (Jan. 1970).

38 **Crisis Text Line (CTL) is a company:** Nancy Lublin, "Crisis Text Line," Crisis Text Line, 2013, www.crisistextline.org.

40 **Myers-Briggs Type Indicator:** Katharine Cook Briggs and Isabel Briggs Myers, "Myers-Briggs Type Indicator," MBTI Basics, Myers & Briggs Foundation, www.myersbriggs.org.

40 **sometimes use the Enneagram:** George Gurdjieff, "The Enneagram Personality Test," Truity, Jan. 8, 2021, www.truity.com.

40 **the Big Five personality test:** Lewis Goldberg, "Big Five Personality Test," Open Psychometrics, Aug. 2019, openpsychometrics.org.

42 **High neuroticism scores:** Benjamin R. Karney and Thomas N. Bradbury, "Neuroticism, Marital Interaction, and the Trajectory of Marital Satisfaction," *Journal of Personality and Social Psychology* 72 (1997): 1075–92.

42 **if a couple is having a lot of sex:** V. Michelle Russell and James K. McNulty, "Frequent Sex Protects Intimates from the Negative Implications of Their Neuroticism," *Social Psychological and Personality Science* 2 (2011): 220–27.

42 **In more than one study, neuroticism:** Terri D. Fisher and James K. McNulty, "Neuroticism and Marital Satisfaction: The Mediating Role Played by the Sexual Relationship," *Journal of Family Psychology* 22, no. 1 (Feb. 2008): 112–22.

42 **High levels of conscientiousness and agreeableness:** David P. Schmitt and Todd K. Shackelford, "Big Five Traits Related to Short-Term Mating: From Personality to Promiscuity Across 46 Nations," *Evolutionary Psychology* 6, no. 2 (2008).

42 **In a meta-analysis:** Noam Shpancer, "How Your Personality Predicts Your Romantic Life," *Psychology Today,* Aug. 2, 2016, www.psychologytoday.com.

42 **Openness to experience seems:** Schmitt and Shackelford, "Big Five Traits."

44 **To experts like Celia Klin:** Celia Klin, interview with author, June 18, 2020.

44 **extroverts use the word "mouth":** Tal Yarkoni, "Personality in 100,000 Words: A Large-Scale Analysis of Personality and Word Use Among Bloggers," *Journal of Research in Personality* 44, no. 3 (2010): 363–73.

46 **IBM came up with:** Tanya Lewis, "IBM's Watson," *Business Insider,* July 22, 2015, www.businessinsider.com.

47 **MIT researchers trained a computer:** Rob Matheson, "Model Can More Naturally Detect Depression in Conversations," *MIT News,* Aug. 29, 2018, news.mit.edu.

47 **One study looked at 6,202 Twitter users:** Sharath Chandra Guntuku et al., "Studying Expressions of Loneliness in Individuals Using Twitter: An Observational Study," *BMJ Open* 9, no. 11 (2019).

47 **A Czech study asked 124 female students:** Jana M. Havigerová et al., "Text-Based Detection of the Risk of Depression," *Frontiers in Psychology* 10 (March 2019).

48 **Mentions of money can indicate lack of agreeableness:** Yarkoni, "Personality in 100,000 Words."

49 **those who bandy about negations:** Ibid.

51 **Jessica Bennett suggests:** Jessica Bennett, "When Your Punctuation Says It All (!)," *New York Times,* Feb. 27, 2015, www.nytimes.com.

51 **Big Five assessments has shown question marks:** Jennifer Golbeck et al., "Predicting Personality from Twitter," IEEE International Conference on Privacy, Security, Risk, and Trust, and IEEE International Conference on Social Computing, 2011, www.demenzemedicinagenerale.net.

52 **Celia Klin's research group:** Danielle N. Gunraj et al., "Texting Insincerely: The Role of the Period in Text Messaging," *Computers in Human Behavior* 55 (Feb. 2016): 1067–75.

52 **F. Scott Fitzgerald reportedly said:** F. Scott Fitzgerald, "An Exclamation Point Is Like Laughing at Your Own Joke," Quote Investigator, Jan. 6, 2019, quoteinvestigator.com.

52 **One study showed that overuse:** Golbeck et al., "Predicting Personality from Twitter," 153.

54 **In her book of essays:** Elena Ferrante, *Incidental Inventions,* trans. Ann Goldstein (Brentwood, Calif.: Europa Editions, 2019), 60.

55 **Gretchen McCulloch has elaborately documented:** Gretchen McCulloch, *Because Internet: Understanding the New Rules of Language* (Waterville, Maine: Thorndike Press, 2020).

55 **Americans, for instance, smile:** Olga Khazan, "Why Americans Smile So Much," *Atlantic,* June 1, 2017, www.theatlantic.com.

56 **A large-scale study:** Weijian Li et al., "Mining the Relationship Between Emoji Usage Patterns and Personality," arXiv, April 14, 2018, arxiv.org.

58 **For instance, extroverts will be more:** Ibid.

CHAPTER 3: WORKING OUT THE KINKS

63 **A large-scale study of forty-one thousand:** Queensland University of Technology, "Online Daters Ignore Wish List When Choosing a Match," *Science News,* Feb. 21, 2017, www.sciencedaily.com.

64 **In his seminal book:** Timothy D. Wilson, *Strangers to Ourselves: Discovering the Adaptive Unconscious* (Cambridge, Mass.: Belknap Press of Harvard University Press, 2004), 6.

65 **"To be is to do":** Kurt Vonnegut, *Deadeye Dick* (New York: Dial Press, 2010), 253.

71 **In a famous experiment:** Michael Norton and Zoë Chance, " 'I Read *Playboy* for the Articles': Justifying and Rationalizing Questionable Preferences," Harvard Business School Working Paper 10-018, Sept. 24, 2009, hbswk.hbs.edu.

74 **Research by the professor:** Rick Harrington and Donald A. Loffredo, "Insight, Rumination, and Self-Reflection as Predictors of Well-Being," *The Journal of Psychology* 145, no. 1 (2010): pp. 39–57.

74 **By contrast, the psychologist Anthony Grant:** Anthony M. Grant, John Franklin, and Peter Langford, "The Self-Reflection and Insight Scale: A New Measure of Private Self-Consciousness," *Social Behavior and Personality: An International Journal* 30, no. 8 (2002): 821–35.

74 **Tasha Eurich outlines in her book:** Tasha Eurich, *Insight: The Surprising Truth About How Others See Us, How We See Ourselves, and Why the Answers Matter More Than We Think* (New York: Currency, 2018), 135–42.

78 **When the difference is quantified:** Simine Vazire and Mitja D. Back, "Knowing Our Personality," in *Handbook of Self-Knowledge,* ed. Simine Vazire and Timothy D. Wilson (New York: Guilford Press, 2012), 137.

79 **As the therapist James Hollis:** James Hollis, *Living an Examined Life: Wisdom for the Second Half of the Journey* (Boulder, Colo.: Sounds True, 2018).

80 **The University of Virginia psychologist:** Timothy D. Wilson et al., "Just Think: The Challenges of the Disengaged Mind," *Science* 345, no. 6192 (July 2004): 75–77.

81 **Both feedback and mindfulness can run up:** Timothy D. Wilson and Daniel T. Gilbert, "Affective Forecasting: Knowing What to Want," *Current Directions in Psychological Science* 14, no. 3 (June 2005).

85 **our own biographers:** Wilson, *Strangers to Ourselves,* 16.

85   **"Students achieving Oneness":** Woody Allen and Linda
     Sunshine, *The Illustrated Woody Allen Reader: Prospectus* (New
     York: Alfred A. Knopf, 1993), 53.

CHAPTER 4: TEXTING WITH STRANGERS

87   **Eighty-four percent of users:** Plenty of Fish, "Pressure Points
     Report 2019" (Egnyte, 2019), 1–8, craftedcom.egnyte.com.
87   **A 2019 white paper:** Ibid.
92   **In the early days of dating apps:** Isabel Thottam, "The History of
     Online Dating (US)," eHarmony, 2018, www.eharmony.com.
93   **A Harvard Business School study:** Rachel Layne, "Asking
     Questions Can Get You a Better Job or a Second Date," HBS
     Working Knowledge, Oct. 30, 2017, hbswk.hbs.edu.
93   **Data science has shown:** OkCupid, "Online Dating Advice:
     Optimum Message Length," *The OkCupid Blog,* Medium, Aug. 7,
     2019, theblog.okcupid.com.
96   **Research out of Cornell:** Jason Dou et al., "What Words Do We
     Use to Lie? Word Choice in Deceptive Messages," arXiv, Sept.
     2017, arxiv.org.
100 **Neuroscientists have speculated:** Lindsay M. Oberman, "Broken
     Mirrors: A Theory of Autism," *Scientific American,* June 1, 2007,
     www.scientificamerican.com.
102 **The writer and storyteller David Sedaris:** David Sedaris,
     Facebook, Dec. 3, 2019, www.facebook.com.
108 **The professor of psychology Rod Martin:** Rod A. Martin
     and Thomas E. Ford, *The Psychology of Humor: An Integrative
     Approach* (London: Academic Press, 2018).
110 **self-enhancing humor:** Paul Frewen et al., "Humor Styles and
     Personality-Vulnerability to Depression," *Humor* 21, no. 2 (2008):
     179–95.
111 **aggressive humor:** Rod A. Martin et al., "Individual Differences
     in Uses of Humor and Their Relation to Psychological Well-
     Being: Development of the Humor Styles Questionnaire," *Journal
     of Research in Personality* 37, no. 1 (2003): 48–75.
113 **In data analyzed by OkCupid:** OkCupid, "Online Dating Advice."

114　**John Bowlby was the first:** Lumen Learning and Diana Lang, "1950s: Harlow, Bowlby, and Ainsworth," Iowa State University Digital Press, May 18, 2020, iastate.pressbooks.pub.

115　**Research suggests that half the human:** Amir Levine, *Attached: The New Science of Adult Attachment and How It Can Help You Find—and Keep—Love* (New York: TarcherPerigee, 2012), 4.

CHAPTER 5: COMMUNICATION STYLES

127　**In 2013, *The New York Times* ran:** Alex Williams, "The End of Courtship?," *New York Times,* Jan. 11, 2013, www.nytimes.com.

129　**In focus groups for his book *Modern Romance:*** Aziz Ansari, "The Power of Waiting," in *Modern Romance,* with Eric Klinenberg (New York: Penguin Press, 2015), 59–64.

130　**Helen Fisher—an anthropologist with expertise:** Helen E. Fisher, *Anatomy of Love: A Natural History of Mating, Marriage, and Why We Stray* (New York: W. W. Norton, 2017).

135　**"language-style matching":** James W. Pennebaker, *The Secret Life of Pronouns: What Our Words Say About Us* (New York: Bloomsbury, 2013), 200.

135　**James Pennebaker, a professor of psychology:** Ibid., 206.

135　**In his book *The Secret Life of Pronouns:*** Ibid., 1–17.

136　**Pennebaker told me:** Pennebaker, phone interview with author, Aug. 26, 2020.

139　**A study in Germany showed:** Silke Anders et al., "A Neural Link Between Affective Understanding and Interpersonal Attraction," *PNAS,* March 31, 2016, www.pnas.org.

142　**"It's no good pretending":** Nick Hornby, *High Fidelity* (New York: Riverhead Books, 1996), 117.

151　**When talking about work:** Pennebaker, *Secret Life of Pronouns,* 170–95.

152　**In his analysis of function words:** Ibid.

152　**"In short":** Pennebaker, phone interview with author.

152　**Even pack animals behave:** Enikő Kubinyi and Lisa J. Wallis, "Dominance in Dogs as Rated by Owners Corresponds to Ethologically Valid Markers of Dominance," *PeerJ* 7 (May 2019).

153 **Men use more articles:** Pennebaker, *Secret Life of Pronouns,* 170–95.

155 **Some of these behaviors are encouraged:** Ellen Fein and Sherrie Schneider, *The Rules* (New York: Grand Central Publishing, 2008).

155 **men are taught the art of "negging":** Neil Strauss, *The Game* (Edinburgh: Canongate Books, 2016).

156 **"The very essence of romance":** Oscar Wilde, *The Importance of Being Earnest* (London: Renard Press, 2021), act 1, p. 3.

157 **As a cognitive neuroscientist at Brown:** Rachel Herz, *The Scent of Desire: Discovering Our Enigmatic Sense of Smell* (New York: HarperCollins, 2009).

CHAPTER 6: TEXTING TOWARD INTIMACY

159 **"Love seems the swiftest":** Mark Twain, *Mark Twain's Notebook,* ed. Albert Bigelow Paine (London: Hesperides Press, 2006).

160 **"Love rests on two pillars":** Esther Perel, *Mating in Captivity* (London: Hodder & Stoughton, 2007), 25.

161 **"Love is giving something":** Allan Gois, "The Perfect Imperfections of Love," *The Psychotherapist Blog,* March 3, 2014, www.allangois.co.uk.

161 **Erikson, a renowned psychologist:** Erik H. Erikson, *Identity and the Life Cycle: Selected Papers* (New York: Norton, 1980).

161 **Much attention has been given:** Gary D. Chapman, *The Five Love Languages: How to Express Heartfelt Commitment to Your Mate* (Chicago: Northfield, 1995).

171 **The psychologist and relationship expert:** Kubinyi and Wallis, "Dominance in Dogs."

172 *language of attunement:* John M. Gottman and Nan Silver, *What Makes Love Last? How to Build Trust and Avoid Betrayal* (New York: Simon & Schuster Paperbacks, 2013), 83–90.

173 **Gottman suggests that attunement:** Ibid., 114–28.

175 **As Gottman has followed couples over:** Ibid.

175 **A bid, Gottman explains:** John M. Gottman and Joan DeClaire, *The Relationship Cure: A Five-Step Guide to Strengthening Your Marriage, Family, and Friendships* (New York: Harmony Books, 2002).

176   **As Gottman has studied couples:** John M. Gottman et al., *Eight Dates: Essential Conversations for a Lifetime of Love* (New York: Workman, 2019), 81.

179   **The relationship expert Esther Perel argues:** Perel, *Mating in Captivity.*

180   **Recall the classic "Soup Nazi":** "Soup Nazi," *Seinfeld,* season 7, episode 6, aired Nov. 2, 1995.

180   **"If intimacy grows through repetition":** Perel, *Mating in Captivity,* 37.

181   **"are more than you":** E. E. Cummings, "Because It's," All Poetry, 2005, allpoetry.com.

CHAPTER 7: PEACE, LOVE, AND UNDERSTANDING

182   **"All happy families are alike":** Leo Tolstoy, *Anna Karenina,* trans. Richard Pevear and Larissa Volokhonsky (New York: Penguin Books, 2002), 1.

184   **"Passionate Love Scale":** Elaine Hatfield, "Passionate Love, Companionate Love, and Intimacy," in *Intimacy,* ed. Martin Fisher and George Stricker (Boston: Springer, 1982).

184   **When a person scoring high:** Hongwen Song et al., "Love-Related Changes in the Brain: A Resting-State Functional Magnetic Resonance Imaging Study," *Frontiers in Human Neuroscience* 9, no. 71 (Feb. 2015).

185   **As the psychologist Jonathan Haidt:** Jonathan Haidt, *The Happiness Hypothesis: Putting Ancient Wisdom and Philosophy to the Test of Modern Science* (London: Random House Business Books, 2021), 126.

185   **"power of seeing through its own enchantments":** C. S. Lewis, *A Grief Observed* (London: CrossReach Publications, 2016), 72.

186   **The British psychologist Edward Titchener:** Richard M. Frankel, "The Many Faces of Empathy," *Journal of Patient Experience* 4, no. 2 (May 2017).

189   **In a paper titled "What Do You Do When Things Go Right?":** Shelly Gable et al., "What Do You Do When Things Go Right? The Intrapersonal and Interpersonal Benefits of Sharing Positive

Events," *Journal of Personality and Social Psychology* 87, no. 2 (2004): 228–45.

194 **"Respect is like air":** Kerry Patterson et al., *Crucial Conversations: Tools for Talking When Stakes Are High* (New York: McGraw-Hill, 2012), 79.

195 **To do that, Gottman emphasizes:** John M. Gottman and Nan Silver, *The Seven Principles for Making Marriage Work* (London: Cassell Illustrated, 2018).

195 **Nicholas Epley, a professor of behavioral science at the University of Chicago:** Nicholas Epley, *Mindwise* (New York: Vintage Books, 2015), 10.

202 **The sex columnist Dan Savage:** Amy Muise, "Are You GGG?," *Psychology Today*, Aug. 31, 2012, www.psychologytoday.com.

202 **In a study of long-term couples:** Amy Muise et al., "Keeping the Spark Alive: Being Motivated to Meet a Partner's Sexual Needs Sustains Sexual Desire in Long-Term Romantic Relationships," *Social Psychology and Personality Science* 4, no. 3 (2013).

204 **"Jealousy feeds on doubts":** François de La Rochefoucauld, *Maxims* (New York: Penguin Classics, 1982), 41.

206 **5 percent of Americans practice polyamory:** Elisabeth Sheff, "Updated Estimate of Number of Non-monogamous People in U.S.," *Psychology Today*, May 27, 2019, www.psychologytoday.com.

206 **A 2016 study found:** Jessica Kegu and Jason Silverstein, "'Things Are Opening Up': Non-monogamy Is More Common Than You'd Think," CBS News, Oct. 27, 2019, www.cbsnews.com.

206 **jealousy is no more prevalent among CNMs:** Elaine Hatfield, Richard L. Rapson, and Jeanette Purvis, *What's Next in Love and Sex: Psychological and Cultural Perspectives* (New York: Oxford University Press, 2020), 151–68.

207 **Estimated prevalence rates for CNM:** Ethan Czuy Levine et al., "Open Relationships, Nonconsensual Nonmonogamy, and Monogamy Among U.S. Adults: Findings from the 2012 National Survey of Sexual Health and Behavior," *Archives of Sexual Behavior* 47, no. 5 (July 2018).

207 **Infidelity has higher reported rates:** Hatfield, Rapson, and Purvis, *What's Next in Love and Sex,* 151–68.

207   **Yet when married couples are asked:** Michael W. Wiederman and Elizabeth Rice Allgeier, "Expectations and Attributions Regarding Extramarital Sex Among Young Married Individuals," *Journal of Psychology and Human Sexuality* 8, no. 3 (1996): 21–35.

209   **"We cross our bridges":** Tom Stoppard, *Rosencrantz and Guildenstern Are Dead* (Stuttgart: Reclam, 1993), 47.

CHAPTER 8: TOXIC TEXTING

217   **The person who stonewalls:** Gottman and Silver, *What Makes Love Last?*, 40.

220   **The psychologist Sue Johnson developed an approach:** Sue Johnson, *Hold Me Tight: Your Guide to the Most Successful Approach to Building Loving Relationships* (London: Piatkus, 2011), 32.

235 _ **"Life is pleasant. Death is peaceful":** Laura Ward, *Famous Last Words: The Ultimate Collection of Finales and Farewells* (London: PRC, 2004), 14.

CHAPTER 9: CROSSROADS

236   **"Love never dies a natural death":** Anaïs Nin, *The Four-Chambered Heart* (Denver: Swallow Press, 1959), 48.

237   **One data scientist tracked the word content:** Alice Zhao, "Text Messaging," A Dash of Data, Sept. 5, 2017, adashofdata.com.

243   **"a constant challenge":** Rainer Funk, *Erich Fromm: His Life and Ideas: An Illustrated Biography* (New York: Continuum, 2000), 138.

244   **One study, led by Lori Schade:** Lori Cluff Schade et al., "Using Technology to Connect in Romantic Relationships: Effects on Attachment, Relationship Satisfaction, and Stability in Emerging Adults," *Journal of Couple & Relationship Therapy* 12, no. 4 (2013): 314–38.

258   **"Truth, like gold, is to be obtained":** Tolstoy, *Anna Karenina,* 8.

260   **His notion of love was of a ladder:** Emrys Westacott, "Discover What Plato Means About the Ladder of Love in His 'Symposium,'" ThoughtCo, Aug. 2020, www.thoughtco.com.

261   **"This is a gang":** N.W.A, "Gangsta Gangsta," on *Straight Outta Compton,* 1988.

Bibliography

Allen, Woody, and Linda Sunshine. *The Illustrated Woody Allen Reader: Prospectus.* New York: Alfred A. Knopf, 1993.

Anders, Silke, Roos de Jong, Christian Beck, John-Dylan Haynes, and Thomas Ethofer. "A Neural Link Between Affective Understanding and Interpersonal Attraction." *PNAS,* March 31, 2016. www.pnas.org.

Anderson, Monica, Emily A. Vogels, and Erica Turner. "The Virtues and Downsides of Online Dating." Pew Research Center: Internet & Technology, Oct. 2, 2020. www.pewresearch.org.

Ansari, Aziz. *Modern Romance.* With Eric Klinenberg. New York: Penguin Press, 2015.

Bennett, Jessica. "When Your Punctuation Says It All (!)." *New York Times,* Feb. 27, 2015. www.nytimes.com.

Carman, Ashley. "Tinder Says It No Longer Uses a 'Desirability' Score to Rank People." *Verge,* March 15, 2019. www.theverge.com.

Chapman, Gary D. *The Five Love Languages: How to Express Heartfelt Commitment to Your Mate.* Chicago: Northfield, 1995.

Cloninger, Robert. "A Systematic Method for Clinical Description and Classification of Personality Variants." *Archives of General Psychiatry* 44, no. 6 (1987).

Cummings, E. E. "Because It's." All Poetry, 2005. allpoetry.com.

Dimoka, Angelika, Paul A. Avalou, and Fred D. David. "NeuroIS: The Potential of Cognitive Neuroscience for Information Systems Research." *Information Systems Research* 22, no. 4 (Dec. 2011): 1–16.

Dou, Jason, Michelle Liu, Haaris Muneer, and Adam Schlussel. "What Words Do We Use to Lie? Word Choice in Deceptive Messages." arXiv, Sept. 2017. arxiv.org.

Ekman, Paul. "Micro Expressions: Facial Expressions." Paul Ekman Group, Feb. 6, 2020. www.paulekman.com.

Epley, Nicholas. *Mindwise.* New York: Vintage Books, 2015.

Erikson, Erik H. *Identity and the Life Cycle: Selected Papers.* New York: Norton, 1980.

Eurich, Tasha. *Insight: The Surprising Truth About How Others See Us, How We See Ourselves, and Why the Answers Matter More Than We Think.* New York: Currency, 2018.

Fein, Ellen, and Sherrie Schneider. *The Rules.* New York: Grand Central Publishing, 2008.

Finkel, Eli J., Paul W. Eastwick, Benjamin R. Karney, Harry T. Reis, and Susan Sprecher. "Online Dating: A Critical Analysis from the Perspective of Psychological Science." *Psychological Science in the Public Interest* 13, no. 1 (2012).

Fisher, Helen E. *Anatomy of Love: A Natural History of Mating, Marriage, and Why We Stray.* New York: W. W. Norton, 2017.

Fisher, Terri D., and James K. McNulty. "Neuroticism and Marital Satisfaction: The Mediating Role Played by the Sexual Relationship." *Journal of Family Psychology* 22, no. 1 (Feb. 2008): 112–22.

Frankel, Richard M. "The Many Faces of Empathy." *Journal of Patient Experience* 4, no. 2 (May 2017).

Freud, Sigmund. "Volume 2, Studies in Hysteria." Edited by Carrie Lee Rothgeb. Psychoanalytic Training Institute of the Contemporary Freudian Society, 1971. instituteofcfs.org.

Frewen, Paul, Jaylene Brinker, Rod A. Martin, and David Dozois. "Humor Styles and Personality-Vulnerability to Depression." *Humor* 21, no. 2 (2008): 179–95.

Funk, Rainer. *Erich Fromm: His Life and Ideas: An Illustrated Biography.* New York: Continuum, 2000.

Gable, Shelly L., Harry T. Reis, Emily A. Impett, and Evan R. Asher. "What Do You Do When Things Go Right? The Intrapersonal and Interpersonal Benefits of Sharing Positive Events." *Journal of Personality and Social Psychology* 87, no. 2 (2004).

Gladwell, Malcolm. *Blink: The Power of Thinking Without Thinking.* New York: Back Bay Books, 2019.

Gois, Allan. "The Perfect Imperfections of Love." *The Psychotherapist Blog,* March 3, 2014. www.allangois.co.uk.

Golbeck, Jennifer, Cristina Robles, Michon Edmondson, and Karen Turner. "Predicting Personality from Twitter." IEEE International Conference on Privacy, Security, Risk, and Trust, and IEEE International Conference on Social Computing, 2011. www.demenzemedicinagenerale.net/.

Goldberg, Lewis. "Big Five Personality Test." Open Psychometrics, Aug. 2019. openpsychometrics.org.

Gottlieb, Lori. *Marry Him: The Case for Settling for Mr. Good Enough.* New York: New American Library, 2011.

Gottman, John M. "Love Lab." Gottman Institute, Sept. 10, 2019. www
.gottman.com.

Gottman, John M., Kim T. Buehlman, and Lynn Katz. "How a Couple
Views Their Past Predicts Their Future: Predicting Divorce from an Oral
History Interview." *Journal of Family Psychology* 5, no. 3 (Jan. 1970).

Gottman, John M., and Joan DeClaire. *The Relationship Cure: A Five-Step
Guide to Strengthening Your Marriage, Family, and Friendships.* New
York: Harmony Books, 2002.

Gottman, John M., Julie Schwartz Gottman, Doug Abrams, and Rachel
Carlton Abrams. *Eight Dates: Essential Conversations for a Lifetime of
Love.* New York: Workman, 2019.

Gottman, John M., and Nan Silver. *The Seven Principles for Making Marriage
Work.* London: Cassell Illustrated, 2018.

Grant, Anthony M., John Franklin, and Peter Langford. "The Self-Reflection
and Insight Scale: A New Measure of Private Self-Consciousness." *Social
Behavior and Personality: An International Journal* 30, no. 8 (2002):
821–35.

Gunraj, Danielle N., April M. Drumm-Hewitt, Erica M. Dashow, Sri Siddhi
N. Upadhyay, and Celia M. Klin. "Texting Insincerely: The Role of the
Period in Text Messaging." *Computers in Human Behavior* 55 (Feb. 2016):
1067–75.

Guntuku, Sharath Chandra, Rachelle Schneider, Arthur Pelullo, Jami
Young, Vivien Wong, Lyle Ungar, Daniel Polsky, Kevin G. Volpp, and
Raina Merchant. "Studying Expressions of Loneliness in Individuals
Using Twitter: An Observational Study." *BMJ Open* 9, no. 11 (2019).

Gurdjieff, George. "The Enneagram Personality Test." Truity, Jan. 8, 2021.
www.truity.com.

Haidt, Jonathan. *The Happiness Hypothesis: Putting Ancient Wisdom and
Philosophy to the Test of Modern Science.* London: Random House
Business Books, 2021.

Harrington, Rick, and Donald A. Loffredo. "Insight, Rumination, and Self-
Reflection as Predictors of Well-Being." *The Journal of Psychology* 145,
no. 1 (2010): 39–57.

Hatfield, Elaine. "Passionate Love, Companionate Love, and Intimacy." In
Intimacy, edited by Martin Fisher and George Stricker. Boston: Springer,
1982.

Hatfield, Elaine, Richard L. Rapson, and Jeanette Purvis. *What's Next in
Love and Sex: Psychological and Cultural Perspectives.* New York: Oxford
University Press, 2020.

Havigerová, Jana M., Jiří Haviger, Dalibor Kučera, and Petra Hoffmannová. "Text-Based Detection of the Risk of Depression." *Frontiers in Psychology* 10 (March 2019).

Herz, Rachel. *The Scent of Desire: Discovering Our Enigmatic Sense of Smell.* New York: HarperCollins, 2009.

Hollis, James. *Living an Examined Life: Wisdom for the Second Half of the Journey.* Boulder, Colo.: Sounds True, 2018.

Iqbal, Mansoor. "Tinder Revenue and Usage Statistics (2020)." *Business of Apps,* Oct. 30, 2020. www.businessofapps.com.

Ireland, Molly E., Richard B. Slatcher, Paul W. Eastwick, Lauren E. Scissors, Eli J. Finkel, and James W. Pennebaker. "Language Style Matching Predicts Relationship Initiation and Stability." *Psychological Science* 22, no. 1 (Jan. 2011): 39–44.

Jensen, David G. "Tooling Up: First Impressions—Are Interview Results Preordained?" *Science,* Aug. 20, 2004.

Johnson, Sue. *Hold Me Tight: Your Guide to the Most Successful Approach to Building Loving Relationships.* London: Piatkus, 2011.

Karney, Benjamin R., and Thomas N. Bradbury. "Neuroticism, Marital Interaction, and the Trajectory of Marital Satisfaction." *Journal of Personality and Social Psychology* 72 (1997): 1075–92.

Kegu, Jessica, and Jason Silverstein. " 'Things Are Opening Up': Non-monogamy Is More Common Than You'd Think." CBS News, Oct. 27, 2019. www.cbsnews.com.

Khazan, Olga. "Why Americans Smile So Much." *Atlantic,* June 1, 2017. www.theatlantic.com.

Kubinyi, Enikő, and Lisa J. Wallis. "Dominance in Dogs as Rated by Owners Corresponds to Ethologically Valid Markers of Dominance." *PeerJ* 7 (May 2019).

Laeng, Bruno, Oddrun Vermeer, and Unni Sulutvedt. "Is Beauty in the Face of the Beholder?" *PLoS ONE* 8, no. 7 (2013).

La Rochefoucauld, François de. *Maxims.* New York: Penguin Classics, 1982.

Layne, Rachel. "Asking Questions Can Get You a Better Job or a Second Date." HBS Working Knowledge, Oct. 30, 2017. hbswk.hbs.edu.

Learning, Lumen, and Diana Lang. "1950s: Harlow, Bowlby, and Ainsworth." Iowa State University Digital Press, May 18, 2020. iastate.pressbooks.pub.

Levine, Amir. *Attached: The New Science of Adult Attachment and How It Can Help You Find—and Keep—Love.* New York: TarcherPerigee, 2012.

Levine, Ethan Czuy, Debby Herbenick, Omar Martinez, and Brian Dodge. "Open Relationships, Nonconsensual Nonmonogamy, and Monogamy Among U.S. Adults: Findings from the 2012 National Survey of Sexual Health and Behavior." *Archives of Sexual Behavior* 47, no. 5 (July 2018).

Lewis, C. S. *A Grief Observed.* London: CrossReach Publications, 2016.

Lewis, Tanya. "IBM's Watson." *Business Insider,* July 22, 2015. www
.businessinsider.com.

Li, Weijian, Yuxiao Chen, Tianran Hu, and Jiebo Luo. "Mining the
Relationship Between Emoji Usage Patterns and Personality." arXiv,
April 14, 2018. arxiv.org.

Lieberman, David J. "Award-Winning Lie Detection Course: Taught by FBI
Trainer." Udemy, Jan. 7, 2021. www.udemy.com.

Martin, Rod A., and Thomas E. Ford. *The Psychology of Humor: An
Integrative Approach.* London: Academic Press, 2018.

Martin, Rod A., Patricia Puhlik-Doris, Jeanette Gray, Kelly Weir, and Gwen
Larsen. "Individual Differences in Uses of Humor and Their Relation
to Psychological Well-Being: Development of the Humor Styles
Questionnaire." *Journal of Research in Personality* 37, no. 1 (2003): 48–75.

Matheson, Rob. "Model Can More Naturally Detect Depression in
Conversations," *MIT News,* Aug. 29, 2018, news.mit.edu.

McCulloch, Gretchen. *Because Internet: Understanding the New Rules of
Language.* Waterville, Maine: Thorndike Press, 2020.

Muise, Amy. "Are You GGG?" *Psychology Today,* Aug. 31, 2012. www
.psychologytoday.com.

Muise, Amy, Emily Impett, Alexsandr Kogan, and Serge Desmarais.
"Keeping the Spark Alive: Being Motivated to Meet a Partner's Sexual
Needs Sustains Sexual Desire in Long-Term Romantic Relationships."
Social Psychology and Personality Science 4, no. 3 (2013).

Nakazato, Taizo. "Striatal Dopamine Release in the Rat During a Cued
Lever-Press Task for Food Reward and the Development of Changes over
Time Measured Using High-Speed Voltammetry." *Experimental Brain
Research* 166, no. 1 (Sept. 2005).

Nin, Anaïs. *The Four-Chambered Heart.* London: Peter Owen, 2004.

Norton, Michael, and Zoë Chance. " 'I Read *Playboy* for the Articles':
Justifying and Rationalizing Questionable Preferences." Harvard Business
School Working Paper 10-018, Sept. 24, 2009. hbswk.hbs.edu.

Norton, Michael, Jeana H. Frost, and Dan Ariely. "Less Is More: The Lure of
Ambiguity, or Why Familiarity Breeds Contempt." *Journal of Personality
and Social Psychology* 92, no. 1 (2007): 97–105.

Oberman, Lindsay M. "Broken Mirrors: A Theory of Autism." *Scientific
American,* June 1, 2007. www.scientificamerican.com.

Ohadi, Jonathan, Brandon Brown, Leora Trub, and Lisa Rosenthal. "I Just
Text to Say I Love You: Partner Similarity in Texting and Relationship
Satisfaction." *Computers in Human Behavior* 78 (Sept. 2017).

OkCupid. "Online Dating Advice: Optimum Message Length." *The
OkCupid Blog,* Medium, Aug. 7, 2019. theblog.okcupid.com.

Patterson, Kerry, Joseph Grenny, Ron McMillan, and Al Switzler. *Crucial Conversations: Tools for Talking When Stakes Are High*. New York: McGraw-Hill, 2012.

Pennebaker, James W. *The Secret Life of Pronouns: What Our Words Say About Us*. New York: Bloomsbury, 2013.

Perel, Esther. *Mating in Captivity*. London: Hodder & Stoughton, 2007.

Plenty of Fish. "Pressure Points Report 2019." Egnyte, 2019. craftedcom .egnyte.com.

Queensland University of Technology. "Online Daters Ignore Wish List When Choosing a Match." *Science News*, Feb. 21, 2017. www.sciencedaily .com.

Reis, Harry, Peter A. Caprariello, Michael R. Maniaci, Paul W. Eastwick, and Eli J. Finkel. "Familiarity Does Indeed Promote Attraction in Live Interaction." *Journal of Personality and Social Psychology* 101, no. 3 (March 2011): 557–70.

Russell, V. Michelle, and James K. McNulty. "Frequent Sex Protects Intimates from the Negative Implications of Their Neuroticism." *Social Psychological and Personality Science* 2 (2011): 220–27.

Schade, Lori, Jonathan Sandberg, Roy Bean, Dean Busby, and Sarah Coyne. "Using Technology to Connect in Romantic Relationships: Effects on Attachment, Relationship Satisfaction, and Stability in Emerging Adults." *Journal of Couple & Relationship Therapy*, 12, no. 4 (2013): 314–38.

Schmitt, David P., and Todd K. Schackelford. "Big Five Traits Related to Short-Term Mating: From Personality to Promiscuity Across 46 Nations." *Evolutionary Psychology* 6, no. 2 (2008).

Schwartz, Barry. "More Isn't Always Better." *Harvard Business Review*, Aug. 1, 2014. hbr.org.

———. *The Paradox of Choice*. New York: Ecco, 2004.

Sheff, Elisabeth. "Updated Estimate of Number of Non-monogamous People in U.S." *Psychology Today*, May 27, 2019. www.psychologytoday .com.

Shpancer, Noam. "How Your Personality Predicts Your Romantic Life." *Psychology Today*, Aug. 2, 2016. www.psychologytoday.com.

Smullyan, Raymond M. *Gödel's Incompleteness Theorems*. New York: Oxford University Press, 2020.

Song, Hongwen, Zhiling Zou, Juan Kou, Yang Liu, Lizhuang Yang, Anna Zilverstand, Federico d'Oleire Uquillas, and Xiaochu Zhang. "Love-Related Changes in the Brain: A Resting-State Functional Magnetic Resonance Imaging Study." *Frontiers in Human Neuroscience* 9, no. 71 (Feb. 2015).

Stoppard, Tom. *Rosencrantz and Guildenstern Are Dead*. Stuttgart: Reclam, 1993.

Strauss, Neil. *The Game*. Edinburgh: Canongate Books, 2016.

Thottam, Isabel. "The History of Online Dating (US)." eHarmony, 2018. www.eharmony.com.

Tolstoy, Leo. *Anna Karenina*. Translated by Richard Pevear and Larissa Volokhonsky. New York: Penguin Books, 2002.

Twain, Mark. *Mark Twain's Notebook*. Edited by Albert Bigelow Paine. London: Hesperides Press, 2006.

Vazire, Simine, and Mitja D. Back. "Knowing Our Personality." In *Handbook of Self-Knowledge*, edited by Simine Vazire and Timothy D. Wilson. New York: Guilford Press, 2012.

Vedantam, Shankar. "The Choices Before Us: Can Fewer Options Lead to Better Decisions?" NPR, May 4, 2020. www.npr.org.

Vonnegut, Kurt. *Deadeye Dick*. New York: Dial Press, 2010.

Ward, Laura. *Famous Last Words: The Ultimate Collection of Finales and Farewells*. London: PRC, 2004.

Westacott, Emrys. "Discover What Plato Means About the Ladder of Love in His 'Symposium.'" ThoughtCo, Aug. 2020. www.thoughtco.com.

Wiederman, Michael W., and Elizabeth Rice Allgeier. "Expectations and Attributions Regarding Extramarital Sex Among Young Married Individuals." *Journal of Psychology and Human Sexuality* 8, no. 3 (1996): 21–35.

Wilde, Oscar. *The Importance of Being Earnest*. London: Renard Press, 2021.

Williams, Alex. "The End of Courtship?" *New York Times*, Jan. 11, 2013. www.nytimes.com.

Wilson, Timothy D. *Redirect: Changing the Stories We Live By*. New York: Back Bay Books, 2015.

———. *Strangers to Ourselves: Discovering the Adaptive Unconscious*. Cambridge, Mass.: Belknap Press of Harvard University Press, 2004.

Wilson, Timothy D., David A. Reinhard, Erin C. Westgate, Daniel T. Gilbert, Nicole Ellerbeck, Cheryl Hahn, Casey L. Brown, and Adi Shaked. "Just Think: The Challenges of the Disengaged Mind." *Science* 345, no. 6192 (July 2004): 75–77.

Wilson, Timothy D., and Daniel T. Gilbert. "Affective Forecasting: Knowing What to Want." *Current Directions in Psychological Science* 14, no. 3 (June 2005).

Yarkoni, Tal. "Personality in 100,000 Words: A Large-Scale Analysis of Personality and Word Use Among Bloggers." *Journal of Research in Personality* 44, no. 3 (2010): 363–73.

Zhao, Alice. "Text Messaging." A Dash of Data, Sept. 5, 2017. adashofdata.com.